North-So
on Marine Policy

North-South Perspectives on Marine Policy

EDITED BY
Michael A. Morris

Westview Press
BOULDER & LONDON

Westview Special Studies in Ocean Science and Policy

Copyright © 1988 by Westview Press, Inc.

Published in 1988 in the United States of America by Westview
Press, Inc., 5500 Central Avenue, Boulder, Colorado 80301

Library of Congress Cataloging-in-Publication Data
North-South perspectives on marine policy.
   (Westview special studies in ocean science and
policy)
   Includes index.
   1. Marine resources--Government policy. 2. Marine
resources--Government policy--Developing countries.
I. Morris, Michael A. II. Series.
HC92.N67 1988   333.95'2   87-31711
ISBN 0-8133-7428-6

Printed and bound in the United States of America

The paper used in this publication meets the requirements
of the American National Standard for Permanence of Paper
for Printed Library Materials Z39.48-1984.

6   5   4   3   2   1

Contents

PART THREE
NORTH-SOUTH PERSPECTIVES

Tables, Figures and Maps

1

Introduction

Michael A. Morris

NORTH-SOUTH CONFLICT AND COOPERATION AT SEA

Management of the world's oceans is often competitive and untidy, because of the dynamics of national politics and the rudimentary nature of the international order. Ocean uses for both peace and war have increased, and membership of the international community has greatly expanded including attendant multiplication of competitive national marine policies. Every coastal country aspires to pursue national interests at sea through marine policy, which involves varying degrees of competition with well over a hundred other coastal states. In addition, land-locked states, most of which are in the Third World, acquired greater influence in ocean affairs through the Third United Nations Conference on the Law of the Sea (UNCLOS), 1973-1982.

International pressure may be exerted in a variety of ways by one state on another to alter national marine policy, but the backdrop for conflictive interaction between countries in the realm of ocean affairs is naval power. New weaponry technologies have enhanced the destructive power of established navies and have become more accessible to Third World navies. The superpower naval arms race, to which various alliance members make important naval contributions, continues unabated. The proliferation of independent Third World states in the postwar period brought in its train a belated awareness of the promise of offshore resources and

1

the need for maritime defense and led, in due course, to a fairly general, if uneven, naval expansion.[1]

UNCLOS did alter the overall context of ocean politics, especially by codifying a global consensus about expanded national ocean zones. General agreement was reached on expanded national ocean zones including a 12-mile territorial sea, over which coastal states are sovereign save for a foreign state right of innocent passage, and a 188-mile exclusive economic zone (EEZ) further seawards where coastal states have jurisdiction over natural resources and related matters.

However, UNCLOS did not resolve a fundamental split between developed and developing states over the deep seabed, which is located seawards of the national ocean zones. The United States and a few other developed states have refused to sign or ratify the 1982 UNCLOS Convention because of its deep seabed provisions restricting private mining enterprises. After long resistance, the developed states did accept expanded national ocean zones. In contrast, the developing countries of the Third World were the original instigators of expanded national ocean zones, and they also championed an international deep seabed regime at UNCLOS.

Military competition at sea fell largely outside the aegis of UNCLOS, so East-West naval rivalry continues unabated. This conflict pits most of the First World or West (United States, Western Europe and allies) against the Second World or East (Soviet Union, Eastern Europe and allies).

The two major power blocs (East and West) include most of the developed states, and are referred to collectively as "the North." Usually the Third World or "the South" includes developing countries in Africa, Asia, Latin America and the Middle East, although there is some ambiguity about membership of a few countries in this grouping such as Israel, South Africa and Turkey.

North-South relationships in the new ocean setting often remain troubled. UNCLOS did help defuse the protracted North-South confrontation over expanded national ocean zones, but did not ease the counterpart confrontation over the deep

2

seabed. Friction between developed and developing states at sea continues to be fed by numerous marine as well as non-marine causes. There are nonetheless new opportunities for North-South cooperation including assistance from developed states to help exploit and protect expanded Third World ocean zones.

A number of factors condition the evolving balance between the cooperative and conflictive dimensions of North-South marine relations. The cooperative and conflictive dimensions interact on both the domestic and international fronts.

Domestic politics is generally much more orderly than international politics, because of centralized power and law enforcement at the national level. Multiple ocean uses in coastal areas still pit a variety of domestic interests against one another. While governments can impose solutions on competing domestic actors when necessary, even authoritarian governments often prefer not to do so. Complex disputes do not generally admit of clear-cut solutions and in any event well-entrenched domestic actors will continue to pursue their interests on multiple fronts. A recurring tendency for governments is then to defer definitive resolution of domestic disputes as long as a crisis does not arise.

Less efficient governmental institutions and procedures in the South than the North tend to magnify these chronic domestic policy dilemmas. Polities in the South are also generally less stable than those in the North as well as being suspicious of any Northern involvement in their domestic affairs. Even in the best of circumstances, Northern assistance to Southern marine policies will face formidable political and economic obstacles.

North-South marine disputes pose yet additional problems. The domestic policy process generally does not place high priority on reconciling national interests with those of other nations even when foreign policy implications are inevitable, unless serious international complications arise. Since domestic and international affairs, including marine policy, are increasingly interdependent,[2] policy problems on each front easily tend to aggravate those on

3

the other.   The generally troubled nature of
North-South relations tends to accentuate these
recurring problems of international relations.
For example, Southern concessions to the North,
even if reciprocated, will usually evoke hostile
nationalistic feelings at home.
    Marine policy does attempt to resolve
numerous disputes within and between multiple
ocean   uses   domestically   as   well   as
internationally, and thereby encourage more
rational, systematic management of the oceans.
Unfortunately, the strong conflictive dimension of
North-South marine relations tends to overshadow
the cooperative dimension.
    Greater understanding of the complex
opportunities and obstacles facing marine policy
in the new setting can help contain the
competitive dimension and encourage the
conciliatory one.   Toward this end, this book
aspires to contribute to greater understanding of
three major perspectives on marine policy: (1)
developed states' perspectives, (2) developing
states' perspectives, and (3) interaction between
perspectives 1 and 2 or North-South perspectives.
A major section of this book is dedicated to each
of these perspectives.

THREE PERSPECTIVES ON MARINE POLICY

    While the essays in this book cannot aspire
to a comprehensive survey of the extensive subject
matter encompassed by the three perspectives, they
are representative of each perspective.   A variety
of issues in marine policy are analyzed, which
range from:
coastal area to deep seabed issues;
a case study of a strategically-located Third
World area (Southeast Asia) to one on new issues
posed by the European Economic Community (EEC) for
marine policy; and
resource management and protection in the Third
World to hegemonic (northern) leadership in
preventing oil pollution from tankers.
    Comparative   analysis   also   enhances
understanding of the complex, multifaceted marine
policy setting.   A variety of contrasts are made,
including:

vertical (US coastal zone policy) and horizontal
(the mix of EEC and member-state approaches to
marine policy);
functional (impact of extended national marine
jurisdiction) and regulatory (international oil
pollution and deep seabed regulations);
sectoral (fishing, naval affairs, shipping, deep
seabed mining) and geographical (national and
international ocean zones);
national (US ocean policy), cross-
national/regional (EEC, Southeast Asia) and
bloc/global (North-South interaction);
theoretical (Grolin, Laursen, Bowen/Hennessey),
normative (Bailey) and policy-oriented (Morgan and
others); and
conflict dynamics (Larson) and conflict management
(Lowry/Sorensen/Silva).

The variety of disciplines of the
contributors to this volume likewise help reflect
the complexity of marine policy. Disciplines
represented include Agricultural Economics and
Rural Sociology, Environmental Planning,
Geography, International Relations, Political
Science and Urban and Regional Planning.

A protracted planning period also helped
integrate the various essays and parts of this
volume. The Editor met and interacted with most
of the contributors to the volume during a
sabbatical leave from Clemson University at the
Marine Policy and Ocean Management Center of the
Woods Hole Oceanographic Institution (WHOI), 1984-
85. The book grew directly out of a course on
Marine Policy taught by the Editor for the Joint
Graduate Program in Oceanography of WHOI and the
Massachusetts Institute of Technology during the
Fall semester of 1985. The course gave the Editor
the opportunity to develop his own ideas in
dialogue with students and others about different
approaches and perspectives on marine policy. A
number of the eventual contributors to this book
also participated as visiting lecturers in the
course, and they subsequently developed their
lecture notes into articles for the book.

The Editor wishes to express appreciation for
support of this project from Clemson University
and WHOI, as well as the Hatfield Polytechnic
(UK), where he is Fulbright Exchange Professor

5

during the academic year, 1987-88.

While each of the essays and parts of the book may be considered singly, when taken together they reflect the complexity, richness and importance of North-South Perspectives on Marine Policy. An overview of each of the three main divisions of the book is presented below.

Developed States' Perspectives

One reflection of the relatively higher technological level of developed states, in contrast to Third World states, is their generally extensive, multi-sectoral presence at sea. The extensive presence of most developed states at sea and their relatively high level of expertise therein is reflected in the emphasis of the literature on the North. There is a fairly extensive literature about the marine policies of the major developed states, both in terms of general studies and more specific ones about marine sectors. Interaction between developed states has also been examined, particularly security and law-of-the-sea issues, although some other sectors have received much less attention from this perspective of international relations. Comparative studies are few and nearly all focus on developed states.[3]

The articles in Part 1 of this volume by Jesper Grolin and Finn Laursen combine domestic, comparative and international perspectives, and together indicate that even the extensively researched marine policies of developed states can benefit from careful attention to new approaches and issues. The traditionally dominant position of developed states is central to the article by Jesper Grolin on hegemonic leadership in preventing oil pollution from tankers. Implications for lesser states especially those in the Third World are noted. While European states have a long marine policy tradition, Finn Laursen assesses how the EEC has posed new problems and opportunities for marine policy. In both articles, US ocean policy bulks large either as that of the current global hegemon (Grolin) or as a federal model contrasting in distinctive ways with the EEC approach (Laursen).

Developing States' Perspectives

Third World marine policies have generally been sparsely represented in the literature, although there have been a few major studies in recent years about the marine policies of the larger, more prominent Third World states.[4] Comparative studies of developing states' marine policies are even rarer. A 1977 book was unusual in including four out of five marine policy case studies from the Third World (Canada, China, Iran, Nigeria, the Philippines) in a brief chapter (pages 9-52). However, the analysis of each country in just a few pages was necessarily superficial.[5] Another fairly early study in 1979 contrasted African and Latin American law-of-the-sea policies and approaches.[6]

The increasing prominence of Third World states at sea has attracted greater attention to their national marine policies in recent years. The major Third World marine policy sectors have also been receiving more attention.[7]

The article by Morris in Part 2 of this volume synthesizes the implications of the growing Third World presence at sea by identifying stages in the development of Third World marine policies. The following article by Morris and Pomeroy focuses on some recurring problems in Third World offshore resource management and protection, while the last two articles in Part 2 analyze these and related problems in a specific sector (Bailey) and a specific geographic region (Morgan). Bailey proposes ways of overcoming characteristic dilemmas of Third World fisheries, and in so doing shows how North-South interaction can be positive as well as negative. Morgan examines the multiple dimensions of the marine policies of Southeast Asian states, and in so doing he too assesses national, regional and extra-regional interaction.

North-South Perspectives

Just as important areas of marine policies, North and South, remain underexplored or unexplored, so too does North-South interaction at sea require more sustained attention. Some general studies deal to a degree with North-South marine relations,[8] as do more specialized treatments of marine sectors. However, the importance of the topic warrants careful analysis of each leg of the North-South marine relationship singly as well as in interaction. The three parts of the book are oriented by just this logic.

The expansion of national ocean zones, the promise of offshore resources, and the need for maritime defense highlight differing North-South ocean interests and approaches to marine policy. While there are many opportunities for North-South collaboration in developing and protecting offshore resources, considerable dependency of the South on the North infuses a note of discord into this potentially important area for mutual collaboration. Focusing on the problems inherent in the management of a truly international resource -- the oceans -- the contributors examine the potential for conflict and collaboration between and among the developed and developing states.

In Part 3 of this volume, Lowry, Sorensen and Silva show that multiple uses of coastal areas feed domestic disputes, so that emphasis should be placed on conflict management. At the same time, coastal area management reflects a constructive transfer of marine policy techniques and practices from North to South. Bowen and Hennessey examine North-South disputes over the deep seabed especially since the 1982 UNCLOS Convention, and Larson surveys North-South interaction and resulting frictions in naval affairs. The Bowen/Hennessey and Larson articles both suggest the intractability of some North-South disputes.

While all of the articles in the volume reach conclusions relating to the specific topic under discussion, the interlocking nature of the three parts of the book suggests some broader conclusions. A final chapter briefly presents overall conclusions of the book.

NOTES

1. Michael A. Morris, Expansion of Third-World Navies (London, England: The Macmillan Press, 1987 and New York: St. Martin's Press, 1987).

2. Robert O. Keohane and Joseph S. Nye, Power and Interdependence: World Politics in Transition (Boston: Little, Brown and Company, 1977).

3. Center for Ocean Management Studies, University of Rhode Island Comparative Marine Policy: Perspectives from Europe, Scandinavia, Canada and the United States (New York: Praeger, 1981). Timothy M. Hennessey was chairman of the conference whose proceedings were subsequently published as this 1981 book, and he is also a contributor to the present volume.

4. Michael A. Morris, International Politics and the Sea: The Case of Brazil (Boulder, Colorado: Westview Press, 1979).

5. John King Gamble, Jr., Marine Policy: A Comparative Approach (Lexington, MA.: Lexington Books, 1977).

6. Michael A. Morris, ed., special, double-length issue of Ocean Development and International Law: The Journal of Marine Affairs on "Influence and Innovation in the Law of the Sea: Latin America and Africa," vol. 7 (1979); follow-up materials in vol. 9 (1981).

7. Morris, Expansion of Third-World Navies.

8. Keohane and Nye, Power and Interdependence; Stephen D. Krasner, Structural Conflict: The Third World Against Global Liberalism (Berkeley: University of California Press, 1985); and Barry Buzan, "A Sea of Troubles? Sources of Dispute in the New Ocean Regime," Adelphi Papers No. 143 (London: IISS, 1978).

PART 1

Developed States' Perspectives

2

Environmental Hegemony, Maritime Community and the Problem of Oil Tanker Pollution

Jesper Grolin

INTRODUCTION

Oil pollution from tankers has plagued coastal states since the beginning of this century, and since the mid-1920s attempts have been made to eliminate oil tanker pollution through international regulation. Yet, it was not until the mid-1970s that decisive and adequate steps in this direction were taken. After decades with regulations that merely sought to ensure that tankers did not discharge oil too close to land, the 1973 MARPOL convention and its 1978 amendments introduced a broad array of costly requirements for the construction and equipment of tankers -- requirements that will radically reduce the discharge and spillage of oil everywhere on the oceans. Hence, the MARPOL convention constituted a true turning point in the fight against tanker pollution. In fact, of all sources of marine pollution, tanker shipping has probably become the source which is subjected to the most stringent international regulation.[1]

This tremendous progress in oil tanker pollution control in the 1970s was due primarily, if not exclusively, to the persistent environmentalist pressure and leadership provided by the United States within the International Maritime Organization (IMO). This much is clear from recent political analyses of oil tanker regulations.[2] What is less clear is why U.S. leadership as such was necessary to achieve adequate protection against oil pollution; and why nations could not just cooperate to solve a problem that after all affected them all as coastal states. This is the main question to be analyzed in this chapter. To do so requires going back to the very beginning, to the very first international oil pollution conference in Washington D.C. in 1926, and then tracing the exasperatingly slow development of regulations through the 1935 League of Nations conference, the 1954 London conference and the consideration of oil tanker pollution in IMO since its establishment in 1958.[3] The aim is not just to provide a fuller historical analysis than is usually given, but to apply some newer contributions from the theory of collective action, which I believe to be particularly useful in understanding problems of international management of common resources.[4]

TANKERS AND OIL POLLUTION

The marine environment has a limited capacity to cleanse itself of pollutants. It may happen either through biological degradation of the substance, dilution in seawater, or more or less permanent storage of the substance through sedimentation at the bottom fo the ocean. Together, these mechanisms constitute what is usually referred to as the assimilative capacity of the marine environment. The existence of such a capacity means that the marine environment is a renewable resource and that -- within its limits -- it may be used legitimately for waste disposal purposes. Pollution occurs, however, when the combined load of contamination exceeds what the assimilative and regenerative mechanisms can handle.

Oil contamination from tankers is caused either by accidents such as groundings, collisions and explosions, or by operational discharges in connection with normal ballasting procedures whereby empty oil-cargo and fuel tanks are filled with seawater. The purpose of ballasting is both to clean tanks and to maintain sufficient propeller immersion and stability of the tanker itself. At some point on the trip to the loading port, the dirty ballast water, mixed with whatever

14

oil residues remain in the tanks, will be discharged and clean ballast water taken on board. Tankers were responsible for approximately 1.5 million tons (or 70%) of the more than 2 million tons of ship-generated oil discharges in 1973. Of these 1.5 million tons of oil, 87% came from operational discharges and only 13% from accidents.[5]

Oil is bio-degradable, but only gradually and, in some cases, only incompletely. Large spills in connection with tanker accidents will lead to acute, but usually only short-term pollution effects, whereas the smaller, but continuous operational discharges along the major tanker routes can lead to chronic oil pollution. Most shipping routes lie close to shore, and most of the oil discharged or spilled by ships will therefore affect coastal states. Even small and infrequent spills in polar regions can have serious, long-term effects due to the slowness of biological processes at low temperatures.

Oil pollution has well-known, adverse visual effects such as dirty beaches and tainting of seafood, and it can have pathogenic effects affecting the survival or reproductive capacity of fish and sea birds. Oil also contains carcinogenic components which may accumulate in the marine food-chain and, thus, possibly affect human health. Finally, oil pollution may have ecomorphic effects if species of fish or sea birds become either extinct or permanently reduced so that the composition of the ecosystem is altered.

THE REGULATION OF OIL TANKER POLLUTION

Regulation of oil tanker pollution developed slowly from sporadic national laws and unsuccessful attempts at international regulation in the 1920s and 30s to the successful adoption of international conventions in the post war period which gradually tightened the requirements for tankers' ballasting procedures and later their construction. These developments will be described and interpreted with some reference to theory.

The History of Oil Tanker Regulation

Around the turn of the century, a major transition from coal to oil as the primary source of energy had begun. This meant not only that more ships used oil-fueled engines, but also that oil became a commodity transported by ship in increasing quantities. With this development, oil pollution of sea, coastlines and ports inevitably followed as a result of both accidents and operational discharges. The latter was then, as it is now, the bigger problem, and until the late 60s it was the only problem explicitly addressed by international oil pollution regulations.

As became clear already at the 1926 Washington conference on oil pollution, there are basically three ways of dealing with the problem of operational discharges. One can especially seek to control and minimize adverse visual effects by stipulating that oil may only be discharged beyond coastal prohibition zones of a certain breadth. Alternatively, one can seek to eliminate oil pollution altogether by requiring ships to separate the oily ballast water and retain the oily waste on board, or by requiring ports to provide reception facilities where ships can unload their oily ballast mixtures.

The zonal solution was clearly the simplest and the cheapest one, and it is, therefore, not surprising that it was the first to be chosen. After initial, but utterly ineffective attempts by local port authorities to appeal to shipmasters to avoid oil discharges in ports, the U.K. and the U.S. prohibited all oil discharges in their 3 mile territorial seas in 1922 and 1924. These narrow zones alleviated the worst oil pollution problems in ports, but only at the expense of beaches and coastal areas close to ports where oil pollution now increased.

As a consequence, the 1926 Washington conference on oil pollution and the 1935 League of Nations conference proposed an expansion of the prohibition zones to 50 miles and in special areas to 100 or 150 miles. These zones, it was emphasized, were to be special prohibition zones of a functional nature. They were not to be territorial seas, and they were not to alter or in

16

any way affect the traditional law-of-the-sea principle of flag-state enforcement. Coastal states could report and provide evidence of violations of the discharge prohibition, but it would be up to the flag-state to prosecute the shipmasters according to its own laws, i.e., if it deemed it possible and necessary to do so.

Due to inertia and the subsequent interruption of all international cooperation during the Second World War, these prohibition zones were not formally accepted until 1954 when the first International Convention for the Prevention of Pollution of the Sea by Oil (OILPOL) was adopted at a conference in London. However, by then, the adequacy of the zonal solution was increasingly being questioned. When in 1962 IMO adopted the goal of eliminating all operational discharges on the oceans, other types of measures had to be considered.

The option of using port reception facilities was actually considered already in connection with the British Act of 1922, but it was turned down then as well as later in 1926 and 1935. Port authorities were unwilling to pay for the installation of reception facilities, and tanker-owners for their part were unwilling to spend the extra 3-4 days it would take to clean tanks in ports rather than at sea. At the 1954 conference, the U.K. did manage to sway the majority of states to adopt a binding obligation for ports to provide reception facilities for non-tankers, but the obligation turned out to be a major obstacle to many countries' ratification of OILPOL, and it was therefore eliminated again at the 1962 conference.

The alternative of ship-board retention of oily wastes had also been considered in the prewar period. Oil separating mechanisms were in fact used by some non-tankers already in the 1920s, and at the 1926, 1935 and 1954 conferences, the British pressed with increasing vigour to have such oil separators made compulsory at least for non-tankers. They failed all three times, partly because of the economic costs involved and partly because of uncertainty about the efficiency of the technology.[6]

In the 1960s, the British -- much encouraged and assisted by BP and other oil companies --

17

began to focus on the Load on Top system, which was based on the simple fact that crude oil is lighter than water. By letting the lighter oil accumulate on top of the water, it was possible to decant fairly clean ballast water from the bottom of the tank, and then pump the oily residues into a separate slop tank, where new oil cargo could simply be "loaded on top". The system had two great advantages -- it saved oil and it was fairly inexpensive. So in the late 1960s and early 1970s, oil companies voluntarily installed Load on Top on their tankers, and the 1973 MARPOL convention made it compulsory for existing tankers as a means of reducing operational discharges.

While the Load on Top system was an improvement, it could in no way fulfill the goal of total elimination of operational discharges adopted by IMO in 1962 and again in 1971. To achieve that, the United States now pressed for the adoption of the far more expensive solution of segregated ballast tanks. While it still left a problem of cleaning cargo tanks, it did eliminate the problem of oily ballast water since the separate ballast tanks would never be used for the carriage of oil. The solution was made compulsory for all new tankers in 1973.

Later in 1978, the U.S. managed to push things a step further despite strong resistance from the U.K. and European shipping nations. The Load on Top system was completely abandoned. Instead, existing tankers were given a choice between being retrofitted with segregated ballast tanks or installing a new technique of crude oil washing developed by the oil companies. Crude oil can dissolve its own residues, and the technique was therefore able to clean cargo tanks almost completely by means of high pressure jets of crude oil. Since segregated ballast tanks did not solve the problem of cleaning cargo tanks, a combination of the two methods was clearly preferable, and exactly this was the costly requirement stipulated in 1978 for new tankers. To minimize procrastination in the ratification process, the 1978 MARPOL amendments also recommended that the new requirements should be applied to new tankers ordered after the middle of 1979 irrespective of whether the amendments had entered into force.

As for accidental pollution, the principal response was the establishment of rules of liability and compensation. Thus, after the grounding of the tanker Torrey Canyon in 1967, causing a spillage of about 100,000 tons of crude oil off the coast of Cornwall, a Civil Liability Convention was adopted in 1969, and an International Fund to supplement compensation payments was established in 1971. After the even more disastrous grounding of the tanker Amoco Cadiz in 1978, causing a spillage of no less than 220,000 tons of crude oil off the coast of Brittany, the liability and fund conventions were revised in 1984, raising the total compensation per incident from $36 million to $135 million.

As more preventative measures, the U.S. pressed at the MARPOL conferences to have tankers built with double bottoms to reduce the outflow of oil in connection with groundings or collisions, and in 1978 the U.S. also demanded the installation of inert gas systems on tankers to reduce the risk of explosions in cargo tanks. The major shipping nations were successful in rejecting the double bottom requirement. Instead, it was accepted that segregated ballast tanks should be placed in protective locations and, despite high costs, it was also accepted that all ships irrespective of size should be built or retrofitted with inert gas systems.

In sum, it can be said that while the U.K. leadership was important in bringing nations out of their complacency and inaction, it took the leadership of the U.S. to press through measures which will reduce accidental oil pollution and virtually eliminate operational discharges. On the basis of this historical outline, an explanation of three phases in the development of regulations of oil tanker pollution will be presented.

First Period: The Weakness of Maritime Community

For cooperation to be rational, joint action must as a minimum contain a positive sum potential so that all participants can hope to gain. This was hardly the case in the first decades of the century when port authorities and shipmasters were the primary actors in the ship pollution game.

Firstly, most ports and coastal communities were highly dependent on shipping and therefore "endeavoured to deter pollution in ways which would not frighten away the very source of their livelihood" in terms of business and supplies.[7] Hence, actions taken by port authorities were mostly limited to verbal appeals to shipmasters, distribution of leaflets or posting of billboards informing about the consequences of oil discharges in ports. Secondly, if, as a last resort, legal action was taken, port authorities often found that their legal powers of prosecution were limited and outdated. Thus, in the U.K., local by-laws pertaining to harbor pollution "dated to King Henry VIII's reign in 1543 and carried a maximum fine of five pounds," which even at the turn of the century was ridiculously low.[8] As for areas outside ports, coastal communities had no powers whatsoever to prosecute ships. Finally, and most importantly, those who could ensure environmental quality, namely the masters of ships and tankers, were not in any significant way consumers of that good and, therefore, had no interest in producing it.

Hence, the strategic structure between individual port authorities and individual shipmasters was more or less that of a zero-sum game. For ships to have stopped using the sea as a waste dump would have been virtually a pure loss. This total asymmetry of power and interests alone meant that no community relations could emerge and thrive between port authorities and masters of oil ships. The fact that these shipmasters were not members of the coastal communities they visited meant furthermore that no social incentives were present to modify this situation of total asymmetry.

This asymmetry was not modified until states, in the early 1920s, entered the stage as the primary actors in the marine pollution game. Because states included port-, coastal- and shipping interests under one hat, they captured to a greater extent both benefits and costs of using the ocean for waste disposal purposes. The change manifested itself in an increasing number of unilateral marine pollution laws of which the British Oil in Navigable Waters Act of 1922 and the U.S. Oil Pollution Act of 1924 were the first.[9]

However, it soon became evident that isolated national action was insufficient. While states -- within their own narrow territorial waters -- could enforce a discharge prohibition against foreign ships, it was clear that any measures beyond the territorial sea would require the agreement and cooperation of other countries to be effective. On the high seas beyond the territorial sea, the flag-state principle applied, and this meant that even the modest measure of pollution prohibition zones of 50 miles was unenforceable without the agreement of other flag states. Furthermore, as British oil and shipping interests pointed out in the preparatory stages of the 1922 Act, it would lead to distortion of competition internationally if they alone had to comply with new regulations -- be they stiffer penalties for discharge violations, compulsory cleaning of tanks at reception facilities in British ports or installation of oily water separators on board.[10] Thus, for reasons of fair competition and effective control of all ship-sources of oil pollution, international action was required.

Yet, international regulation emerged only slowly and after repeated failures which delayed joint action for nearly 30 years from 1926 to 1954. Even then, it took nearly another 20 years until 1973 before measures were adopted that could lead to a total elimination of operational pollution -- a goal that had, in fact, been suggested already at the 1926 conference. The most important reason for this inertia was the fact that community relations between actors were only slightly strengthened by elevating the oil pollution problem to the inter-state level.

Shared values and beliefs among actors is one basic characteristic of community and a necessary requirement for conditional cooperation. Values and beliefs are in some cases closely connected, but nevertheless always distinct factors. While "beliefs" relate to actors' perceptions of reality, "values" relate to the preferences and goals of actors. In the pre-war period, shared values and beliefs about oil pollution of the oceans were hardly present. There was disagreement

21

both about the seriousness of the problem and
about what action to take. Thus, at the 1926
conference, British and American reports about the
oil contamination of their beaches were countered
by German and Dutch claims that oil discharges
were perfectly harmless.[11]

The disagreement seems to have had two
causes. Firstly, the basic split between polluters
and pollutees that had existed between shipmasters
and port- and coastal communities was only
imcompletely overcome by raising the oil pollution
problem to the international level. While almost
all states had both oil ships and coastlines,
states with many ships and short coastlines would
tend to be net polluters while states with few
ships and long coasts would tend to be net
pollutees. Both the U.K., the U.S., Germany and
the Netherlands were big shipping nations, but
whereas Germany and the Netherlands had relatively
short coasts, both the U.K. and the U.S. had long
coasts which were exposed to oil pollution. This
difference naturally led to an asymmetry in the
value attached to a clean marine environment.

A second reason for the disagreement was a
very explicit difference in beliefs about the
biodegradability of oil. This question was the
subject of heated debates in the Committee on
Facts and Causes at the 1926 conference. The Dutch
representative introduced what was for that time
rather sophisticated and advanced scientific
evidence to the effect that crude oil was attacked
and completely decomposed by bacteria in seawater.
The Americans and the British, on the other hand,
maintained that oil tended to persist indefinitely
in the marine environment and, therefore, sooner
or later ended up on the coasts of countries close
to major shipping routes. This difference of
views persisted up to the end of the 1950s.[12] It
meant that all that could be agreed on was an
extension of prohibition zones based on a disputed
assumption that these zones would give the marine
environment enough time to degrade the oil before
it reached coasts and beaches.

As mentioned earlier, oil is biodegradable,
but only incompletely so. Those parts of the crude
oil that are only partially degradable will
gradually form tar-balls that eventually end up on

coasts. This became increasingly clear during the 1960s, and it provided a scientific justification for moving towards a total elimination of all operational discharges. Yet, the emerging scientific consensus on the fate of oil in the marine environment did not automatically translate itself into a new consensus on what means of tanker pollution control should replace the prohibition zones. Shipping nations favoured the fairly inexpensive and ineffective Load On Top system, while the U.S. demanded the installation of the more expensive and effective system of segregated ballast tanks. Clearly, shipping nations were willing to live with a certain amount of continued oil contamination, while coastal states like the U.S. with only a relatively small tanker fleet under its flag found it unacceptable.

Thus, not only did the absence of shared values and beliefs delay effective regulation of oil pollution in the first half of the century, but when shared beliefs finally did emerge, asymmetries in the size of interests of actors blocked their transformation into shared values. This would seem to indicate that in weak communities the integrative effect of consensual knowledge may also be weak.

Many-sided relations among actors is the second fundamental characteristic of community. It is important because it increases the cost of a bad reputation and, hence, the potency of reputational factors as a social deterrent against free-riding. Free-riding in the case under examination will typically take the form of lax enforcement by flag-states both in terms of inspection and certification of the safety and seaworthiness of their fleet and in terms of prosecution of ships and tankers that have violated internationally agreed regulations.

While inspection and certification became an issue only after the construction, design and equipment of ships were subjected to international regulation in the 1970s, the problem of prosecution of ships emerged already with the introduction of prohibition zones beyond the territorial sea. There seems to be little question that flag-states and especially major shipping nations indeed were lax in prosecuting their own

23

ships for violations in foreign waters. According to a 1961 IMO survey, "state-parties to the 1954 Convention reported that out of 92 violations in prohibited zones, none had been prosecuted sucessfully by the flag-state".[13] Canada later reported that out of 80 violations that it had asked various flag-states to prosecute, 39 were not prosecuted, and of the remaining 41 cases only 17 had led to conviction. Judging from other reports to IMO, the experience of Canada was not the exception, but rather the rule.[14] This can only lead to the conclusion that the factor of reputation has been virtually absent in the calculation of individual flag-states. There are three principal reasons for this.

The first is that <u>verification</u> of compliance or rather establishing proof of violations was extremely difficult as long as regulation took the form of prohibition zones. While oil slicks were fairly easy to identify, even with heavy investment in coastal surveillance it was in most cases impossible to prove which ship was responsible or, even worse, to ascertain whether discharges in the prohibition zones exceeded the 100 parts per million that the 1954 OILPOL Convention allowed.[15] With these uncertainties there were plenty of excuses for flag-states not to prosecute or else not to convict ships accused of violations.

At the League of Nations conference, it was suggested that each shipmaster should record in his log book the time, place and quantity of oily ballast water discharged, and the 1954 Convention actually required every tanker to use a special oil record book for the same purposes. Yet, enforcement based on self-reporting is bound to work poorly if there are no effective and independent means of verification. This in fact was the case until regulatory strategies changed from zones to requirements for construction of ships, i.e., segregated ballast tanks or installation of purification systems such as Load On Top and Crude Oil Washing.

The second reason for the virtual absence of reputational considerations was the lack of adequate channels of <u>communication</u>. Questions of violations and prosecution were by nature bilateral matters between coastal states and flag states, and if the incidents of violation were not reported by the press, they were not likely to be known by any other country. This was even more the case with questions of prosecution, which followed much later after the incident. To improve the spreading of information, some common secretariat or organizational forum was needed which could provide the functional equivalent of village gossip and public shaming that are such potent instruments of social control in tribal and traditional peasant communities.[16]

The Washington conference did suggest the establishment of a Central Agency, which would have received and circulated not only technical data but also reports on prosecutions of violations. However, such a forum did not emerge until IMO started operating in 1958, and even then IMO did not automatically produce the "village gossip" since states had to agree to actually provide the necessary information to the organization. British and U.S. proposals in 1962 that would have made it obligatory for states to provide IMO with reports on violations and prosecutions were watered down to a purely voluntary arrangement, and, in fact, IMO received no such voluntary reports until its newly established Marine Environmental Protection Committee asked for them in 1977. Since then, the IMO has kept lists of accidents and violations reported to it, and the accidents and violations are not removed from the list until the flag state has provided a satisfactory report. This is potentially an important step forward because it will increasingly provide the basis for all actors to evaluate the behavior and performance of everyone else.

Yet, it should be emphasized that maritime community gossip and public shaming per se will have a limited effect unless actors' relations are many-sided and different issues so tightly interwoven that the bad reputation of free-riding in marine pollution control affects the actors' reputation as a partner more generally.

This suggests the third reason for the ineffectiveness of reputational factors. No evidence has been found that the bad reputation

25

acquired by particular flag-of-convenience states such as Panama and Liberia has in any way affected these states in other areas of international cooperation. It is doubtful that such evidence can be found.

It does not seem plausible that the ministry of trade or finance in country A will know or, if they do, will care much about the enforcement record of country B in environmental matters. Compartmentalization of states in sectoral bureaucracies entails difficulties of coordination, if not a split personality of the state actor, and this, in turn, impedes issue-linkage.[17] Hence, a bad reputation for lax enforcement of oil tanker regulations is likely to be restricted to the maritime sector, and here it had only a limited effect because of the flag state principle and the associated asymmetry of power in favor of big maritime states.

Thus, to sum up, the weakness of maritime community made regulation of oil tanker pollution slow and difficult, and even to the degree that agreement was reached and verification possible, it was difficult to ensure compliance and proper enforcement. A purely internal solution was impossible at least in a constructive sense of the term "solution". Tit-for-tat retaliation may well have been at work causing lax enforcement by some to be reciprocated by lax enforcement by most others. However, due to asymmetry of interests and lack of shared values, there was no basis on which to strengthen joint action through conditional cooperation. Furthermore, due to the general weakness of international community, social incentives to preserve a good reputation as partner in cooperation were too weak to make any significant contribution towards a solution.

Second Period: British Environmental Leadership

Under these circumstances of weak community, British initiatives were important in ensuring the little progress that did take place from the 1920s until the mid-1960s. Britain was not only the first country to legislate nationally, it was the main force behind the calling of the Washington conference, the League of Nations conference, and

26

the 1954 conference that finally led to the adoption of the OILPOL Convention.[18] At these three occasions as well as the 1962 conference, Britain was also the country to press for the strongest measures. Already at the Washington conference, the head of the British delegation complained that "If we have the zone system, we really cannot enforce it, and we will have this trouble in greater or lesser degree hanging around our necks for an indefinite period, and it is much better for us, and much better for the interests concerned, to settle it definitely once and for all".[19] Britain, therefore, insisted on the need for reception facilities in ports and the installation of oily water separators on board ships to ensure a total elimination of operational discharges.

The British preference for international cooperation and its insistence on strong measures were motivated by two factors. The U.K. had, as earlier mentioned, both strong coastal and shipping interests. It was situated right next to one of the busiest shipping routes, namely the Channel, and it was, after the U.S., the biggest importer of both crude and refined oil and, hence, the largest oil port state in Europe.[20] Furthermore, the U.K. had -- unlike the U.S. -- an extremely active and well-organized environmental movement in the pre-war period, which through the Royal Society for the Protection of Birds and the Royal Society for the Prevention of Cruelty to Animals was well-connected at the elite-level of the British society.[21]

Thus, Britain was caught in a crossfire domestically between environmental interests demanding effective regulation and shipping interests concerned about international competitiveness. Assuming leadership to achieve strong international regulation was a way to escape this cross-fire by pacifying domestic environmentalist pressure without threatening domestic shipping interests.

The pressure for international regulation also served a second British interest of preserving the traditional Law of the Sea with its principle of flag-state enforcement and narrow territorial seas. The traditional Law of the Sea,

27

as it had developed in the 18th and 19th centuries, was very much the product of British interests in maintaining freedom of navigation and dominance in international affairs through its naval power.[22] Yet, at the turn of the century, there were increasingly widespread attempts by smaller coastal states to expand their territorial seas to obtain control especially over fishery resources. The U.K. clearly feared that oil pollution would intensify this emerging trend and lead to attempts to control and limit the free movement of ships.

While Britain had played the role of coercive hegemon in the Law of the Sea, its leadership in international oil pollution regulation does not fit this category. Britain could have played the role of hegemon by unilaterally requiring its ships to install oily water separators and use reception facilities in British ports. Such a unilateral approach was, in fact, what some British environmentalists demanded. Yet, the ships of other countries would have been able to continue polluting, and even unilateral British measures might have been short-lived if distortion of competition had gradually reduced the British commercial fleet. Thus, Lord Runciman in a debate in the House of Lords in 1955, found it counterproductive if Britain "were thought to be the general cleaner-up of other people's doorsteps".[23] To be effective, such benevolent unilateral measures would have had to be combined with coercive measures such as an expansion of the control of ships in coastal waters, but such measures would have run counter to British interests in the freedom of the sea.

Thus British leadership was not hegemonic, but rather what in collective action theory is called political entrepreneurship. What is distinctive about a political entrepreneur is that he seeks to solve collective action problems by attempting to "change individual preferences..., beliefs ... or inject resources (very probably knowledge or new technology ...) into the group so as to make its members' efforts more productive".[24] Britain did exactly that through its initiatives and very active participation in conferences and through its investment in research

28

especially in oily water separators. Yet, in the end, Britain only had the power of good arguments and persuasion. Britain could not force regulations beyond what was at any given time the least common denominator, and even by the early 1960s that did not amount to more than a system of protection zones.

The Perceived Threat of a New Law of the Sea

In such a situation, communitarian relations among actors were virtually absent, tit-for-tat retaliation was ineffective, benevolent hegemony was impossible, and the persuasiveness of political entrepreneurs was insufficient to change the wayward behavior of free-riders. The use of selective incentives of a material nature constitutes a last possibility, i.e., if they are available and within reach in terms of costs.

There were relevant selective incentives at hand, namely the extension of territorial seas or, alternatively, a strengthening of the jurisdiction of port states. This would leave the initiative to a greater extent in the hands of the pollutees, and hence lead to more energetic enforcement as well as potentially lead to more potent sanctions. Flag state prosecution, when it was undertaken and when it led to conviction, typically resulted in fines. Yet, fines had a limited deterrent value not only because they were on the whole quite modest in size, but also because the fines were covered by the ships' insurances.

An expansion of the jurisdiction and the rights of coastal- and port-states to stop, inspect and possibly detain ships was a far more serious threat, because it would cause delays and thereby disrupt the efficient and smooth operation of the shipping industry. And the costs of delays were not covered by the insurances of ships. An even more serious threat connected with expanded coastal jurisdiction was the possibility of unilateral coastal state legislation regarding the construction, design and equipment of ships. Not only would that mean that flag states would lose control over the cost-levels of such requirements, but international shipping as such would be greatly hampered if ships had to comply with

29

different and perhaps contradictory standards. As
a U.S. official put it, there would, in the
extreme, be "not only 120 different construction
standards, all perhaps quite reasonable, but in
addition to that .... all of those standards could
be changed through time .... there simply would be
anarchy in trying to construct ships that would be
able to ply the world's oceans".[25]

The use of such material incentives was not
beyond imagination even in the 1950s. The coastal
zone extensions that began in the early part of
the century continued in the post-war period
especially among developing countries. The
marine capabilities of these countries were
limited to their local coastal waters, and the
coastal zone extensions came very much as a
response to increasing competition over fishery
resources. As before the war, the dominant trend
was extensions of territorial seas to 12 miles,
but at the end of the 1940s, more radical demands
of 200 mile zones emerged in Latin America and
they later spread to other developing countries.
Like the territorial sea extensions, the 200 mile
zones were very broadly defined extensions of
coastal state control including not only exclusive
access to resources but also a right to protect
the environment.

Nevertheless, none of the developing
countries with 200 mile claims appear to have made
unilateral ship pollution laws or attempted to
prosecute violations of international rules in
their extended zones. They had a full plate just
trying to enforce their claims of exclusive access
to fishery resources, which the U.S. and other
distant-water fishing nations adamantly refused to
accept. To have taken on the extra burden of
enforcing national marine environmental
legislation against foreign ships would have
increased costs considerably and probably exceeded
these poorer countries' perceived value from a
cleaner marine environment.

The first step to increase coastal states'
rights to protect their marine environments
against foreign ships only came after the
grounding of the tanker Torrey Canyon in 1967. The
fact that the grounding had occurred outside the 3
miles territorial sea had delayed British actions

to counter the spread of oil by 10 days while the owner made an attempt to salvage the ship.[26] The Intervention Convention adopted in 1969, therefore, gave coastal states a right to take necessary measures beyond their territorial seas "to prevent, mitigate or eliminate grave and imminent danger" of pollution of their coastlines from accidents. Yet, the convention was by no means a carte blanche for coastal state interference with the free movement of ships. Intervention could only happen after an accident or incident threatening to cause pollution had taken place, and even then, the coastal state intervention had to be "proportionate" to the actual or threatened damage. This, in turn, meant that coastal states would be liable for the costs of unwarranted delays. Hence, the Intervention Convention constituted only a small modification of the flag state principle.

The Civil Liability Convention, which was also adopted at the 1969 conference, added another small modification of the flag state principle. The Convention required tankers to carry insurance for oil pollution accidents, and parties to the convention were obliged to require such insurance for all vessels entering their ports irrespective of whether the flag state of the vessel had ratified the convention. This put non-complying states and their vessels at a competitive disadvantage and as a result, all major maritime states quickly ratified the convention, and even countries that had not ratified the convention complied with it.[27]

A far more radical step was taken in 1970, when Canada adopted its Arctic Pollution Prevention Act whereby it arrogated the powers to make and enforce national norms both with regard to discharges and the construction of ships navigating within a 100 mile broad pollution control zone off the Canadian coasts.[28] The Act was only partially motivated by environmental problems. At the end of the 1960s, U.S. oil companies were planning to take their tankers through the Canadian Northwest Passage with oil from the Alaskan continental shelf. This raised the sensitive issue of whether the Arctic archipelago was Canadian internal waters under

31

full Canadian sovereignty or -- as the Americans maintained -- international straits with a right of innocent passage for foreign ships. Rather than making a direct claim of sovereignty, Canadian chose an indirect strategy via the environment, perhaps because it provided valid arguments due to the high vulnerability of Arctic waters, and because such arguments -- given the generally rising environmentalism in Western countries -- were likely to have broader international appeal than mere nationalistic expansionism.

Whatever the reasons, Canada began an aggressive diplomatic campaign to gain international recognition of its claims, and this made it for some time a strong environmentalist leader of the coastal state movement, supported by such other developed coastal states as Australia and New Zealand. At the U.N. Seabed Committee and at the Stockholm Conference on the Human Environment in 1972, it effectively gathered support from developing coastal states, and it was successful in persuading a large number of these countries to participate in the 1973 IMO conference -- so successful, in fact, that developing countries for the first time constituted a majority in IMO.

Yet, Canada's experience in trying to implement its Arctic Act also showed the potential limitations of coastal state unilateralism. With very few tankers of its own, Canada was dependent on the services of the international shipping industry, and, with only a moderate share of the international oil trade, it was not in a position to make radical demands. Thus, Canada had to spend two years consulting and negotiating with international maritime insurers and industries before it could implement the Act in 1982, and by then Canadian demands on foreign ships navigating in their waters had been reduced more or less to what was accepted internationally.

To have been effective in its environmental demands, Canada would have had to coordinate its unilateral ship pollution legislation with ship pollution legislation of the many developing coastal states. That never took place, if it were ever considered. The sheer costs of organization would have been considerable. In addition,

developing coastal states were more interested in
extending their general rights of regulation than
in implementing specific, let alone, radical
environmental legislation that implied costly
requirements for their own ships and possible
constraints on the development of their own
commercial fleet.[29]

Thus, the coastal state group faced a
collective action dilemma in actually turning
their coastal state power into effective sanctions
against ship pollution. Their environmental
values alone were too different for there to be
any solid basis of community to overcome this
dilemma by themselves.

Third Period: The U.S. Takes the Lead

The environmental leadership of the U.S.
brought about the substantial improvements in
international oil pollution regulation in the
1970s. U.S. leadership was not based on coastal
state expansionism, but rather on its power as a
port state. The possibility of a radical
expansion of coastal state jurisdiction remained a
threat at least in the minds of maritime states.

The U.S. did have all the makings of a
powerful coastal state. It had, potentially, the
largest 200 mile zone in the world,[30] and it was
the largest maritime trading nation both in oil
and all other goods.[31] At the same time, it was
not hampered by strong shipping interests. The
U.S. share of the total world tanker fleet was
relatively small -- in fact, it had fallen by
nearly 50% from 1966 to 1974.[32] As a consequence,
tankers under U.S. flag carried less than 7% of
the crude and petroleum imported and exported by
the U.S.[33] It is true that a substantial part of
the tanker fleet under Liberian and Panamanian
flags of convenience was American-owned, but that
only meant that the U.S. did not have a direct and
significant income from shipping to protect.

The U.S., however, had other prominent
maritime interests which made it a strong opponent
of the coastal state movement. As mentioned
earlier, the U.S. had interests in distant-water
fishing, and this brought it in direct conflict
with Chile, Peru and Ecuador in the 50s, when

33

these countries sought to enforce their claims of exclusive access to fishery resources. Far more important, however, was the fact that the global military leadership of the U.S. was based partially on naval power and, hence, on the free movement of naval vessels.

The gradual extensions of the territorial sea to 12 miles were unsettling to the U.S., particularly because they threatened to bring more than 100 international straits of less than 24 miles under coastal state sovereignty. While ships had a right of "innocent passage" in the territorial sea, the concept of innocence of passage was vague and it was uncertain whether the passage of warships would be considered innocent. What was clear, however, was that airplanes had no right of overflight above the territorial sea and that submarines had to navigate on the surface and show their flag. This, in turn, meant that the relative undetectability of submarines on which the US strategic nuclear deterrent depended heavily would be endangered. Similarly, the idea of 200 mile territorial seas which would enclose areas such as the Mediterranean Sea was completely unacceptable to the U.S.

At the Law of the Sea conference in the 1970s, the U.S. accepted a 12 mile territorial sea, but only because a separate legal regime guaranteeing the basic high seas freedoms of navigation was established for international straits. The U.S. also accepted 188-mile exclusive economic zones (EEZs) beyond, but succeeded in limiting the jurisdictional content of these zones so that free movement of both naval and commercial vessels was left unaffected. Coastal state rights of intervention against polluting ships stipulated in the 1982 Law of the Sea Convention are basically those which were already established in the 1969 Intervention Convention.

Instead, the Law of the Sea Convention increased the jurisdiction of port states. Port states can not only prosecute ships in their ports for discharge violations committed in their internal and territorial waters, but also for violations committed in their EEZs and on the high seas. Furthermore, port states can -- as has always been the case -- demand that special construction, design and equipment requirements be fulfilled by ships entering their ports. Flag states can preempt port state prosecution of discharge violations beyond the territorial sea, but only if the flag state itself institutes proceedings against the ship and if the port (or coastal) state proceedings do not "relate to a case of major damage". Finally, the flag state has no right of preemption if it "has repeatedly disregarded its obligation to enforce effectively the applicable international rules and standards in respect of violations committed by its vessels" (art. 228. 1.).

The latter provision is interesting because it shows that while individual flag states had not been negatively affected by their lax enforcement, flag states as a group had clearly acquired a bad reputation. When a reform of the traditional law of the sea finally took place, this bad reputation did result in port and coastal states tightening the conditions for future cooperation. One may wonder why flag states did not anticipate and avoid this, but despite British leadership they were as a group as helplessly caught in a dilemma of collective action to preserve the good name of flag states as coastal states were in collectively countering their irresponsible behaviour. Furthermore, with the cut-throat competition characteristic of the shipping market, future benefits were probably at all times discounted at a very high rate.

The somewhat greater strengthening of port state enforcement was to the shipping industry the lesser of two evils because it minimized the potential interference of coastal states whose waters they were merely passing through. At the same time, however, this solution maximized the power of the U.S. Due to its status as the world's single most important port state, the U.S. had an effective threat of unilateral legislation. Unlike Canada with only 0.8% of the world's oil trade, the U.S. could, with 8% of all traded oil going through its ports, not be disregarded by the shipping industry.[34] Ships that were not constructed and equipped so that they could enter U.S. ports would be unable to participate in the competition for nearly one tenth of the oil shipping market, and since four out of the five biggest tanker flag states were the major competitors in that market, the U.S. port state power was considerable.[35]

The United States had used the threat of unilateral legislation for ships entering its ports in connection with the 1973 and 1978 IMO conferences. Thus, in July 1972, the U.S. Congress passed the Ports and Waterways Safety Act which gave the U.S. Coast Guard the right (but not the obligation) to require ships entering U.S. ports to be fitted with both segregated ballast tanks and double bottoms. While Congress had left some leeway for negotiation, the U.S. delegation made it perfectly clear to all that if it was not reasonably satisfied with the new convention, unilateral action would follow. In a similar way, President Carter stated in 1977 that if improvements of the MARPOL convention could not be achieved internationally through IMO, then the U.S. would act alone.[36] In neither case did the U.S. achieve all it wanted, but U.S. pressure was definitely responsible for the major steps forward that were taken.

The one important demand that the U.S. did not manage to press through was the requirement for tankers to be built with double bottoms to reduce the risk of accidental pollution. One important reason for this was the widespread doubt about the cost-effectiveness of this added requirement. Not only were double bottoms more expensive than segregated ballast tanks. It could be argued that double bottoms, in some cases, would increase rather than reduce accidental pollution because double bottoms would make it more difficult to salvage a grounded tanker, and it might increase the chance of explosions.[37]

In any event, the U.S. had, with the demand for segregated ballast tanks, reached the bargaining limit of what access to its one tenth of the oil trade was worth, and like a political entrepreneur, it could achieve no more if additional measures were not clearly in the enlightened self-interest of other actors. Double bottoms were not, and "in the absence of more convincing technical arguments the American initiative lost" its supporters.[38] The U.S. could have chosen to act unilaterally, but the maintenance of international regulation of ship pollution was <u>per se</u> of value to the U.S. since it restrained coastal state unilateralism which might have followed a break-down at IMO.

This leaves the question of how to characterize the U.S. environmental hegemony on the basis of what it did achieve, notably the requirement of segregated ballast tanks. The U.S. hegemony was clearly of a coercive nature. External threats relating to the business of shipping were used to achieve progress in the protection of the marine environment. What is less clear is what the international distributional consequences will be. The costs will through higher freight rates affect countries proportionately to their import of oil, whereas benefits will depend on a multitude of more or less quantifiable factors such as length of coastlines, proximity to major tanker routes, economic value of coastal fishery and the economic, aesthetical and health value of less oil-polluted coastal waters for recreational purposes.

On the basis of quantifiable costs and gains only, some U.S. economists have concluded that the added benefits from segregated ballast tanks do not justify the extra costs. For every dollar spent on segregated ballast tanks as compared to the Load on Top system, the added benefits have been calculated to be in the range from $ 0.002 to 0.213.[39] If this is true and if we assume that the U.S. has acted rationally in forcing through the requirement for segregated ballast tanks, it means that very strong, non-quantifiable environmentalist values must have motivated the U.S.. And if this is so, it follows that countries -- to the degree that such strong environmentalist values are not present, especially in developing countries -- may well end up spending more on oil pollution control than their immediate benefits justify. Thus, strictly speaking, it could be said that U.S. environmental leadership will have exploitative consequences distributionally.

The cost-benefit ratios cited above bring out a perennial problem in environmental policy making, namely how to evaluate those many immediate as well as future benefits from a healthy environment that -- unlike the costs -- cannot be quantified. It is precisely because many environmental benefits are "soft" and non-quantifiable that they are often disregarded. Therefore, the true significance of U.S. environmental leadership may be that it has given full value to the non-quantifiable benefits of marine environmental protection. In that case, "far-sighted" rather than "exploitative" may be a more appropriate label to attach to U.S. environmental leadership in the 1970s.

CONCLUDING REMARKS

From this perspective, the possible weakening of the U.S. leadership role in IMO becomes a crucial problem. While U.S. hegemonic capabilities as one of the largest oil port states in the world have remained unchanged, U.S. environmental priorities have not. With the election of Reagan as president in 1980, a downgrading of U.S. environmental priorities took place. Both the Republican platform and Reagan's acceptance speech in 1981 made it clear that environmental protection was a goal secondary to that of economic growth.[40]

In spite of resistance in the U.S. Congress, the Reagan administration has managed to some degree to change U.S. environmental policy internationally as well as domestically. In some cases, there has been an explicit reversal of earlier policies. This has been the case with U.S. financial contributions to UNEP, cooperation with Canada to reduce acid rain, and control of export of hazardous substances especially to developing countries. In other areas, international cooperation has been permitted to continue because "there was no conspicuous conflict with high-level administration ideology" or U.S. economic interests, but the role of the U.S. has, on the whole, been a fairly passive one.[41]

The U.S. commitment to work in IMO seems to have been largely unaffected by the general environmental policy upheaval under Reagan. The U.S. has ratified the MARPOL convention and is presently in the process of implementing one of its optional annexes, namely annex V on discharge of garbage from ships.[42] Furthermore, the U.S. supported the amendment of the Civil Liability Convention and the Fund Convention in 1984, and with the higher levels of compensation adopted here, the Reagan administration has now recommended U.S. ratification of the two conventions.[43]

However, the 1980s have not been a decade of innovation in IMO, but rather a period when implementation of the major initiatives of the 1970s has been started. So, even if the United States under Reagan has remained active within IMO and not rescinded earlier commitments, it is far from certain that it would be willing to provide leadership to solve future problems of vessel-source pollution. It is therefore appropriate to end this chapter by briefly reviewing the possibility of non-hegemonic cooperation as it has developed in the period analysed.

In the pre-war period and the immediate post-war period, the basis for cooperation was very weak. Differences in the size of interest in reducing oil pollution and the lack of shared beliefs about the assimilative capacity of the marine environment made prohibition zones the only measure on which agreement could be reached. Compliance with this minimal protection measure was extremely difficult to verify and enforce. Even when violations were detected, social incentives were too weak to ensure an effective flag-state prosecution of the accused shipmaster. And, given the lack of material incentives with which to threaten flag-states, there was little that could be done to improve the system of oil tanker regulations.

A number of factors affecting the possibility of non-hegemonic cooperation have changed in a favorable direction since the 1950s and early 1960s. First, with a 535% increase in oil transported by sea from 1953 to 1978, the size and urgency of the oil pollution problem grew significantly, and this, no doubt, has increased the level of shared interests in the sense of raising the least common denominator. Second, the change in regulatory strategy from prohibition zones to construction and equipment standards has made verification of compliance easier. Third, the gathering and circulation of information on flag-state enforcement by IMO have made reputational considerations somewhat more significant, although the information still remains very much within the maritime community itself. Last, the recent changes in the traditional Law of the Sea and especially the modifications of the principle of flag-state enforcement have provided coastal- and particularly port-states with potentially effective material sanctions.

These changes have improved the possibilities of enforcing MARPOL and other IMO conventions, and, in fact, a considerable intensification in enforcement activities has taken place in Europe. In January 1982, the Scandinavian and EEC countries signed a Memorandum of Understanding on Port State Control according to which they undertook to increase the number of inspections to 25% of all foreign merchant ships calling at their ports. The memorandum specified that inspectors are to ensure that "no more favourable treatment" is given to non-Convention ships. This means that European port-states will require foreign ships to comply with MARPOL and other IMO conventions irrespective of whether the ship's flag-state has ratified these conventions. In case sub-standard ships are detected, action by the port-state may include detention of the ship until deficiencies are remedied. Finally, to assist each other in selecting the most likely violators for inspection, an on-line information system has been established to exchange data on ships inspected in the ports of the participating states.[44] Considering that Holland, the U.K., Italy, France and West Germany alone have 20% of the world's total amount of sea-transported goods and oil loaded and unloaded in their ports,[45] strengthened European port-state cooperation will almost certainly make a big contribution towards ensuring wide-spread implementation of MARPOL and other IMO conventions.

Whether the European countries' port-state cooperation would also be capable of providing leadership in solving future vessel-source pollution problems in IMO is, however, far less certain. European countries remain fairly conservative maritime states with large merchant fleets, and environmental cooperation within, for instance, the Paris Commission on Land-based Sources of Marine Pollution has shown rather marked differences in environmental values.[46] Of course, if the merchant fleets of Europe were increasingly transferred to flags of convenience, European states might find it easier to demand new costly requirements for ships if that should be necessary. However, if such radical changes do not take place in the registry of ships, future innovative regulations to solve new problems of ship pollution will very likely have to depend on a possible re-strengthening of U.S. environmental priorities in the post-Reagan era.

NOTES

I wish to thank a number of colleagues and friends for the help and encouragement they have given me in writing this chapter. They are Morten Ougaard, J. Dige Pedersen, Nikolaj Petersen, J. Poulsen and Mette Skak of the University of Aarhus, Finn Laursen of the London School of Economics, the editor of this book, Michael Morris, and last, but not least, Michael Taylor of the University of Washington.

1. For a comparative evaluation of the stringency and effectiveness of the regulation of ship pollution (within the International Maritime Organization), dumping (within the London Dumping Convention) and land-based sources of marine pollution (within the Paris Convention) I refer to earlier works of mine such as Jesper Grolin, "Marine Environmental Regulation and the Dilemma of Collective Action", (Florence, Italy: European University Institute, 1985, unpublished paper), and Jesper Grolin, "The Politics of International Marine Pollution Control", Occasional Papers, vol. 2 (1985), Institute for Global Policy Studies, Amsterdam.
2. See especially R. M. M'Gonigle and M.W. Zacher, Pollution, Politics and International Law: Tanker at Sea (Berkeley: University of California Press, 1979), and A.B. Sielen and R.J. McManus,

"IMCO and the Politics of Ship Pollution", in D.A. Kay and H.K. Jacobson, eds., Environmental Protection: The International Dimension (Totowa New Jersey: Allanheld, Osmun Publ., 1983), pp. 140-183.

3. Up to May 1982, IMO's name was the Inter-Governmental Maritime Consultative Organization (IMCO). I shall only use the new name of the organization.

4. The original work by Mancur Olson, The Logic of Collective Action (Cambridge, MA.: Harvard University Press, 1971), has been further developed by Russell Hardin, Collective Action (Baltimore, Maryland: The Johns Hopkins University Press, 1982), and especially by Michael Taylor in his two works Community, Anarchy and Liberty, (Cambridge: Cambridge University Press, 1982), and The Possibility of Cooperation, (Cambridge: Cambridge University Press, 1987).

5. Petroleum in the Marine Environment (Washington, D.C.: National Academy of Sciences, 1975), p. 6.

6. Sonia Zaide Pritchard, Oil Pollution Control (London: Croom Helm, 1987), pp. 90-91.

7. Pritchard, p. 2.

8. Ibid.

9. Pritchard, pp. 2-7, 25-30.

10. Pritchard, p. 3.

11. Pritchard, p. 19.

12. Prichard, pp. 16-18, 88-89.

13. Pritchard, p. 112.

14. M'Gonigle & Zacher, Pollution..., p. 334 incl. fn. 46.

15. M'Gonigle & Zacher, Pollution..., pp. 218-223.

16. Taylor, Community..., p. 84.

17. Keohane acknowledges sectoral boundaries as a serious obstacle to bargaining linkages, but strangely enough he does not consider the possibility of similar obstacles in his analysis of reputational linkages. R. Keohane, After Hegemony (Princeton, New Jersey: Princeton University Press, 1984), pp. 91, 103-105.

18. Pritchard, pp. 7-9, 45-49, 72-75.

19. Quoted from Pritchard, p. 21.

20. A. C. Hardy, Oil Ships and Sea Transport

(London: G. Routledge and Sons, 1931), pp. 24, 25.

21. Pritchard, pp. 11-14.

22. J. Grolin & F. Laursen, Ret eller Magt pa Havet (Copenhagen, Denmark: FN-forbundet, 1982), pp. 8-14.

23.Quoted from Pritchard, p. 110.

24. Taylor, The Possibility..., p. 24.

25. John N. Moore, "Report on the Course of Negotiations at Caracas -- Commentary" in F.T. Christy et al., eds., Law of the Sea: Caracas and Beyond (Lexington, MA.: Proceedings, Law of the Sea Institute, 9th Annual Conference, Ballinger Publishing Co., 1975), pp. 11-12.

26. Pritchard, pp. 154-157.

27. M'Gonigle & Zacher, Pollution..., p. 318.

28. The analysis of Canadian policy draws heavily on R. M. M'Gonigle and M. W. Zacher, "Canadian Foreign Policy and the Control of Marine Pollution" in B. Johnson and M. W. Zacher, eds., Canadian Foreign Policy and the Law of the Sea (Vancouver, Canada: University of British Columbia Press, 1977), pp. 100-157.

29. M'Gonigle & Zacher, Pollution, pp. 294-298.

30. G. J. Mangone, Concise Marine Almanac (New York: Reinhold, 1986), pp. 31-35.

31. United Nations Statistical Yearbook: 1975 (New York: United Nations, 1976).

32. Ibid.

33. R. J. Stewart, "Tankers in U.S. Waters," Oceanus, vol. 20 (1977), p. 78.

34. United Nations Statistical Yearbook: 1975.

35. Ibid. Also R.J. Stewart, "Tankers...".

36. M'Gonigle and Zacher, Pollution..., pp. 111, 129-130.

37. Sielen and McManus, pp. 168-171.

38. M'Gonigle and Zacher, Pollution, p. 119.

39. R. D. Eckert, The Enclosure of Ocean Resources: Economics and the Law of the Sea (Stanford: Stanford University Press, Hoover Institution, 1979), p. 181.

40. M. E. Kraft, "A new environmental policy agenda: The 1980 Presidential campaign and its aftermath", in N.J. Vig and M.E. Kraft, eds., Environmental Policy in the 1980s: Reagan's New

Agenda (Washington D.C.: Congressional Quarterly Press, 1984), pp. 29-50, esp. pp. 34-37.

41. L.K. Caldwell, "The world environment: reversing U.S. policy commitments", in Vig and Kraft, Environmental..., pp. 319-338, cit. p. 326.

42. Council on Ocean Law, Ocean Policy News, (Oct./Nov. 1987), pp. 11-12.

43. Council on Ocean Law, Ocean Policy News, (Jan./Febr. 1985) p. 8, and (Dec. 1985), p. 6.

44. I. Matthiesen, "The Role of the Government Nautical Surveyor", in Ship Safety and Marine Surveying (Malmo, Sweden: International Conference, The World Maritime University, May 8-9, 1986), pp. 18-61, esp. 33-37.

45.United Nations Statistical Yearbook: 1975.

46. Grolin, "Marine Environmental...", pp. 31-34, 72-75.

3

Marine Policies of
the European Community

Finn Laursen

INTRODUCTION

The purpose of this chapter is to identify the extent to which the European Community (EC) has developed its own marine policies and to explain the emergence of such policies. Indeed, the EC has in recent years become a new marine political actor. The centerpiece is the Common Fisheries Policy (CFP), but the Community also has a common shipping policy and to some extent a common marine environmental policy. In other respects, especially continental shelf resources, the EC has been less successful, even if it did try. Finally there are issues in marine policy which have been left largely untouched by the EC, especially security matters and delimitation problems. So one of the questions which we will be investigating is why there is such a variance in marine political integration within the EC across functional issue areas.

The questions posed also involve a case study in international integration. The EC is the most advanced example of regional international integration. It started with the European Coal and Steel Community (ECSC) in 1952. A European Defence Community was tried, but failed when the French National Assembly declined to ratify in 1954. European integration continued with the European Economic Community (EEC) as well as the European Atomic Energy Community (EURATOM) in 1958. These three communities originally had six members -- Belgium, France, the Federal Republic of Germany,

Italy, Luxembourg, and the Netherlands. The first enlargement took place in 1973 when Denmark, Eire, and the United Kingdom joined. Greece followed in 1981, and Spain and Portugal in 1986.

The three original communities each had a Council of Ministers where national governments were represented, and an independent executive known as the Commission (or High Authority in the case of the ECSC). They also had a common parliamentary assembly and a Court of Justice. The Councils and Commissions were merged in 1967. Since 1970 the Community countries have also had some general foreign policy cooperation, known as European Political Cooperation (EPC). The whole setup was to some extent consolidated with the European Single Act in 1987, which gave the EPC a treaty basis, although decisions within the EPC still will be based on consensus. The Act also gave the meetings of the heads of state or governments, the European Council, a juridical basis, and it reinforced the role of the Parliament in the decision-making process. Much of it deals with the internal market, economic cooperation and research. The environment was brought within the treaty framework, too.

It seems fair to say that the EC has expanded in domain (new members) and scope (new functions). However, has it also expanded in respect to the level of integration, and has the decision-making capacity of the EC increased? This question is more controversial, since it is linked with the sensitive question of supranational powers and majority decisions instead of unanimous decisions. Many of the founding fathers wanted the Community to develop towards a European federal state, but member countries have hesitated and tried to claim a right to veto decisions if important national interests were at stake. One of the ideas behind the European Single Act is that majority decisions shall be used increasingly in the Council.

In respect to marine policy the scope of the EC has clearly expanded over the years, starting with the first Common Fisheries Policy in 1970, then revised because of the first enlargement of membership in 1973 and later because of the introduction of 200-mile fishing zones in 1977. A comprehensive CFP was finally agreed in January

46

1983. A common shipping policy has also been developed gradually, from the mid-70s until 1986. A few problems remain in respect to shipping. Some member countries still reserve coastal traffic for their own flag vessels (known as cabotage). Strictly speaking this is against the concept of non-discrimination between nationals of different member states within the Community, which is one of the central ideas of the EC. More timidly, elements of a common marine pollution policy have also developed since the early 1970s. However, environmental policy remains very much a shared responsibility between the EC and its member states.

THE LOGIC OF INTEGRATION VERSUS STATIST GOALS
AND DOMESTIC POLITICS

Efforts among political scientists to understand and explain the process of European integration coincided with the origins of the process itself in the 1950s. Ernst Haas analyzed the ECSC in The Uniting of Europe (1958).[1] His major contribution was the concept of spill-over, the idea that once supranational cooperation begins in one area it perforce gradually extends to other areas. He borrowed from earlier functionalists, especially David Mitrany, who had argued that international cooperation should start in technical, non-controversial areas and then gradually expand to create a sense of international community thus in a way undermining national sovereignty.[2] But whereas early functionalists had believed that traditional intergovernmental cooperation would be sufficient, the neofunctionalists, like Haas, and the founding fathers of the EC, such as Jean Monnet, saw the creation of common supranational institutions as important. The aim of neofunctionalism clearly was to transcend the nation-state.[3] A common independent institution, like the Commission, would contribute actively to the process of integration by helping to form the necessary political coalitions.

Neofunctionalists of the 1950s were rather optimistic. They saw integration, once started, as a fairly automatic process. But when the process

47

ran into problems in the 1960s, partly because of General de Gaulle's European policies, some political scientists took a second critical look at the process and the early theories. Especially Leon Lindberg and Stuart Scheingold reformulated neofunctionalist integration theory to take account of political leadership -- or lack of same.[4] They made the theory more voluntaristic. They analyzed the European Community as a political system where demands and leadership are important inputs.

Inputs of demands, support, and leadership are transformed by the system to outputs in the form of decisions and actions, which in turn influence future inputs through a feed-back process. Lindberg and Scheingold had borrowed the systems concept from David Easton,[5] but added leadership among inputs to arrive at a dynamic analysis of the EC. Supranational leadership can be provided by the Commission, and national leadership can be provided by national governments. The authors mentioned four mechanisms as important in a process of integration:

(1) <u>Functional</u> <u>spill-over</u>. Such spill-over takes place because "tasks are functionally related to one another." Especially the economy is seen as a "seamless web." "Governments may be forced from one level of accommodation to another."[6] To do A you sometimes have to do B.

(2) <u>Log-rolling</u> <u>and</u> <u>side-payments</u>. These are bargaining exchanges designed to "gain the assent of more political actors to a particular proposal or package of proposals."[7]

(3) <u>Actor</u> <u>socialization</u>. This is the process whereby the "participants in the policy-making process, from interest groups to bureaucrats and statesmen, begin to develop new perspectives, loyalties, and identifications as a result of their mutual interactions."[8]

(4) <u>Feedback</u>. The term mainly refers to the impact of outputs on the attitudes and behavior of the public at large. If the public finds the output from the system good and relevant, support for the system will increase.[9]

These mechanisms have some explanatory power in respect to EC marine policies. However, external challenges have played a major role in the development of what could be called the Blue Europe. To understand the development of common marine policies within the EC, therefore, it is also necessary to see the EC as a component in a wider international system with a certain degree of interdependence.[10]

But, if there is such a thing as a logic of integration, there is also a logic of diversity which sets limits on integration.[11] The marine geographic situations of the EC member countries vary tremendously. Some of them, such as the UK and Eire, have long coasts and broad continental shelves. Others are geographically disadvantaged, Luxembourg even being land-locked. Some, including Denmark, have well-developed fishing industries, others not. Some have -- or had -- large merchant fleets, others not. Concepts of the national interest, therefore, have sometimes conflicted with the concept of a European interest.[12] To this should be added the role of domestic politics. Parliaments can force governments to take positions which they do not necessarily consider to be in the national interest. Small groups of fishermen have occasionally played large roles in domestic and Community politics. In tightly fought elections their votes can be important.[13]

THE COMMON FISHERIES POLICY

The Treaty of Rome, which established the EEC, included fisheries as part of agriculture for which a common policy was prescribed. But it was only in 1970 that a common fisheries policy was adopted. It happened on the eve of enlargement negotiations with Denmark, Eire, Norway, and the United Kingdom, four countries which could all bring large waters to the EC. What the six original members of the EC did in 1970 was to establish the principle of equal conditions of access to the maritime waters of the member states as well as a free market for fishery products within the EC.[14]

The principle of equal conditions of access applied to territorial seas and national fishing zones, if they existed. Three-mile territorial seas were still predominant, but the 1964 London Fisheries Convention had accepted a 6-mile

49

exclusive national fishing zone plus an adjacent 6-mile zone in which the coastal state could regulate fishing while respecting historic fishing rights. But even then the maritime waters falling under national sovereignty or jurisdiction still constituted a rather narrow belt. The 1970 CFP, incidentally, did include a 5-year transition period in which the members states could reserve a 3-mile zone exclusively for the local fishermen.[15]

The 1970 CFP became an issue in enlargement negotiations, 1970-72, especially in Norway, where fishermen increasingly called for a wider national fishing zone in which they did not want to give access to other Western European fishermen. The result of the enlargement negotiations, found in the Treaty of Accession, established a 10-year transition period in which the member countries could reserve fishing for their own fishermen within a 6-mile zone. For areas where the local population is especially dependent on fishing, including much of Norway's coast, a 12-mile national zone was permitted during the transition period. Norwegian fishermen didn't find this satisfactory. Their negative vote in the referendum about EC membership in 1972 contributed to the Norwegian decision not to join the EC.[16]

After the three applicants joined the EC from 1 January 1973, international fisheries policy developed quickly. Iceland already had established a 50-mile fishing zone in 1972. As in 1958, when Iceland had unilaterally moved from four to 12 miles, it provoked a 'cod war' with the United Kingdom. But when the first negotiating text from the Third UN Conference on the Law of the Sea (UNCLOS III) appeared in the summer of 1975, it included the concept of a 188-mile exclusive economic zone beyond a 12-mile territorial sea. Many EC countries originally opposed this idea at the Conference, but Iceland then quickly introduced a 200-mile fishing zone on 15 October 1975. More importantly, the United States decided early in 1976 to introduce such a zone from 1977. Canada and Norway followed quickly.

The EC countries now faced an external challenge. In May 1976 the British government decided for common EC action. This was an important decision, since the British government had so far been strongly status quo oriented. If distant water fleets increasingly were excluded from Icelandic, Norwegian, Canadian and US waters, then some of these might turn to the North Sea and other EC waters. By taking action in common the EC countries could gain bargaining power with non-members, including distant-water countries like the Soviet Union. Common action would also make it possible to link questions of future access to other countries' fishing zones with the access of these countries to the EC common market. In other words, there was a spill-over effect from the customs union which forms a central part of the EC.

Eventually even the Federal Republic of Germany, which, as a geographically disadvantaged state, had been most strongly against the 200-mile fishing zone, decided for common action within the EC. On 3 November 1976 the Council formally adopted what has become known as the Hague Compromise. The EC member countries would introduce 200-mile fishing zones in the North Sea and the Atlantic from 1 January 1977. The Commission was given a mandate to negotiate fisheries agreements with so-called Third Countries. The compromise also included promises to Eire that it would receive financial and other help to develop its fisheries.[17] Clearly, log-rolling played its part. During the negotiations, the member of the Commission in charge, Finn Gundelach, worked actively to put the package together, so there was also an element of supranational leadership.

After the decision to introduce the 200-mile fishing zone, the EC still faced the problem of developing a management policy for the new common waters. It was decided in principle to establish Total Allowable Catches (TACs) for the most important species and divide the TACs into national quotas. But with increased pressure on the resources and overcapitalization in the fishing industry, this turned out to be extremely difficult in practice.

An internal EC battle for access and larger quotas resulted. The British and Irish started by demanding a national zone of up to 50 miles within the 200-mile zone. The Commission was willing to

51

accept a national 12-mile zone within the 200 miles. However, especially the French wanted to be able to continue to fish up to 6 miles from the English coast as they had been able to do under the 1964 London Fisheries Convention. The Commission tried to gain British and Irish acceptance of its proposal by offering larger quotas and a licensing system whereby larger vessels could be kept out of some coastal areas. This got the Irish to accept the Commission proposals at an informal meeting of the Council in Berlin in January 1978, but the British remained intransigent. If the EC waters were divided into national zones, about 60% would become British. The UK government, therefore, did not find the 25-30% of the TACs offered by the Commission to be sufficient.[18]

Fisheries had become politicized in the UK during the so-called renegotiation of membership of the EC in 1974-75. The 18 most important fishing towns in the UK at the time had 22 parliamentary seats, many of which were tightly contested in elections. Perceived weaknesses of the government could easily be exploited by the opposition. This situation set limits on what the government could accept.[19]

Only after the election of the Thatcher government in 1979 did the negotiations start moving. Eventually the UK accepted the Commission's quota proposals, and the French access problem within the 6-to-12-mile zone off the UK coasts was also solved. Suddenly in 1982 Denmark was the only country having problems with the Commission's proposals. Again domestic politics played a role.

Danish governments must have their EC policies accepted by a powerful commission in the national parliament, the Market Committee. Towards the end of 1982 Denmark had a minority coalition government of four center-right parties, including the Liberal party. The chairman of the Market Commission, a member of the Liberal party, also happened to be chairman of one of Denmark's two associations of fishermen. At the same time, the Social Democratic opposition was not eager to help the government. Gradually the EC Commission offered slight improvements in the Danish quotas, and eventually the government was able to get an agreement with the Social Democrats that assured parliamentary acceptance of the Commission proposals in January 1983. A rough estimate of the national quotas for the most important species was: Belgium 2%, Denmark 24.5%, the Federal Republic of Germany and France each about 13%, Eire 4.5%, the Netherlands 7%, and the United Kingdom 36%. These quotas did not deviate significantly from the average catches during the 1973-78 reference period. Only Eire improved its share -- as promised during the negotiations. The Federal Republic took the largest loss.[20]

THE COMMON SHIPPING POLICY

Article 84(2) of the Treaty of Rome stipulates that the Council, by a unanimous vote, can decide to introduce measures for sea transport. But at the time of the first enlargement in 1973 nothing had happened in that respect.[21]

In 1974 the EC Court, the European Court of Justice in Luxembourg, decided that the general principles of the Treaty of Rome apply to shipping. These include free movement of labor, capital and services. But it took external challenges before the EC started developing a genuine shipping policy.

It was the competition from Eastern European socialist countries in the international shipping market which got the EC to introduce a consultation procedure in 1977. This was the first application of article 84(2). The state-owned commercial fleets of the COMECON countries were offering rates which EC shipowners considered unfair. The EC might have to consider countermeasures, so that again common action could give more bargaining power.[22]

There was another external challenge. The developing countries were fighting for a greater share of international shipping. In 1974 they succeeded in getting a Code of Conduct for Liner Conferences adopted by the UN Conference on Trade and Development (UNCTAD). It proposed, inter alia, to divide the cargo according to the formula: 40% to the exporting country, 40% to the importing country, and 20% to third countries, so-called cross-traders. This, it was thought, would assure developing countries of at least 40% of their exports for their own shipping industries.

Originally the EC countries had rather different attitudes to the UNCTAD Code. Belgium, the Federal Republic of Germany, and France had voted for it. Italy and the Netherlands had abstained. Denmark and the United Kingdom, which have both traditionally engaged a lot in cross-trade, voted against. Since this happened just after the decision by the Court that the general principles of the Treaty of Rome apply to shipping, the Commission could legitimately exercise supranational leadership. It insisted that consultations should take place in view of establishing a common attitude to the Code among the EC countries. After four years of difficult negotiations, it was agreed in the so-called Brussels package that the EC countries must ratify the Code, but with certain reservations. The cargo-sharing formula should not be applied among developed countries, and EC shares of north-south trade should be divided commercially between EC shipping companies.[23]

A special problem faced in connection with the development of an EC shipping policy was the question of the application of the competition rules of the Treaty of Rome. Liner conferences are a special problem because they are agreements between companies that do limit competition. After long negotiations the Council finally agreed on four regulations in December 1986. These include the following measures:

(1) Freedom to provide services. The EC countries must gradually abolish all restrictions in shipping. Restrictions have to be abolished by 31 December 1989 for trade between EC countries. For trade between EC countries and third countries on EC member state flag vessels the restrictions must be abolished by 31 December 1991, and for third country flag vessels by 1 January 1993. (Cabotage, as mentioned earlier, is not yet covered).

(2) Application of Articles 85 and 86 of the Treaty of Rome to maritime transport. The EC competition rules, which endeavour to promote competition between firms, will, with various

exceptions, be applied to shipping in the future. The major exemption is liner conferences, but certain conditions and obligations are attached to the exemption. For instance, liner conferences cannot apply rates and conditions of carriage which are differentiated solely by reference to the country of origin or destination of the goods carried.

(3) Redressive action against unfair pricing practices. The EC will be able to introduce anti-dumping measures against shipowners from third countries conducting unfair rate policies. This includes the state-owned Eastern European commercial fleets.

(4) Coordinated action to safeguard free access to cargoes in ocean trades. The EC will be able to introduce countermeasures against third countries engaging in various forms of flag discrimination.[24]

The clear implication of points 3 and 4 is increased bargaining power for EC shipping vis-a-vis third countries. Again we see the importance of external challenges to European integration.

TOWARDS A COMMON MARINE ENVIRONMENTAL POLICY

The Treaty of Rome did not mention environmental problems until it was amended through the European Single Act in 1987. When the treaty was negotiated in the mid-50s the environment was not a political issue, but a meeting of EC heads of state and government in Paris in 1972 decided to put the environment on the EC agenda. The Council adopted the first environmental program in November 1973 and during the following years various recommendations and directives were adopted.[25]

In respect to land-based pollution the Commission took part in the Paris conference, 1973-74, which negotiated the Paris Convention for the Prevention of Marine Pollution arising from Land-Based Sources. In 1975 the EC as such became a party to the convention. The following year the Council adopted a directive on pollution caused by certain dangerous substances discharged into the aquatic environment of the Community. In 1976 the EC Commission took part in the Barcelona

Conference which adopted the Barcelona Convention for the Protection of the Mediterranean Sea. The EC has become a party to this convention as well as the 1980 Athens protocol dealing with land-based pollution of the Mediterranean.

The Barcelona Convention also has a protocol on dumping to which the EC has been a contracting party since 1977. But dumping is the environmental area where the EC has been least successful. Due to differing political perspectives among the member countries, the EC has not been able to accede to the London and Oslo conventions on dumping, both signed in 1972. Nor has the EC been able to accede to the Helsinki Convention on the Baltic Sea, which also covers dumping. And efforts to adopt an EC directive on dumping, first proposed by the Commission in 1976, have so far not been successful.[26]

Although oil pollution is not necessarily the most dangerous kind of marine pollution, it is the most visible one. This may partly explain why this is the area where most action has been taken internationally.[27] It was the blow-out on the Bravo drilling rig in the Norwegian Ekofisk field in April 1977 that compelled the EC to start thinking about pollution in connection with resource exploitation. Before that the Torrey Canyon disaster on the U.K. Cornish coast in 1967 had stimulated the North Sea states to conclude the Bonn Agreement in 1969 on cooperation in dealing with pollution of the North Sea by oil. It took another major disaster, the Amoco Cadiz disaster off Britanny in March 1978, before the EC finally took important decisions. On the proposal of President Valery Giscard d'Estaing of France, the EC summit (now called the European Council) in Copenhagen in April 1978 decided that the EC should make the prevention of marine pollution, especially by hydrocarbons, a major objective. The summit called for "swift implementation of existing international rules, in particular those regarding minimum standards for the operation of ships," and coordinated action by member states to assure "a satisfactory functioning of the system of compulsory shipping lanes" and "more effective control over vessels which do not meet the standards."[28]

In June 1978 the Council adopted an Action Programme on the control and reduction of pollution caused by oil and proposed various studies. The Council also adopted a recommendation to the member states to accelerate ratification of the 1973 Convention for the Prevention of Pollution from Ships (MARPOL) as amended by its 1978 protocol, the 1974 Safety of Life at Sea (SOLAS) Convention, and the ILO convention no. 147 of 1976 on Minimum Standards in Merchant Ships.[29]

In December 1978 the Council finally adopted the first two directives relevant for vessel-source pollution. One set minimum standards for tankers entering or leaving EC ports and the other dealt with pilotage in the North Sea and the English Channel.[30] In addition, the EC acceded to a new Bonn Agreement for the North Sea in 1983, now also covering other harmful substances than oil.

However, the most effective fight against substandard ships in West Europe today may well be via port state control, which now takes place on the basis of the Paris Memorandum of Understanding of 1982. The non-EC countries of Norway and Sweden are also parties.[31]

EC decisions in the marine environmental area have been limited to recommendations and directives. Directives set certain objectives and are addressed to member states, but it is up to the member states to decide how they will attain those objectives. Recommendations also permit member state discretion in implementation. Regulations are different in resembling laws in national legislation. They are also addressed to individuals and are directly applicable. As we saw earlier, a number of regulations have been adopted in the fisheries area and some in the shipping area. This contrast constitutes another reason why it has to be concluded that integration has gone further in those two areas than in the marine environmental area.

THE EC AT UNCLOS III

During the Third UN Conference on the Law of the Sea (UNCLOS III), 1973-82, the EC member states had regular meetings to try to coordinate their policies. But it was clear from the beginning that the EC countries viewed many law-of-the-sea problems in different ways. The Commission had proposed to the Council that the EC countries should present common positions at the conference. It was proposed that the EC should support a 12-mile territorial sea and an adjacent zone up to 200 miles where the coastal state should have certain rights of an economic character, but which should remain free for navigation. For the area outside national jurisdiction an international authority should be created to regulate deep seabed mining, but according to the Commission's proposal in 1974 that authority should not itself engage in deep seabed mining. The proposal also emphasized regional fisheries cooperation.[32] The Commission proposal was based on a conception of the EC as a developed and coastal community.

The Commission's effort to become the law-of-the-sea spokesman of a Community speaking with one voice failed. The member countries were of the view that most issues on the UNCLOS agenda were national, not community matters. Such EC matters were largely limited to fishing and to some extent environmental policy. Political matters not covered by the Treaty of Rome could of course be discussed within the EPC.[33] But the reality of the matter was that eight of the nine member countries presented national positions at the plenary of the Caracas session in 1974. (Land-locked Luxembourg did not).

Marine geography was clearly visible in sustaining national positions. The Federal Republic of Germany and the Benelux countries, which regard themselves as geographically disadvantaged in relation to access to marine resources, wanted to limit coastal state jurisdiction over coastal resources like oil and fish as much as possible. Coastal states like Denmark, Eire, France, and the United Kingdom found it easier to accept coastal state jurisdiction, at least over continental shelf resources. For Eire, which only had coastal fishing it was not difficult to accept the idea of a 200-mile exclusive fishing zone.

Both Denmark and the UK had special problems

in relation to fisheries. The United Kingdom still had important distant water fishing in the North Atlantic. Denmark's position was complicated by peculiarities involving Greenland and the Faroe Islands, which are parts of the Kingdom of Denmark.

Despite the different national interests, coordination did start at Caracas. But the EC proposal on fishing reached through this coordination did not get UK support, and the proposal reached on deep seabed mining did not get Eire's support. Most agreement among the EC countries existed in respect to freedom of navigation, the high seas, international straits, and settlement of disputes.

The EC member states had a special problem in respect to a law-of-the-sea convention. In areas where powers have been transferred to EC institutions, such as fisheries, the EC countries cannot on their own accept treaty obligations. These belong to the EC as such. For this reason the EC fought for a provision in the convention allowing the EC as such to accede. This battle succeeded, since the UN Convention on the Law of the Sea adopted in 1982 has an annex which makes it possible for international organizations which have competence in the areas covered by the convention to accede to it. This presupposes that a majority of the members of the organization accede to the convention, and that the organization specifies the areas where transfer of competence has taken place.

When the Convention was opened for signature in 1982 only five of the ten EC members signed it, namely Denmark, Eire, France, Greece, and the Netherlands. The deep seabed mining aspects of the convention made the other member countries hesitate. However, Belgium, Italy, and Luxembourg did decide to sign in 1984. Since the two countries which still withheld signature, the Federal Republic of Germany and the UK, did not oppose EC signature, the EC as such was able to sign the UN Convention on the Law of the Sea in December 1984. This was an important step towards making the EC a marine political actor.

A blue Europe thus has gradually emerged. But certain areas have not been touched by EC legislation or policy harmonization. The coordination of policy at UNCLOS III did not cover security or delimitation aspects. Differing national interests set certain limits.

The most important area where integration has remained very limited is that of continental shelf resources. The Treaty of Rome, which antedates the 1958 Convention on the Continental Shelf, does not mention the shelf.

A Commission memorandum in 1970 did conclude that the general principles of the Treaty of Rome apply to the continental shelf. These include the customs union, free movement of labor and capital, and non-discrimination on the basis of nationality. It is debatable whether the member states have always respected these principles regarding the continental shelf. It can be argued, for instance, that Labour governments in the UK in the 1970s discriminated in favour of the British National Oil Corporation (BNOC). Since the question of continental shelf resources became an issue during the British renegotiation in 1974-75, the Commission did not want to press the issue.[34]

In any event, it is clear that there is no common EC continental shelf today in the way there is a common EC fishing zone. The Commission does not play the key role in respect to offshore oil that it plays in respect to marine fishing. Moreover, the energy crisis strengthened national demands for security of supply of energy resources. The one big energy producer in the EC, the UK, wanted to remain in charge of its own offshore oil and natural gas resources.

CONCLUSIONS: MARINE FUNCTIONALISM AND MARINE FEDERALISM

Despite the limits of integration in some areas, especially in respect to offshore hydrocarbon resources, we have to conclude that a Blue Europe, a marine political EC, has emerged since 1970. The neofunctionalist theory mentioned at the outset can help us understand part of the process. Theoretically this is interesting because it questions the common view that European integration has stopped and that neofunctionalism was erroneous. This is far from the truth. The Blue Europe can partly be seen as a spill-over from the Common Agricultural Policy, the so-called Green Europe, and from the customs union. Coalition-making has played an important role, as envisaged by neofunctionalist theory. There was log-rolling, and there were side-payments. Various package deals constituted major steps forward, such as the Hague Compromise in respect to fishing in 1976, the Brussels Compromise in respect to the UNCTAD Liner Code in 1979, and the packages that put the Common Fisheries Policy in place in 1983 and the Common Shipping Policy in place in 1986.

However, we have also suggested early on that neofunctionalism cannot by itself explain everything. Time and again external challenges were of decisive importance. The 200-mile fishing zone was very much forced upon the EC, and in the shipping area it was Third World demands and COMECON competition that pushed the EC countries together. The aim of common policies has often been to gain bargaining power vis-a-vis the outside world. This is interesting, too, from a theoretical point of view, because such factors are mentioned as important in the origin of federal states by some authors.[35] A major EC difference from the classical federal states, like the United States and Switzerland, however, is the importance of the security motive in the origin of those states. Integration among modern welfare states with long histories is a slower and more difficult process, where 'low politics' seems to come before 'high politics.' Yet, some of the events that have made the EC move forward in the marine political area did take on aspects that resembled 'high politics.'

If we make a more static comparison between the EC and existing federal states like the United States, we notice great similarities in respect to fisheries. The federal or Community level is in both cases responsible for fisheries policy outside the territorial sea or some similar relatively narrow zone where the states remain responsible. The major difference exists in

61

respect to the continental shelf where the US shelf outside the territorial sea is regulated by the federal authorities while European shelves are regulated by the member states in the EC.

If we compare the actual policies chosen by the United States and the EC after the creation of 200-mile offshore zones, we will find some similarities but mainly differences. The regional councils that play an important role in fisheries management in the United States do not exist in the EC. Here TACs are proposed by the Commission in Brussels on the basis of scientific advice, and national quotas are proposed by the Commission on the basis of political criteria established between 1976 and 1983. The final decision is made by the Council of Fisheries Ministers, but a decision must be based on a Commission proposal. Fishermen lobby their national governments as well as the Commission. Since 1983 this process has worked better than predicted. The EC has been able to take unpopular decisions, for instance, cutting down on cod quotas in the North Sea when overfishing threatened. The role of an independent Commission, which has the right of initiative, has proven its value. Compared with the period before the CFP when North Sea states tried to manage the resources through a weak North East Atlantic Fisheries Commission (NEAFC), which, for instance, was unable to hinder the collapse of the herring stock, a giant step forward has been taken.[36] Since fishermen find it difficult to understand the need for regulations, the EC does not always get the credit it deserves in this respect.

In respect to offshore licensing there are also differences between the United States and Western Europe. The United States uses competitive bidding, which is supposed to maximize revenue. The UK, and most other European countries, have normally used discretionary licensing, which gives more political control.[37]

Clearly the European Community is not yet a federal state, if it ever will be. Nor is it a confederation. It is <u>sui generis</u>. It is an interesting experiment in regional cooperation. It is increasingly getting its own marine policies, among other common policies. And it has taken over certain powers from the member states in the marine political area. Those interested in the future of the seas must therefore include it in their studies.

NOTES

1. Ernst B. Haas, The Uniting of Europe (Stanford: Stanford University Press, 1958).
2. David Mitrany, A Working Peace System (Chicago: Quadrangle Books, 1966).
3. For a good overview of the theories, see Charles Pentland, International Theory and European Integration (London: Faber and Faber, 1973).
4. Leon N. Lindberg and Stuart A. Scheingold, Europe's Would-Be Polity: Patterns of Change in the European Community (Englewood-Cliffs: Prentice-Hall, 1970).
5. David Easton, A Systems Analysis of Political Life (New York: Wiley, 1965).
6. Lindberg and Scheingold, Europe's Would-Be Polity, p. 117.
7. Ibid., pp. 118-19.
8. Ibid., p. 119.
9. Ibid., p. 120.
10. R.J. Harrison, Europe in Question: Theories of Regional International Integration (London: Allen & Unwin, 1974), pp. 132-51. On international interdependence, see also Robert O. Keohane and Joseph S. Nye, Power and Interdependence (Boston: Little, Brown, 1977).
11. Stanley Hoffmann, "Obstinate or Obsolete? The Fate of the Nation-State and the Case of Western Europe," Daedalus, vol. 95 (1966), pp. 862-915.
12. On the idea of statist interests, see especially Stephen Krasner, Defending the National Interest (Princeton: Princeton University Press, 1978).
13. Donald J. Puchala, "Domestic Politics and Regional Harmonization in the European Communities," World Politics, vol. 27 (1974-75), pp. 496-520. See also James N. Rosenau (ed.), Domestic Sources of Foreign Policy (New York: The

Free Press, 1967).

14. Yves van der Mensbrugghe, "The Common Market Fisheries Policy and the Law of the Sea," Netherlands Yearbook of International Law, vol. 6 (1975), pp. 199-228.

15. See also Rosemarie Allen, "Fishing for a Common Policy," Journal of Common Market Studies, vol. 19 (December 1980), pp. 123-39.

16. Angelika Volle and William Wallace, "How Common a Fisheries Policy," World Today, vol. 33 (February 1977), pp. 62-72.

17. EC Bulletin, No. 10 (1976), pt. 1501-1505.

18. Evelyne Peyroux, "Les difficultes actuelle de la politique commune des peches," Revue trimestrielle de droit europeen, vol. 15 (1979), pp. 269-289.

19. Allen, "Fishing for a Common Policy," p. 136.

20. Michael Leigh, European Integration and the Common Fisheries Policy (London: Croom Helm, 1983), pp. 88-99.

21. Daniele Rizzi, "The EEC Treaty and the Merchant Fleets of the Member States," Marine Policy, vol. 2 (October 1978), pp. 268-74.

22. Anna E. Bredimas, "The Common Shipping Policy of the EEC," Common Market Law Review, vol. 18 (February 1981), pp. 9-32.

23. A.D. Couper, "Shipping Policies of the EEC," Maritime Policy and Management, vol. 4 (1977), pp. 129-39; and Anna E. Bredimas and John G. Tzoannos, "In Search of a Common Shipping Policy for the E.C.," Journal of Common Market Studies, vol. 20 (1981), pp. 95-114.

24. Official Journal of the European Communities, No. L 378 (31 December 1986).

25. Stanley P. Johnson, The Pollution Control Policy of the European Communities (London: Graham & Trotman, 1983).

26. Jonathan Side, "The European Community and Dumping at Sea," Marine Pollution Bulletin, vol. 17, No. 7 (1986), pp. 290-94.

27. Jesper Grolin, "The Politics of International Marine Pollution Control," Occasional Papers, vol. 2 (1985), Institute for Global Policy Studies, Amsterdam. Also see Chapter 2 of this volume.

28. EC Bulletin, No. 44 (1978), pp. 21-22.

29. EC Bulletin, No. 5 (1978), pp. 42-43; EC Bulletin, 6-1978, pp. 45-46.

30. Henri-G. Nagelmackers, "Aftermath of the Amoco Cadiz: Why must the European Community Act?" Marine Policy, vol. 4 (January 1980), pp. 3-18.

31. "A Move against Substandard Shipping," Marine Policy, vol. 6 (October 1982), pp. 326-30.

32. EC Commission, Dritte Seerechtskonferenz, Mitteilung der Kommission an den Rat, SEK (74) 862 endg., Brussels, 20 March, 1974.

33. Tullio Treves, "La Comunita Economica Europea e la Conferenza sul Diritto del Mare," Revista di Diritto Internazionale, vol. 59 (1976), pp. 445-67.

34. Alain Wenger, "La C.E.E. et le plateau continental," Revue du Marche commun, vol. 12 (1975), pp. 7-26.

35. Finn Laursen, "Etudes federalistes aux Etats-Unis," L'Europe en formation, No. 190-92 (January-March 1976), pp. 181-99.

36. D.J. Driscoll and N. McKellar, "The Changing Regime of North Sea Fisheries," in C.M. Mason (ed.), The Effective Management of Resources: The International Politics of the North Sea (London: Frances Pinter, 1979), pp. 125-67.

37. Kenneth W. Dam, Oil Resources: Who Gets What How? (Chicago: The University of Chicago Press, 1976); and Oeystein Noreng, The Oil Industry and Government Strategy in the North Sea (London: Croom Helm, 1980).

PART 2

Developing States' Perspectives

4

Stages in the Development
of Third World Marine Policies

Michael A. Morris

INTRODUCTION

Certain broad characteristics of the historical evolution of the Third World presence at sea help distinguish marine policies, North and South. Until recent years, development of Third World marine policies was largely neglected. Many Third World states now have enhanced appreciation of the importance of the seas, but numerous policy problems loom ahead.

On the basis of these and other overall similarities, the evolution of Third World marine policies may be divided roughly into three stages or periods. While the three stages overlap in part, they are generally quite distinct and in considerable measure are logically and organically consecutive.

STAGE ONE: PROMOTION OF A NEW OCEAN ORDER

The roots of contemporary Third World marine policies lie in the early postwar period. Some Third World states can trace the origins of national marine policy back to the nineteenth century, especially in Latin America where political independence was achieved at a relatively early date. However, even for them, the formative stage of contemporary marine policy was in the years immediately following World War II.   During the early part of the postwar era, a growing number of developing countries became concerned with establishing a new, global legal

69

framework for marine policy more compatible with Third World needs. A first stage in the evolution of Third World marine policies primarily involved promotion of this kind of new ocean order. A new ocean order was achieved in a second stage and is now being implemented in a third stage.

The first stage began shortly after the end of World War II and continued to the late 1960s-early 1970s. Latin American states, which had gained political independence at a relatively early date and had established at least a tentative presence at sea, played the predominant role in this phase. In the late 1940s and early 1950s, Chile, Ecuador and Peru (the CEP states) made the first 200-mile claims off the west coast of South America.

Unregulated foreign exploitation of rich fisheries resources spurred the CEP states to try to bring hitherto international waters off their shores under national control. Seizures of foreign fishing vessels resulted, but enforcement was not effective. Meagre local naval capabilities made it imperative that political and legal channels, rather than military ones, be emphasized to promote policy change.

Sustained CEP efforts were made to generate opposition to the established freedom-of-the-seas legal doctrine supported by the maritime powers. This CEP politico-legal strategy for change emphasized recruitment of additional Third World allies for the alternative 200-mile doctrine. At first, other South American states were targeted in the name of Latin American solidarity. Images of abundant offshore resources exploited rapaciously by the maritime powers were evoked to mobilize coastal state opposition to the freedom-of-the-seas doctrine. Growing strains in US-Latin American relations also made regional states more susceptible to change.

Latin American practice began to encroach on the traditional freedom-of-the-seas doctrine in other ways. Many Latin American states had replicated the 1945 US continental shelf proclamation, and a few went well beyond the US measure in extending state prerogatives to waters superjacent to the shelf. Argentina's so-called epicontinental sea was a case in point.

70

The Third World campaign for expanded national ocean zones or "national enclosure" was rocky and protracted. The CEP states largely stood alone in advocating 200-mile offshore limits at the 1958 and 1960 First and Second United Nations Conferences on the Law of the Sea (UNCLOS I and II). Even as late as UNCLOS II, many Latin American states echoed the freedom-of-the-seas doctrine favored by the maritime powers.

Differences in Latin American marine interests and positions contributed to the protracted delay in forging regional unity. While Ecuador and Peru experienced recurring clashes with the United States over offshore fishing rights, other Latin American states were neither faced with such pressing bilateral maritime differences nor were they as willing to risk confrontation over legal principle.

Over the years an increasing number of Latin American states did come to adhere to one version or another of the 200-mile doctrine. Most South American states joined the 200-mile movement during the 1960s through supporting national legislation as well as joint declarations at regional law-of-the-sea conferences and meetings (i.e., Montevideo and Lima conferences). The 1970 Santo Domingo conference and resulting law-of-the-sea declaration added many Caribbean basin states to the growing 200-mile movement.

However, Caribbean basin states were generally inclined toward a more qualified assertion of coastal state powers 200 miles offshore (a patrimonial sea) than were South American states (a territorial sea or some version thereof). That is, a patrimonial sea limits coastal state control out to 200 miles to jurisdiction over resources and related matters (most Caribbean basin states), while a 200-mile territorial sea asserts sovereignty for all purposes far offshore (most South American states to one degree or another). While there was a broad contrast between Caribbean basin and South American states along patrimonialist and territorialist lines, there were dissidents within each group. Regional divisions were evident in still other ways. Landlocked states in South America (Bolivia and Paraguay) emphasized their

71

rights in adjoining seas and some Caribbean states favored a matrimonial sea, which would have involved sharing of offshore resources among all states bordering the Caribbean basin.

Many Third World states only gained political independence from the 1960s, so that they did not participate in either UNCLOS I in 1958 or UNCLOS II in 1960. Colonial rule for still others continued until the 1970s or 1980s. Marine policy was generally neglected in the first years of political independence and often much longer. Domestic disorder and other pressing land-based issues often threatened national survival in the early years of political independence and required priority attention before new ocean vistas could be systematically explored and developed. Technical constraints further impeded development of an integrated, multifaceted marine policy.

Several factors aggravated North-South confrontation during the first stage. The ability of developed states to invoke and enforce existing law in support of their own national interests fuelled resentment of Third World states, which in many cases had only recently been emancipated from their colonial masters. In response, Third World nationalism increasingly tended to regard extended offshore areas as part of the national patrimony. The lack of Third World means to protect the claimed offshore patrimony from alleged foreign predators often seemed to lead to a compensating crescendo of nationalistic rhetoric.

While offshore disputes often tended to polarize along North-South lines, Third World nationalism was easily deflected toward neighbors as well. Increasing Third World awareness and sensitivity about extended offshore areas tended to give rise to or aggravate already existing marine disputes with neighbors.

STAGE TWO: ACHIEVEMENT OF A NEW OCEAN ORDER

The deliberations of the UN Seabed Committee, 1967-1973, may be considered as a bridge between the first and second periods. On the one hand, Third World states made a sustained effort to promote a new law of the sea through the Seabed Committee discussions (first period). At the same time, the discussions constituted a decisive step toward eventual achievement of the new ocean order (second period). These discussions were originally to have been limited to the deep seabed issue and not to have been the prelude to a new law-of-the-sea conference. Third World states pressured successfully to broaden the agenda and membership of the Committee, and thereby were able to use it as a launching pad for a new conference for revising all of the law of the sea.

The second stage, encompassing the period of achievement of the new law of the sea, roughly coincides with the Third United Nations Conference on the Law of the Sea (UNCLOS III), 1973-1982. A global consensus on national enclosure emerged in principle early in the conference, although North-South negotiations and trade-offs about specific rights and responsibilities in extended ocean zones continued over the next decade. The de facto agreement early in UNCLOS III on the broad nature of revised rules about an important part of the law of the sea marks the commencement of the second stage.

Over the decade from 1973 to the 1982 treaty, the new rules about expanded national ocean zones gained legal stature through absorption into customary international law. The 1982 law-of-the-sea Convention further reinforced the legal standing of the major Third-World goals of national enclosure, especially a 12-mile territorial sea, a 188-mile exclusive economic zone (EEZ), and an expansively defined continental shelf. Inclusion of these Third-World sponsored planks in the 1982 Convention marks the end of the second stage.

The decade-long negotiating process helped reshape marine relations between and among countries of both the North and South. For example, protracted UNCLOS III negotiations helped specify and reinforce the consensus among Third World coastal states about the fundamentals of national enclosure. Concessions on all sides tended to sublimate the differences between Third World patrimonialists and territorialists, and bring more Third World states and regions into a comprehensive law-of-the-sea consensus. The Latin American consensus built up first and encouraged

73

and became associated with a counterpart African consensus. Asian states gradually aligned with the emerging Afro-Latin American law-of-the-sea consensus.[1]

UNCLOS III also played a key role in enhancing Third World awareness of the importance of ocean management and hence of marine policy. Reform of the international law of the sea through national enclosure, it was increasingly recognized, could complement national policy aims for offshore development and security.

In a sense, achievement of the UNCLOS Convention in 1982 vindicated Third World nationalism. Third World nationalism had helped push the North into a compromise with the South about national enclosure as expressed through the 1982 Convention.

At the same time, important interests within the North eventually began to lobby for national enclosure, while Third World nationalism evoked counterproductive northern responses. While national enclosure was of Third World origin and complemented many Third World aims, developed states made concomitant gains.

Since expanded national ocean zones benefited both groups of states, a detailed global consensus about national enclosure eventually was able to emerge during UNCLOS III. Even nonsignatories to the 1982 treaty such as the United States accepted the legitimacy of its national enclosure provisions, since US objections focused on UNCLOS deep seabed provisions.

UNCLOS III was only a qualified success for the South. North-South polarization over the deep seabed issue continued during and after UNCLOS, and tended to poison the broader political climate for North-South marine relations. North-South views even continue to diverge on a series of national enclosure issues. The North has tended to regard the EEZ as high seas and hence free for military activities by all, while Third World countries have tended to define coastal state EEZ powers expansively. Similar North-South splits over national enclosure issues, all with military implications, include the permissible scope of foreign state passage rights through straits, archipelagos and territorial seas.[2] Within the

74

South, UNCLOS rules for maritime boundary delineation did not resolve many disputes. In sum, some important North-South problems remain unresolved, intra-South problems continue, and new challenges are emerging for individual Third World marine policies.

STAGE THREE: POLICY IMPLEMENTATION AND INTEGRATION

A third stage involves the implementation and integration of Third World marine policies. While in some respects this phase overlaps the previous two phases, the thrust of the first and second stages is politico-legal in nature while the final stage is primarily technical in orientation. With the culmination of UNCLOS in the 1982 law-of-the-sea Convention, Third World politico-legal marine goals were achieved to a considerable extent. In the new, post-UNCLOS ocean setting, technical challenges of implementing Third World marine policies are more prominent.

The impact of the first and second stages on the third one has both positive and negative aspects. The Third World effort to use the Seabed Committee and UNCLOS III to promote shared objectives was largely successful, with the major exception of the deep seabed. This did help establish a global legal framework compatible with subsequent national marine policy development of relatively weak states. However, longstanding Third World politico-legal emphasis on the marine front tended to defer the hard, largely technical task of developing and implementing multi-pronged, integrated national marine policies. The prominent role played by lawyers and diplomats in international fora during the early stages of development of many Third World marine policies may have been necessary in the historical context, but this tended to divert much talent and attention away from concrete measures required at the national level to develop and protect offshore resources.

Uncertainty about whether ambitious national enclosure goals would be consolidated in law also tended to blunt and deflect incentives for committing scarce national resources to marine policy. While protracted law-of-the-sea negotiations did help alert many Third World states to the importance of benefiting from ocean resources through national marine policies, the complexity and uncertainty of the negotiations tended to defer implementation of these policies.

Deferral was especially marked in the case of Antarctica, since this issue was consciously excluded from UNCLOS III. Third World policy fragmentation and neglect tended to result. There was little Third World interest in Antarctica during the UNCLOS negotiations except for Argentina and Chile, which under the aegis of the Antarctic Treaty sustained territorial claims to overlapping Antarctic sectors. In recent years some additional Third World states have acceded to the Antarctic Treaty. Still other Third World states began pressuring in the 1980s for greater participation in Antarctic affairs through an international common heritage regime resembling that provided for the deep seabed in the UNCLOS Convention.

Military issues were largely excluded from the UNCLOS negotiations and will certainly pose sticky North-South problems as the implementation stage of Third World marine policies gains momentum. Straits are a case in point. In a basic UNCLOS trade-off, the maritime powers insisted successfully at an early date in the negotiations that their acceptance of national enclosure would depend on treaty recognition of assured transit through straits. At the same time, many Third World straits states have favored greater coastal state control of straits. The post-UNCLOS setting remains fluid in this respect, especially since the United States insisted from an early date in the negotiations on navigational guarantees through straits but later did not sign the treaty. Critics of US policy argue that nonsignatories should not benefit from UNCLOS treaty rights, in which case implementation of the new UNCLOS straits regime could lead to constraints on US vessels.

Third World states which achieved political independence at relatively early dates, like more affluent or advanced Third World states, enjoyed certain advantages. They have had the greatest

76

opportunity to address some of the technical challenges required for marine policy implementation and integration. However, even in these relatively favored cases, effective marine policy implementation has only occurred in at most a few sectors. Overall results have been mixed, since numerous marine sectors were neglected until a fairly recent date.

Marine policy instead requires sustained, integrated technical efforts in multiple sectors. Such multifaceted Third World marine policies have only begun to emerge in some cases in the 1980s.

For example, Brazil is large, has been independent since the last century, and has generally been recognized as a Third World leader in overall industrialization as well as more specifically in marine affairs. However, concerted national efforts to develop a variety of marine sectors only date from the 1960s or later, and mixed results have required renewed commitment to specific sectors as well as to overall policy coordination and integration in recent years.[3] Other prominent Third World states, such as Argentina and India, have also made some notable progress in implementing individual marine policy sectors. However, sector-by-sector surveys of Argentine and Indian marine policy have concluded that sustained national interest in the sea only began late in the postwar period and that important shortcomings in policy implementation and integration remain.[4]

Less advanced Third World states have not yet moved meaningfully into the third implementation/integration stage of marine policy. An African diplomat who played a prominent role at UNCLOS recently acknowledged the general failure to develop and implement national marine policies in the region.

> Yet hardly any African country -- for that matter the OAU [Organization of African Unity] -- is doing anything to realize the immense resources potential of the seas around Africa, which are its economic zone. Apart from the various legislations establishing various national EEZs, there are hardly any regulations at national,

regional or continental level for the
exploration, exploitation or conservation
of the zone.[5]

North-South marine policy contrasts are still
only relative, not absolute. The ocean setting
poses similar challenges for all countries. Like
Third World states, developed states have faced
recurring problems in shaping effective marine
policies. The North-South contrast regarding
marine policy implementation and integration is
nonetheless stark. Developed states have long
recognized the need to commit sizable resources
and bring sophisticated technologies to bear on
multiple ocean sectors while forging a unified
policy, and their potential for meeting such a
complex challenge has been much greater than that
of Third World states.

Policy coordination among Third World
countries can help overcome obstacles. Third
World countries, in aspiring to mobilize the
oceans more effectively for national development
and to protect newly acquired offshore areas, do
have certain common ocean interests. These common
interests have been expressed especially through
the Third World Group of 77 at UNCLOS. To a
certain extent, Third World states have acted in
unison in other marine areas such as shipping.

However, as the thrust of Third World marine
policies has moved from promotion of legal
abstractions to implementation of specific
measures, new difficulties for coordination of
Third World marine policies have emerged. In
particular, it is easier to achieve and sustain
Third World unity over principles than details.
Lack of interest and diversity of Third World
interests make it much harder to forge unity
around specific policy measures.

The technical requirements of the third stage
for effective Third World marine policies are also
hard to mesh with the legacy of nationalism from
the first two stages. Nationalism has influenced
Third World marine policies throughout all three
stages, but is least well adapted to the third
stage. Nationalism has emphasized Third World
dependency under the old ocean order, and has long
portrayed achievement of a new ocean order as

tantamount with control of the offshore national patrimony. In fact, offshore dependency is likely to continue and even increase in many cases under the new order, since foreign expertise and assistance are needed in exploiting and protecting newly-acquired offshore zones. Continuing Third World offshore dependency may trigger new, unpredictable outbursts of nationalism. Moreover, UNCLOS did not resolve a host of North-South and intra-South marine disputes, which continue to feed nationalism at sea.

There are parallels to the above-mentioned Third World approaches to international negotiations and policy implementation in marine affairs. A study of North-South bargaining concluded that debates about the principle of individual commodity agreements rarely raised the question of implementation, in the belief that agreement in principle would solve all the practical difficulties.[6] While the ocean setting is distinctive, these parallels suggest that problems of Third World marine policies are deeply rooted in the structure of international affairs.

SUMMARY AND CONCLUSIONS

The pursuit and eventual achievement of a new ocean order -- the first and second stages in the development of Third World marine policy -- helped forge Third World unity around abstract yet fairly clear national enclosure concepts. Sustained, quite unified Third World efforts produced impressive political victories in these initial policy stages. In contrast, coordinated management of complicated technical matters in multiple marine sectors by a variety of highly qualified members of the national marine community is required in the third stage of policy implementation/integration. Each marine policy sector poses distinctive challenges, and even the largest, most advanced Third World states have been hard pressed to forge viable policies for individual sectors and integrate these sectors into an overall marine policy. Coordination among Third World states also tends to be more difficult in the third stage.

After the impressive achievements of stages

one and two, it would be tragic if national marine policies in the Third World failed to meet the specific, technical challenges of implementation and integration in the third stage. Long-standing nationalistic goals did help achieve de jure control of extended national ocean zones (stages one and two), but achievement of de facto control of these zones on the economic and military fronts will require more pragmatic policies (stage three). So while nationalism helped generate Third World unity in support of a new ocean order, it is ill-designed to guide policy implementation. The nationalist desire for decreased dependency nonetheless remains attractive, although ironically the most appropriate means to that end appears to be less emphasis on nationalism and more on meeting technical challenges.

While UNCLOS helped fan Third World nationalism especially with regard to the deep seabed, the protracted negotiating process promoted Third World pragmatism as well. Territorialists and patrimonialists compromised within the South, and much of the UNCLOS treaty hangs on North-South compromises. Where there was North-South confrontation over legal principle, there is now a significant area of North-South consensus about national enclosure. The UNCLOS experience with compromise across an array of marine issues should help Third World policy-makers meet the emerging challenges of policy implementation and integration. It remains to be seen whether the ideological or pragmatic skein of Third World marine policies will predominate.

NOTES

1. Michael A. Morris, Editor, special double-length issue of Ocean Development and International Law: The Journal of Marine Affairs on "Influence and Innovation in the Law of the Sea: Latin America and Africa," 7: 1-2 (1979) and also Editor of follow-up materials in Volume 9: 1-2 (1981).
2. Michael A. Morris, Expansion of Third-World Navies (London, England: The Macmillan Press, 1987 and New York: St. Martin's Press,

1987), especially Chapter 5, "Ocean Zone Characteristics and Conflicts."

3. Michael A. Morris, International Politics and the Sea: The Case of Brazil (Boulder, Colorado: Westview Press, 1979).

4. S.N. Kohli, Sea Power and the Indian Ocean: With Special Reference to India (New Delhi, India: Tata McGraw-Hill, 1978); and Carlos Noe Alberto Guevara, "Panorama general de los intereses maritimos," Revista de la Escuela de Guerra Naval, vol. 11 (Feb. 1979), pp. 55-84.

5. Frank X. Njenga, "Historical Background of the Evolution of the Exclusive Economic Zone and the Contribution of Africa," in Giulio Pontevorvo (ed.), The New Order of the Oceans: The Advent of a Managed Environment (New York: Columbia University Press, 1986), 147.

6. Robert L. Rothstein, Global Bargaining: UNCTAD and the Quest for a New International Economic Order (Princeton, New Jersey: Princeton University Press, 1979), pp. 18-19.

5

Third World Offshore Resource Management and Protection

Michael A. Morris and Robert S. Pomeroy

INTRODUCTION

General dilemmas of security and development
faced by Third World states impinge on marine
policy, although the ocean setting does shape
these dilemmas in distinctive ways. Marine policy
encompasses a complex gamut of interrelated
sectors cutting across both development and
security, with different possibilities and
constraints in each sector. The distinctive
challenges of each sector need to be met and the
parts blended into a unified whole. Even
developed states experience many difficulties in
responding to these interrelated challenges. It
is all the more difficult for less advantaged
nations to muster sufficient expertise and
resources to shape viable approaches to both
offshore security and development.
Another recurring challenge for developing
countries involves sustaining an adequate balance
in marine affairs between costly and often
inefficient policies emphasizing self-sufficiency
and those which would lean too heavily on foreign
expertise. Even the maritime powers do not aspire
to autarky in ocean affairs. A prudent balance
will depend on the peculiarities of the particular
ocean sector as well as capabilities and resource
endowments of individual Third World states.
Third World marine policies tailored to specific
circumstances can do much to meet the interlocking
challenges of offshore development and security,
especially if a mutually productive relationship

with developed states can be fashioned.

THIRD WORLD OFFSHORE RESOURCE DEVELOPMENT

Until recent times, ocean politics and law reserved the world's oceans as open space. The number of ocean demands and uses were relatively few and uncomplicated in relation to the perceived endless supply of space and resources contained in the seas. It made no sense economically either to divide the oceans generally or to restrict access (except in a few, selected fishing grounds and a narrow band of "territorial sea" adjacent to coastlines).

The pressure of increasing population, technological advances for exploiting ocean resources, and heightened expections for national economic development throughout the world have led to greater demands being placed on the oceans. New ocean uses have emerged, such as deep sea mining, oil extraction from deeper areas and increasing volume of international shipping; as have new ocean disputes, such as conflicts in more extended offshore zones over fishing rights and marine pollution. There is also increasing competition for ocean resources among and between developed and developing countries. These demands and competition, when left unresolved, often result in economic externalities and displacement or destruction of certain highly valued activities, which can lead to economic inefficiency in resource use.

The open access nature of ocean resources and common property rights in their use are economically appropriate only if the bounty of the oceans is virtually limitless relative to demands, or if demands are static or growing only slowly. We have become aware that we no longer live in a time of abundance for many resources, and that resource scarcity even applies to the oceans.

The acknowledgement of ocean resource scarcity and the continuing search for food and mineral resources in the ocean to feed growing populations and growing economies have contributed to a redefinition of property rights of ocean uses. This redefiniton is away from common ownership to what can generally be considered to

84

be private property and an expansion of the concept of territoriality of ocean resources.

The first major private structure of property rights over ocean resources or "national enclosure" was initiated in 1945 when the United States asserted an exclusive right to control oil and gas and other minerals on or under the continental shelf near its coastline and to regulate fisheries well offshore for conservation purposes. Subsequently, the majority of the world's coastal nations have forwarded and established claims to fish, minerals, hydrocarbons and other resources usually within 200 miles of their coast. These enclosures are normally established with economics in mind, that is, most of the claims emphasize the resources of the ocean and only a handful claim ownership of the ocean itself or the right to restrict navigation.

This situation offers mixed prospects for Third World offshore resource development. On the one hand, the expanded ocean zones open new possibilities for boosting Third World development. Third World states championed 200-mile zones, which in some cases enclose substantial offshore resources. On the other hand, Third World marine policies generally have not effectively harnessed offshore resources. Consequently, most developing countries remain heavily dependent on the industrialized states for exploitation of these resources. Moreover, offshore resources are very unevenly distributed among Third World states, and developed states have gained the largest portion of newly enclosed 200-mile offshore areas.

The so-called new law of the sea can be of substantial assistance to Third World states in managing and protecting ocean resources, even though there is often continuing dependence on developed states. Offshore areas out to 200 miles are recognized by the 1982 law-of-the-sea Convention as belonging for resource purposes to coastal states, including those in the Third World. (The Third United Nations Conference on the Law of the Sea or UNCLOS III produced the Convention.) Legal recognition of expanded national ocean zones provides a firm foundation for supporting subsequent development of Third

World offshore areas, which in a number of cases are large and resource-rich. Without this new, legal imprimatur, the maritime powers would have been justified in continuing to exploit resources offshore Third World states without constraint through the freedom-of-the-seas doctrine.

THIRD WORLD OCEAN SECURITY AND RESOURCE PROTECTION

Enhanced Third World awareness of the promise of offshore resources brought with it more concerted efforts to provide for maritime defense. In the wake of consequential naval expansion, a few regional powers with powerful navies have emerged and a Third World naval hierarchy has begun to be discernible.[1] Potent, relatively inexpensive naval weaponry with bee-sting capabilities in constricted waters helps deter great power gunboat diplomacy and local aggressors as well as protect offshore resources.

However, naval expansion is capital-intensive and tends to be open-ended. Once naval expansion begins, it is difficult to avoid a pull toward successively more ambitious weaponry increments. For example, there is a pull from fast patrol boats toward corvettes and then on to frigates and submarines. Third World naval expansion also may stimulate counterpart expansion by a local rival, which can generate yet another round of weaponry growth.

The enclosure of offshore resources out to 200 miles propels a related drive to develop lower-level military capabilities for resource protection. Resource protection capabilities include coastal patrol craft, fast patrol craft, maritime patrol aircraft and helicopters. Such specialized vessels and aircraft are well designed for resource protection and, while not cheap, they can help economize on acquisition of much more expensive surface warships and/or submarines. At the same time, acquisition of modest capabilities for offshore protection may whet the coastal state appetite for more potent naval weaponry, and thereby help trigger national rivalries and/or expansive aims of territoriality.

Expansion of both naval power and offshore resource protection capabilities are often desired, but it is difficult for Third World states to respond adequately to both kinds of offshore security needs. More potent and expensive naval weaponry is generally given priority as resources permit. All too often the result does not enhance national security nor provide efficient offshore resource protection. The objective of self-sufficiency is not achieved either, since sophisticated naval weaponry as well as specialized equipment for offshore resource protection require imports from developed states.

For example, Brazil's navy has been ranked as one of the top three in the Third World, although the Brazilian navy has remained heavily dependent on foreign imports of sophisticated warships in spite of growing national naval production. Naval expansion plans have been successively cut back, while Brazilian capabilities for offshore resource protection have remained deficient.[2] Other leading Third World navies suffer from similar shortcomings, according to a recent study by one of the authors of this article. This study also identified 62 out of 104 Third World navies as "token navies" with no major warships or naval aviation and meagre resource protection capabilities.[3]

NEW CHALLENGES FOR THIRD WORLD MARINE POLICY IMPLEMENTATION

National enclosure can provide for better management and protection of Third World ocean resources. This may occur either by reducing the exploitation of the resource to manageable levels or by making a more careful assessment of the impacts of imcompatible uses. Enclosure allows the coastal nation to limit fishing effort when the survival of a species is threatened from a variety of users and to determine who will utilize the resource. Enclosure also allows the coastal nation to capture some of the previously foregone economic rent from the resource, such as that from foreign fishing fleets which had previously exploited the offshore fishery without restraint.

Implementation of policy in part involves designing a mechanism to promote more rational management and utilization of ocean resources. The implementation of marine policy is especially difficult due to the need to design a program to reconcile often conflicting objectives and priorities while competing against other economic sectors for limited public sector resources.

To meet the challenges of successfully implementing marine policy, several major requirements exist for a country:

1) a skilled bureaucracy with training in specialized marine areas and in policy analysis;

2) a scientific, technical and information gathering network;

3) an enforcement capability; and

4) the willingness to cooperate on ocean issues globally, regionally and bilaterally.[4]

These requirements are technical in nature and call for the establishment of new institutions or the overhaul of existing ones to fulfill the functions of ocean resource management and development. Several of these requirements will already exist in some Third World countries or can be easily fulfilled, while others will require more formalized government action and/or outside assistance.

As Third World countries act to organize or reorganize their institutions and fulfill the requirements for ocean resource management and development, they will have to make many choices related to the development of expertise, the type of administrative framework and the commitment of resources. Some countries, due to their size and past involvement in these areas, will be able to adjust their institutions effectively to meet the needs of the new marine policy. Others will need to develop expertise and/or rely on outside assistance, either through foreign expertise or multi- or bilateral cooperation, to manage and develop their ocean resources effectively. Each country will need to make decisions concerning whether expertise will be developed internally or whether and how much they will rely on outside assistance. These decisions will be influenced by the abilities of the citizenry and available financial resources. All of these ocean resource issues and requirements must be balanced in terms of competing demands from other sectors of the economy for limited resources.

While this paper does not propose to address all the issues of implementing a new marine policy directly, it is of interest to address some key aspects of the establishment and operation of the institutions and requirements of the new policy. Of specific interest are the prospects for self-reliance or outside assistance or some mix of both by Third World countries in establishing and operating these institutions and meeting the requirements of various marine sectors.

This autonomy-dependency continuum is likely to vary considerably by sector as well as by Third World country. Marine fisheries and hydrocarbons will be used to illustrate some opportunities and constraints along the continuum. As developing countries move to implement new ocean resource management and development regimes, there are a variety of ways in which states might organize themselves in creating institutions to deal with the functions of research, regulation, and enforcement.

SCIENTIFIC RESEARCH

This function includes conducting research, the collection and analysis of data and information, and the provision of such data and analyses to decision-makers for use in management and development of ocean resources.[5] Goals of this function include the development of sufficient data to make informed decisions; the acquisition of information in a timely, reliable, and acceptable manner so as to be effective; and the minimization of costs in acquisition and provision.

Historically, primary responsibility for the collection, analysis and provision of data for fishery management has rested with the coastal state. Limited coastal jurisdiction often allowed even smaller nations with limited resources to develop a minimal research function. With extended offshore jurisdiction, reliance solely on national means for adequate data is often not possible. Outside technical assistance in research has been provided to developing countries in a number of ways, such as sharing of research information, scholarships for advanced training of scientists, and programs for cooperative research efforts utilizing research scientists, vessels and equipment from developed countries. It is generally felt that this responsibility for providing decision-makers with information should continue to rest with the local fishery staff, although the actual conduct of research and collection and analysis of data may require outside technical assistance.

The increased size of coastal jurisdictions has made the task of providing information much more difficult. The greater diversity of information needs associated with the larger jurisdiction makes relatively few coastal developing nations, or developed nations, capable of undertaking the necessary research alone. Most nations are not capable of maintaining the necessary scientific personnel and specialized equipment to develop sufficient information. Different approaches to meet this more complicated research and information provision function are available.

Larger Third World countries, such as India, for example, may be able to restructure and enlarge their existing research capabilities to some extent. These countries have a relatively large pool of scientific expertise available to them through universities and research facilities that could be expanded with the commitment of additional financial resources. However, "Reliance on the coastal state alone would, in some circumstances, lead to failure to develop sufficient data for conservation, cause failures in the provision of timely data, result in diminished reliability, and, for these reasons, diminish the acceptability of the research results".[6] Unless there were an overriding necessity for a country to undertake an autonomous research effort, such as for national defense reasons or prestige, a large commitment of resources for this purpose would probably not make economic sense.

A number of different approaches seem to be emerging in terms of fishery research. Some nations are entering into bilateral or multilateral arrangements to provide mutual assistance in research. While maintaining national research capabilities, a bilateral arrangement allows a less developed nation not only to conduct more research at less expense but also to gain expertise and strengthen its own scientific personnel. For example, exploratory fishing of highly migratory species has been conducted off Chile through joint investigation by Chilean and Japanese researchers.

Some nations are working with international agencies to conduct research on specific fish stocks or on a particular geographic area. Through these arrangements the international agency either undertakes the research itself with approval of the coastal nation or coordinates the research effort of several coastal states. For example, the Food and Agriculture Organization (FAO) of the United Nations has established several regional bodies worldwide. These regional bodies include the Western Central Atlantic Fishery Commission (WECAFC) and its Committee for the Development and Management of Fisheries in the Lesser Antilles, the Fishery Committee for the Eastern Central Atlantic (CECAF) and the Indo-Pacific Fishery Commission (IPFC).

Another approach is that taken by the Asian Fisheries Social Science Research Network (AFSSRN) located at the International Center for Living Aquatic Resources Management (ICLARM) in Manila, Philippines. The Network is funded by the Ford Foundation and the International Development Research Centre (IDRC) of Canada. The Network was initiated in 1983 to support and assist the development of social science research for fisheries among the participating institutions in Southeast Asia.

Still another approach is to rely on outside expertise employed either directly by the host country or utilized through an international development agency or project, such as the U.S. Agency for International Development. In the Philippines, for example, a fishery information assessment and research program was conducted as part of a large-scale resources development initiative of the U.S. Agency for International Development. Fishery consultants collaborated with Philippine scientists in developing research capabilities.

Many countries will utilize a combination of two or more of these approaches, so that fishery research on enlarged coastal jurisdictions of developing countries will involve a balance of internal research and outside assistance. Smaller coastal states will probably rely more on outside assistance through bilateral arrangements, international regional agencies, or foreign expertise than larger coastal nations. There will still be continued reliance on foreign expertise and resources by most developing countries as they increase their capabilities. Research efforts will be coordinated by scientists in the developing country but with assistance from outside sources. Bilateral research efforts among developing nations and assistance from more scientifically-advanced developing nations will be attractive.

REGULATION

The function of regulation involves establishing control over the total fishing effort within the national fishery. The design of any fishery regulatory program is greatly aided by a clearly stated set of goals for that program. While the precise goals to be achieved will vary from location to location and over time, regulatory measures must aspire to conserve fish stocks throughout the geographic range of the fishery, be economically and socially efficient and equitable, be administratively feasible, be flexible in technique, and be politically acceptable.

The characteristics of the fishery will determine to a considerable extent the appropriate institutional structure and regulatory techniques to be employed. Most fisheries will probably be a mix of different types of fishery, for example, pelagics, tropical multi-species, sedentary species, highly migratory; and thus require the use of several regulatory techniques and possibly more than one institutional authority.

Most developing coastal states will establish their own regulatory mechanism with possible assistance from outside sources. These outside sources can be in the form of hired consultants or experts from international or regional fishery bodies. Regulatory authority will remain with the coastal state.

As an alternative to exclusive coastal state authority, some areas may utilize a regional or international body to manage the resource. A regional or international regulatory body could provide a basis for discussion and resolution of problems among coastal states. For those states having contracts with distant water fleets, the regional body could manage and negotiate contracts. One example of this approach was for tuna by the Inter-American Tropical Tuna Commission. Several Latin American countries participated in activities of this regulatory agency for management of this highly migratory species. The agency has since ceased operation due to an inability to resolve conflicts among member states. For the most part, efforts by regional or international regulatory agencies have not been successful due to conflicts among members and the fact that coastal states are not willing to relinquish authority to such a body.

As a compromise between sole coastal state regulatory authority and a regional or international regulatory body, bilateral or multilateral regulatory activities, with varying degrees of authority, show promise. These regulatory institutions would be managed by several developing countries and be flexible and timely in response to change. Thailand and Malaysia have recently developed such an arrangement to better regulate activities in their fishing zones.

ENFORCEMENT

The primary purpose of enforcement is to provide a credible deterrent to the violation of regulations or laws. The purpose of enforcement is not only to ensure compliance with regulations by nationals and foreigners, but also to prevent unauthorized foreign fishing. Enforcement can also serve to support research by providing information about fishing effort, catch and related matters.

There are four main methods of fishing regulation enforcement: air patrols, sea patrols, special observers on fishing vessels, and inspections in harbors. The type of enforcement method selected will depend on the resources available, the nature of the regulations, and the characteristic of the fishery. Effective regulation enforcement requires a surveillance force that has sufficient size and scope of operation to apprehend violators but does not require disproportionate expenditure of time and resources. An effective enforcement program must be fair in dealing with violators in all regions and all classes of vessels in the fishery.

Enforcement of fishery regulations poses sizable burdens, although coastal states no doubt will try to remain relatively autonomous in the physical task of surveillance because of sensitivity about possible foreign encroachments in offshore zones. Technical assistance still will be required from developed nations or more advanced developing nations in setting up the surveillance program. Assistance also will probably be required by many Third World states in obtaining aircraft and ships specially suited for surveillance purposes.

Again, bilateral or multilateral arrangements will probably see increasing use for enforcement. For example, it has been estimated that to enforce fisheries regulations in the Gulf of Thailand, at least 25 sophisticated patrol vessels would be needed.[8] In 1983 only six such vessels operated in the Gulf of Thailand, and none operated in the Andaman Sea. At the same time, the Royal Thai Navy escorts ships through Burmese waters to avoid incidents initiated by either country. Bilateral or multilateral enforcement, such as the arrangement initiated by Malaysia and Thailand, may be an appropriate means to lessen the amount of illegal fishing occurring in each state's fishery zone.

Global or regional fishery bodies will only serve a minimal role in enforcement, primarily making recommendations for regulatory action and providing technical assistance. No international enforcement body currently exists for fisheries and it appears unlikely that such a body will be acceptable in the near future. A regional enforcement body still might be feasible, since the technical and cost requirements of an enforcement program for extensive offshore zones are beyond the means of many developing countries. It has been estimated that a medium-sized system to protect these zones would cost approximately $1 million per mile of coastline.[9] If the political and administrative problems could be worked out, a shared global, cross-regional or regional enforcement system would appear to offer a sound alternative for many countries.

The Falkland Islands (Malvinas) illustrate the complicated enforcement dilemmas faced by a particular Third World state, Argentina, in the ongoing dispute with a great power, Great Britain. Britain imposed a 150-mile resource zone around the Falklands in 1986, and proceeded to license numerous foreign fishing vessels for the rich fishing grounds. Britain began to enforce the new fisheries regulations in early 1987, which in effect excluded all Argentine fishing craft as being unlicensed. In addition to Argentine concern about exclusion of its vessels, it is feared that proclamation and enforcement of the offshore resource zone reinforce British claims to sovereignty.

Prior to the 1982 Falklands war, Argentina had been particularly concerned about British exploratory efforts around the islands for oil and gas. In recent years, fisheries have emerged as a much more promising source of revenue with the potential to make a continuing British presence on the islands economically viable. Argentina is therefore loath for political and economic reasons to acquiesce to British enforcement of fisheries regulations in offshore zones. Intrusion of Argentine fishing vessels there with possible naval accompaniment could trigger a return to military hostilities.

FISHERY MANAGEMENT IN ST. KITTS/NEVIS, WEST INDIES

Fisheries problems of developing countries may be illustrated graphically in the case of a very small Third World state, St. Kitts/Nevis, West Indies. The small size of the island, the relatively recent date of national independence, and the very limited resources at the disposal of decision-makers all tend to magnify fisheries

95

problems found elsewhere. At the same time, fisheries problems of St. Kitts/Nevis resemble those of other small island-states of the eastern Caribbean. In light of formidable constraints, this mini-state has been responding with some success to national fisheries challenges.

The fishery of St. Kitts/Nevis is still artisanal in nature, with approximately 550 full- and part-time fishermen operating some 300 boats on the two islands. The boats are primarily modified wooden dinghies ranging in size between 12-30 feet in length. The boats are usually powered by outboard engines from 25-40 hp.

The majority of fishermen in both islands are engaged in trap and handline fishing. About 25 boats are used for seine fishing. Roughly 16 vessels specialize in lobster and conch fishing, usually with SCUBA equipment.

A regular fishery statistics program has not been implemented, but it is generally acknowledged that nearshore fishing grounds on leeward coasts of both islands are overexploited, particularly in the case of conch stocks. The windward and deepwater shelf areas, however, are presently underexploited along with migratory stocks and sharks. In addition, there are probably stocks of bivalve and cephalopod mollusks with potential for small-scale exploitation. Access to fishery resources on the outer part of the shelf and beyond are constrained by the small size of the vessels and lack of adequate equipment to exploit the resource. Previous deepwater fishing ventures by foreign nationals in St. Kitts' exclusive economic zone (EEZ) have proven to be successful and local fishermen (especially those on Nevis) have begun to acquire larger boats and equipment to target fishery resources on the outer shelf and beyond.

The Government Fisheries Division operates within the Ministry of Agriculture, Lands, Housing and Development. The staff consists of two Fisheries Assistants (one in St. Kitts and one in Nevis) and one Fisheries Trainee. Support is provided by a fisheries consultant. The division is responsible to the Chief Agricultural Officer. The division has responsibility for management, research, training, program development and enforcement activities related to fisheries.

The national plan of St. Kitts/Nevis includes a variety of fisheries-related activities. Incentives are given to fishermen by the government through duty-free importation of fishing equipment, including outboard engines; through loans for fishermen provided by the Development Bank of St. Kitts/Nevis and the Foundation for National Development; and revocation of annual licensing for boats.

The current fisheries programs established by the Fisheries Division center around five major areas of activity including development of underutilized resources, training and extension services, aquaculture, stock improvement and resource management. There are regulations specifically tailored to the protection of undersized species of fish, lobster, and turtles. Egg-bearing female lobsters are protected and a closed season for turtles exists. Despite these regulations, management of the resource remains a problem due to very limited financial and personnel resources and lack of cooperation by fishermen.

The lack of adequate and trained personnel coupled with a small budget represents the major constraint to fisheries development in St.Kitts/Nevis. The need for trained extension personnel is a particular problem for the small nation. Extension personnel can provide a critical link between development planners, technical personnel, and local fishermen. Since the fisheries staff is very small, when there are several projects operating simultaneously local staff become very thinly spread. It is not possible for the existing fisheries staff to perform all the functions and activities required of them and this exacerbates existing problems of fisheries development. It is doubtful, in the foreseeable future, that the fisheries budget will be increased to support the need for specialized personnel or fisheries research programs.

Management of the resource remains a continuing problem due to inefficient enforcement. Again, lack of personnel makes this task difficult. There is reportedly a great deal of stealing from fishtraps. Enforcement and

97

protection of the fishtraps falls on the
fishermen. One small patrol boat constitutes the
navy of St. Kitts/Nevis and it alone is inadequate
to patrol and enforce laws within the EEZ.

The development of a comprehensive set of
harmonized fisheries regulations for member
countries of the Organization of Eastern Caribbean
States (O.E.C.S.) was established to protect
against unauthorized foreign fishing and to
identify areas of co-operation among neighboring
countries. It has been recognized that areas of
co-operation would include the exchange of
information as some resources transcend boundaries
of member territories, training for fishermen and
fisheries personnel, and delimitation negotiations
for extended fisheries jurisdiction.   St.
Kitts/Nevis is about to begin negotiations with
its neighbor on the west, St. Eustatius, for
delimitation agreements. These types of bilateral
and multilateral arrangements will prove helpful
to understaffed fishery units in the area trying
to manage and develop their fisheries.

DEVELOPMENT AND PROTECTION OF OFFSHORE
HYDROCARBONS

In addition to favorable geological
conditions in a region, the effective development
of offshore hydrocarbon resources will depend on
the financial, regulatory and property rights
conditions which make it feasible to attract the
large investment necessary to exploit the
resource. These factors specifically include
access to financing, issues of resource ownership,
issues of rent sharing, and environmental
concerns.

The amount of capital needed to explore for
and exploit offshore hydrocarbon resources is well
beyond the technical and financial capabilities of
most developing countries. While the World Bank
and Asian Development Bank have made loans
available to developing countries for energy
resource development, the development of offshore
hydrocarbon resources will probably require a
joint venture with an international oil company or
companies to supply investment funds and
technology. This will require the developing

country to balance establishment of a regulatory framework that safeguards national sovereignty over its offshore petroleum resources with protection and encouragement of foreign investors.

The development of offshore hydrocarbon resources has brought about issues of resource ownership. These issues result from conflicts over historical ownership claims, new boundary limits adopted as a result of the law-of-the-sea Convention, and situations where petroleum reservoirs straddle boundaries.

In Southeast Asia, for example, conflicts have arisen in the Natuna Island area between Vietnam and Indonesia. Disputes exist between China and Vietnam over claims in the Gulf of Tonkin, the Paracels, and the Spratlys. A concern that North Korea might make a claim to a potentially rich oil field off the Korean Peninsula may have motivated South Korea unilaterally to lease the offshore area to American oil firms for exploration. Security and political concerns have been a hindrance to the settling of many disputes, although the shared need for oil may override political differences, as in the case of a joint development arrangement between South Korea and Japan.

While leases have been let unilaterally in some disputed areas such as the Gulf of Thailand, the Natuna area, the Spratlys and the Timor Sea, actual unilateral drilling has been undertaken only by Indonesian contract-holders in the Natuna area and by Philippine concession-holders on the Reed Bank. A safe strategy is to explore and develop hydrocarbon resources in undisputed near-shore areas, taking care not to get too close to potentially conflictive international waters. While this does not solve the problem, it can serve as an interim measure as in the Asia-Pacific region until a solution can be reached.[10]

In lieu of a final solution to boundary and territorial disputes, other provisional solutions can be considered. One of the most feasible solutions is a joint agreement to develop the area. This solution calls for putting aside the sensitive problem of territorial sovereignty and pooling efforts to develop offshore hydrocarbon resources for the common good of the countries involved. An agreement of this type was concluded between Malaysia and Thailand in 1979. The 50-year agreement calls for sharing of the expenses and earnings from exploration and production of oil and gas in a 2,100 square-mile area.

The infrequency of joint offshore resource development between Third World neighbors contrasts with the prevalence of joint ventures between Third World and developed states. Third World nationalists lament the paucity of intra-South (South-South) cooperative efforts and the pervasiveness of North-South ties. While joint ventures may not be ideal for political reasons, hard yet pragmatic Third World bargaining can help squeeze economic advantage from them.

Since many offshore hydrocarbon resources will be developed as a joint venture, it will be important at the outset of the venture to establish a mutually acceptable and equitable framework for rent sharing. Disputes often arise over rent-sharing arrangements, with the disagreement revolving around output sharing (the production-sharing formula) or around output pricing. In order for this sensitive issue to be discussed in an environment of mutual respect, the host country must develop sufficient expertise to identify optimal benefits from the development of the resource. Zealous, uninformed protection of national interests often jeopardizes a good project. Mutual understanding of the proper return on investment for both parties in view of the risk and expertise involved in the venture can help optimize development of the resource. Toward this end, it is important that the developing country provide prudent incentives to attract investors and not deter investment with undue regulation.

The importance of the appropriate economic and fiscal framework can be observed in the development of offshore resources in Southeast Asia. The increase in world oil prices in the early 1980s and the attractive production-sharing contract terms in Indonesia allowed commercial development of smaller offshore sites. The more restrictive fiscal framework in Malaysia limited development activity to relatively larger fields. The Philippines, with its attractive terms but limited potential, managed to develop a relatively

100

small oil discovery. Improvements in the service contract by the Philippine government in mid-1982 brought about investment in deeper water contracts.[11]

Oil spills, or blow-outs, are an increasing concern as offshore hydrocarbon resources are developed. Every stage of exploration and development involves some disturbance or potential disturbance of the ocean environment with the potential for long term alteration of the ecosystem. Oil spills in the offshore zones of one country could impact upon the tourist beaches or fishery of a neighboring nation. Governments must make the tradeoffs between the risk of development and the preservation of environmental quality.

The development of offshore hydrocarbon resources by developing countries consequently will require the evaluation of many options. The evaluation of the tradeoffs and benefits of energy development will involve serious consideration of macroeconomic issues, the degree of energy security and reliance on foreign assistance desired, and social preferences of the country.

A distinctive set of issues relating to the protection of on-shore and offshore hydrocarbons has emerged during the Iraq-Iran war, which has continued since 1980. These resource protection issues will be briefly surveyed here, while Chapter 10 will analyze the naval dimension of the war in some detail.

Part of the ground and air war waged by Iran and Iraq, respectively, has targeted on-shore oil installations of the other. When neither side could win the war on the ground or in the air, from mid-1984 each side added an additional maritime dimension to the war by selectively attacking oil tankers. Other countries were subsequently drawn into the so-called tanker war, including local oil-exporting states dependent on unhindered tanker traffic and outside powers recruited to protect that traffic. As coastal, island and offshore oil installations were targeted as well, land-based and naval dimensions of the war increasingly overlapped.

Targeting of coastal, island and offshore oil installations contributed as well to increasing overlap of resource protection and naval activities in the constricted waters of the Persian Gulf. Gradual geographical expansion of the war also tended to have this effect. The small, oil-rich states of the Persian Gulf have not been able to exclude hostile Iranian activities such as minelaying and uninvited inspection of vessels from their territorial seas and EEZs. Their inability to protect national zones helped draw in outside powers for naval protection.

Iran's use of its islands as well as the coastline for deployment of both naval and paramilitary forces involved in the war effort has further blurred the line between resource protection and naval activities. Fortified islands now include those near the mouth of the Gulf at the strategic Strait of Hormuz. From these scattered bases, Iran attempts to sustain a naval as well as paramilitary presence in many parts of the Gulf for pursuit of a variety of belligerent activities without triggering a military response by local or great powers.

SUMMARY AND CONCLUSIONS

The establishment of extended offshore zones has brought both economic benefits and costs for the management and development of offshore resources. Developing countries face many difficult management questions related to these resources. The extent to which developing nations will be able to manage their newly-acquired offshore zones effectively will depend on how well they are able to fashion integrated policy responses to both offshore security and development challenges.

While offshore hydrocarbons may be a source of considerable revenue in a some cases, productive areas are scattered very unevenly off Third World states. Moreover, effective exploitation of offshore hydrocarbons will require considerable reliance on foreign assistance in nearly all Third World cases.

There is greater potential for indigenous management and development of fishery resources by many developing nations with limited outside assistance. The developing country will, however, have to increase its capacity to manage the resource. In many cases, it may be cheaper and more efficient to rely at least in part on foreign assistance or, alternatively, on bilateral or regional cooperation as well as international agencies.

Just as offshore development poses hard choices and pitfalls for developing states, so too does offshore security. Third World naval buildups have often accentuated traditional rivalries, complicated old disputes and generated new ones over offshore resources, and stretched scarce local finances. Even a buildup of more modest capabilities for protecting offshore resources may constitute an initial step up the naval expansion ladder for states with dire developmental needs.

At the same time, offshore development will be impaired by inadequate offshore security. Strategies for protecting offshore resources can complement strategies for developing these resources. They are imperative when resources are in dispute. Naval power can supplement offshore resource protection capabilities and also help deal with local, regional and extra-regional threats.

While offshore security is vital for Third World states and may complement offshore resource development, it is especially important for poorer states to strike a balance emphasizing the latter as much as possible. A balance must be struck as well between expansion of offshore resource protection capabilities and naval power, since developing states can only with great difficulty sustain a buildup of both kinds of offshore security forces. Whichever leg is emphasized, a resulting pull toward naval expansion can easily outstrip scarce national finances. Still another choice involves the extent of reliance on foreign states for weaponry transfers as well as offshore resource protection and ocean security. Hard choices and pitfalls there are, but there is also increasing Third World awareness of the nature of these choices and the dilemmas they pose for marine policy.

NOTES

1. Michael A. Morris, Expansion of Third-World Navies (London: Macmillan and New York: St. Martin's Press, 1987).

2. Ibid., Chapter 9. Also see Michael A. Morris, International Politics and the Sea: The Case of Brazil (Boulder, Colorado: Westview Press, 1979).

3. Morris, Expansion of Third-World Navies, especially Chapter 2 and Part III.

4. T.L. McDorman, "Thailand's Fisheries: A Victim of 200-Mile Zones," Ocean Development and International Law Journal, vol. 16, no. 2 (1986), pp. 183-209.

5. F.T. Christy, Alternative Arrangements for Marine Fisheries: An Overview (Washington, D.C.: Resources for the Future, RFF/PISFA Paper 1, 1973).

6. Ibid.

7. D.J. Clough, Optimization and Implementation Plan for Offshore Fisheries Surveillance (Ottawa, Canada: Department of Fisheries and Oceans, mimeo, n.d.).

8. M.J. Valencia, "Southeast Asian Seas: National Marine Interests, Transnational Issues, and Marine Regionalism," in C.L. Sien and C. MacAndrews, eds., Southeast Asian Seas: Frontiers for Development (Singapore: McGraw-Hill/Institute of Southeast Asian Studies, 1981).

9. Wolfgang T. Muller, "C^3 for the 200 n.m. EEZ," Military Technology, vol. 25 (1981), p. 74.

10. Mark J. Valencia and Masahro Miyoshi, "Southeast Asian Seas: Joint Development of Hydrocarbons in Overlapping Claim Areas?," Ocean Development and International Law Journal, vol. 16 (1986), pp. 211-254.

11. C.M. Siddayao, "Oil and Gas on the Continental Shelf: Potentials and Constraints in the Asia-Pacific Region," Ocean Management, vol. 9 (1984), pp. 73-100.

6

Optimal Development of Third World Fisheries

Conner Bailey

FISHERIES DEVELOPMENT POLICIES

Marine fisheries resources are of vital importance to many tropical developing nations as a source of food, employment, and foreign exchange earnings. Fish provides a high percentage of protein intake in many parts of the world, particularly in Asia, and often is the only affordable source of animal protein for rural and urban poor alike (Kent 1987). Best available estimates indicate that there are 10-15 million full-time fishermen in the Third World, and at least an equal number employed either as part-time fishermen or in fish processing and marketing (Christy 1986; Smith 1979). More recently, the fisheries sector has taken on new importance as a source of foreign exchange earnings for many Third World nations (Floyd 1984).

Fisheries development policies have sought to meet growing demand for fisheries products on both domestic and export markets through the introduction of powerful new fishing technologies. This "blue revolution" has led to increased pressure on fish stocks and open conflict between small- and large-scale fishermen competing for a finite and often dwindling resource. These problems form the crux of development policy in tropical fisheries.

In the process of formulating fisheries policy, competing goals of economic development, resource management and social justice become inextricably mixed. It is the task of those who

105

make fisheries policy to determine what balance between these goals is optimal in a given time and place. In this chapter, the concept of "optimal yield" is presented as a guide to clarify the trade-offs inherent in the decision-making process. This is followed by a discussion of community-based resource management systems, which are presented as an effective mechanism for the management and allocation of fisheries resources.

RETHINKING FISHERIES DEVELOPMENT

Rapid adoption of new production technologies in a context of resource scarcity constitutes the setting for this discussion. Over the last two decades, these technological innovations have greatly increased the capacity of fishermen to exploit biologically renewable fisheries resources. As a consequence, most important fisheries within the Third World are overexploited, limiting future development options in the fisheries sector (Robinson 1982).

Given the power of contemporary fishing technologies and the capacity they provide to overexploit marine stocks, a production-oriented definition of development is dangerously shortsighted. Yet, despite mounting evidence of resource scarcity, national policymakers and international development agencies continue to encourage the expansion of productive capacity. One effect of these policies has been to increase pressure on a biologically renewable resource vulnerable to overexploitation. Additionally, serious economic inefficiencies through overcapitalization and the dissipation of resource rents have been introduced. These policies have led to serious social disruptions due to the concentration of production capacity in the hands of relatively few individuals. As fisheries resources become fully exploited, technological advantages enjoyed by certain fishermen have a direct, negative impact on others. Under these conditions, small-scale fishermen have tended to become marginal producers even though, as shown in Table 6.1, they account for the vast majority of all those employed and contribute substantially to the harvest of fish caught for human consumption

(Bailey 1987; Panayotou 1980; Thomson 1980).

The combination of social disruption and overexploitation of fisheries resources brought about by rapid technological innovation makes it necessary to rethink development policies in a manner consistent with long-term societal interests. This chapter is presented as a small contribution to a larger debate on the future direction of fisheries development in the Third World.[1] The basic argument advanced here is simple: fisheries development must be seen to mean more than an increase in the volume and value of harvests. Fisheries development efforts make little sense unless they are both sustainable over time and socially beneficial. Fisheries development programs must build on resource management policies which promote more than biologically sustainable harvests. They also must provide benefits which are broadly distributed throughout society rather than gains captured by a narrow set of elite interests.

Unfortunately, much of what has passed as fisheries development policy in the Third World fails to meet this basic test of social justice (Bailey 1987; Bailey, Cycon & Morris 1986). Governments and international agencies have sought to promote large-scale fisheries development through the provision of direct and indirect subsidies, but have devoted relatively little attention to the needs of small-scale fishermen (Christy 1987). The capital-intensive nature of most officially sponsored fisheries development efforts have had a negative impact on small-scale fishermen, who lack the means to remain competitive with those who adopt more powerful fishing technologies. Competition for a dwindling resource base has led to declining catches and incomes among small-scale fishermen, who for generations have depended on fisheries resources for their livelihoods. Traditional resource use rights based on historic usage generally have been ignored rather than protected by national governments, who have failed to restrict operators of capital-intensive fishing units from encroaching on coastal fishing grounds where most small-scale fishermen operate (but see Bailey 1986).

107

TABLE 6.1
Comparisons Between Large- and Small-Scale Fisheries

Comparison	Large-Scale	Small-scale
No. fishermen employed	Approx. 450,000	> 12,000,000
Marine fish caught for human consumption (million metric tons/yr)	30-40	> 20
Marine fish caught for reduction to fish meal, fish oil, etc. (million metric tons/yr)	21	Almost none
Annual fuel consumption (million tons)	10-14	1-2
Fish caught per ton fuel (tons of fish)	2-5	10-20
Fishermen employed for each US$ 1 million investment	10-100	1,000 - 10,000

Sources: Thomson (1980:3) and Lawson (1984:236)

The emphasis on large-scale fisheries development stems from a common perception that capital-intensive fishing units are more economically efficient than those of the small-scale subsector.[2] This, however, is by no means always true. At a macro level, large-scale fisheries development generates relatively little employment for the amount of capital invested (Table 6.1), a serious concern in most Third World societies where capital is in scarce supply relative to labor as a factor of production. Large-scale fisheries are relatively energy intensive (Table 6.1), an important consideration for oil importing nations as well as energy exporters seeking to control the growth of domestic fuel consumption. The apparent economic efficiency of large-scale fishing units also is exaggerated by direct or hidden subsidies to large-scale fishermen frequently provided by national governments and international development agencies. These include fuel subsidies, preferred access to credit, infrastructural developments (urban fishing ports, ice plants, and associated facilities), and government sponsored research and gear trials, among other benefits.

At the micro level, we can examine the relative economic efficiency of large- and small-scale fisheries with reference to data from San Miguel Bay, Philippines. In this particular case, a total of 95 trawlers landed roughly half the catch (Pauly and Mines 1982). The remainder was landed by small-scale fishermen whose total investment was double that of the trawl fleet (Table 6.2). Further, trawler owners earned the only pure profits in the fishery (Smith and Mines 1982).

On the face of it, it would appear that these trawlers were far more efficient in economic terms and certainly more effective per unit in production terms. However, the profitability of trawlers in San Miguel Bay depended entirely on government subsidies for diesel fuel (Smith and Mines 1982). Because this subsidy made possible the increased fishing effort by trawlers, it had a direct, negative impact on the catches and incomes of small-scale fishermen in that area. Government fuel subsidies benefited only trawler owners, a total of 25 families out of over 3,500 families directly involved in the fishery (Bailey 1982a). While these owners are responsible for employing roughly ten percent of all fishermen, they have been able to utilize their economic power to impose progressively more onerous sharing systems on their crewmen (Villafuerte & Bailey 1982).

The case of San Miguel Bay is unique only because it is the best documented[3] tropical multispecies fishery in the world. Similar conditions of extreme inequality exist in many other Third World fisheries. Far from being the

109

TABLE 6.2
Comparisons Between Trawlers and Small-Scale
  Fishing Units, San Miguel Bay, Philippines, 1981

Type of Unit	Number of Units	Percent Total Catch	Percent Employment	Percent Investment
Trawlers	95	47.1	8.9	36.5
Small- Scale	948	52.9	91.1	63.5

Source: Bailey (1982: 46-49, Tables 40 & 41).

Note: Data on small-scale fishing units do not include cast nets, scissor nets, and other inexpensive types of gear. Thus, the number of small-scale fishing units is understated, but this has relatively little effect on comparisons of level of investment.

consequence of blind economic fate, such conditions often are the direct or indirect result of official development policy.

OPTIMAL YIELD

Optimal yield (OY) is a conceptual tool for visualizing the trade-offs that often must be made in setting development priorities and goals. The OY concept builds on the concepts of maximum sustainable yield and maximum economic yield which have guided fisheries policymakers over the past 30 years. OY combines the biological and economic parameters of development policy with a broader set of social concerns (Emmerson 1980).
Since passage of the Magnuson Act in 1976, fisheries management decisions in the United States have been guided in principle by OY. More than ten years later, there remain many imperfections in its implementation having to do

with the continued emphasis on biological and economic data and the consequent relegation of social and cultural factors to a status of secondary importance (Fricke 1985). Nonetheless, the principle has been established and is beginning to have an impact on fisheries management in the United States. Third World nations would benefit from explicitly incorporating the broader range of issues addressed under the OY model when designing and implementing their own fisheries policies.[4]

Biological and Economic Parameters

Fish stocks are a biologically renewable resource, potentially a source of almost infinite value for current and future generations. However, beyond a certain point identified as maximum sustainable yield (MSY), increasing levels of fishing effort[5] will not result in any increase in harvests. Simply stated, MSY is that level of fishing effort which produces the highest yields which can be sustained over time.

Figure 6.1 presents a simple model illustrating this point. Once levels of fishing effort have increased to the point where MSY has been reached (C), additional fishing effort will not produce increased harvests. In some cases, the result may be a catastrophic collapse along the curve C -> ->D ->F, as in the case of the Peruvian anchoveta (Paulik 1981) or other single species fisheries. However, most tropical fisheries can be characterized as multi-species resources, whose population dynamics are quite complex (Pauly 1979). Under these circumstances, increased fishing effort does not necessarily lead to a decline in total harvest but rather to a shift in the species composition of the resource. Generally, this involves removal of the larger and more valuable species and their replacement with smaller fish and other marine organisms further down the food chain. Under this common scenario, the value of the catch declines along the curve C ->D ->F even though the volume of landings does not (following instead the curve C ->E).

Society as a whole suffers an economic loss -- the dissipation of resource rents -- if levels

111

FIGURE 6.1
Simple Static Model of an Open Access Fishery

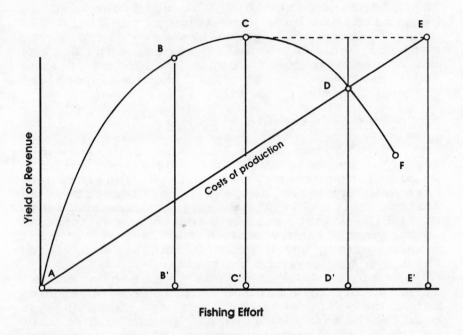

of fishing effort increase to the point where catch value declines, whether this results from reduced harvests or changing species composition. Resource rents to society are the pure profits that accrue to a society through efficient use of its resources. Resource rents are maximized at point B on Figure 6.1, often referred to as the point of maximum economic yield (MEY). Because the slope of the curve A ->B ->C flattens as the level of fishing effort approaches MSY, maximum profits to the industry (and resource rents to society) are earned before MSY is reached. All resource rents are dissipated at the point where total costs (A ->D or A ->E) equal total revenues from the fishery.

The central concern behind the concept of MSY is to protect fish stocks from overexploitation. Arguments advanced in support of MEY stress the importance of economic efficiency. Both sets of goals are valid but incomplete when one considers a broader range of potential social goals associated with the concept "development". The concept of MSY has nothing to say about allocation of access to the resource itself. Similarly, MEY as a concept provides no guidance regarding how resource rents should be distributed through society. Neither concept provides guidance regarding the appropriate balance between labor- versus capital-intensive development.

The concepts MSY and MEY have guided much of the thought regarding fisheries policy since the 1950s, despite the amoral quality and imprecision of the data used for measuring fishing effort and stock assessment. The science of stock assessment is sufficiently inexact that establishing the point at which MSY or MEY is reached involves equal measures of artistic and scientific judgement. This is particularly the case in most tropical fisheries, due to the common absence of adequate data on landings, fishing effort, costs, and revenues. As artifacts of objective science, MSY and MEY have the appearance of rationality. In truth, MSY and MEY often provide a convenient fig leaf of objectivity to cover what is in essence a highly political process. In short, MSY and MEY may more accurately be understood as heuristic devices than as objective conceptual

113

tools of a rational resource management process.

Fishery management is an inherently political process involving difficult choices. In reality, fisheries management decisions are just as likely to be made on the basis of political calculation as they are to hinge on objective measurements of stock abundance (Bailey 1987; McEvoy and Scheiber 1984). The very imprecision of the data upon which fishing effort and stock abundance are measured provides ample opportunity for the introduction of subjective judgement into the fishery management process. More important, however, are the questions that are not asked ("development for whom?") and the data which do not exist ("how are the benefits of development being distributed?").

Social Parameters

The OY concept provides an alternative which incorporates MSY and MEY in a more holistic model of resource management. OY is particularly useful as a conceptual tool in clarifying the often conflicting goals of fisheries development and resource management. The concept of optimal yield makes explicit the fact that fisheries management involves choices and that these choices inevitably are based on competing values.

The OY concept combines social and cultural variables in addition to the biological and economic variables which traditionally have dominated most fisheries policies. The intended effect is to encourage policymakers to combine and balance, as locally appropriate, concerns for resource sustainability and economic efficiency with concerns for employment generation and income distribution, along with other social concerns. Implicit in this concept is the understanding that there may be trade-offs as policymakers attempt to achieve an optimal balance between multiple objectives (Figure 6.2).

Generally, the first consideration in resource management is the sustainability of the resource. Certainly it would be irresponsible to recommend policies that lead to resource depletion or collapse of fish stocks, a result that would be inimical to societal interests. Development that

114

FIGURE 6.2
Optimal Yield: Social, Economic and Biological
  Variables

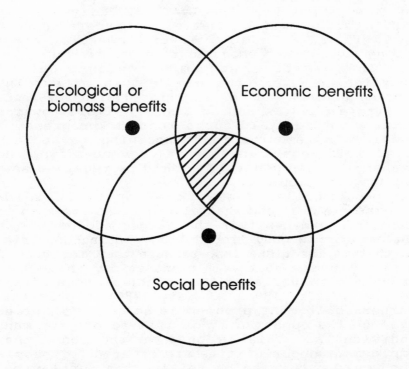

Ecological or
biomass benefits

Economic benefits

Social benefits

 Indicates the point of maximum sustainable
yield or benefit in this ideal situation

Indicates the area of optimal yield or benefit

Source: Fricke (1985)

cannot be sustained because of resource depletion is not development in any meaningful sense of the word. Tropical multispecies stocks, however, generally do not collapse in the face of overexploitation, but rather shift in age and species composition (Pauly 1979; Pauly & Mines 1982). This remains a matter of concern because smaller fish and fish of lower commercial value may generate lower economic returns.

The negative economic consequences of overfishing (i.e., the expenditure of surplus fishing effort) can be illustrated with reference to Figure 6.1. Expanding fishing effort towards point E on the yield curve leads to progressive decline in resource rents accruing to society (i.e., total costs equal total revenues from the fishery). This generally would be regarded as a negative development.

Within the framework of optimal yield, however, we must ask what alternatives are open to these fishermen within the larger economy? The reality within many tropical developing countries is that marine fisheries, because they are an open access resource, act as a giant safety valve that absorbs surplus labor from other sectors of the economy (Bailey 1982a; Christy 1986). Until this larger employment problem is solved, fisheries will be the opportunity of last resort for many individuals. This is good in the sense that employment opportunities are created for people who would otherwise be joining the rural-urban exodus or denuding hillsides. It is bad in that ultimately this increase in pressure on the resource will lead to the dissipation of all resource rents and shared poverty among large numbers of fishermen. In the meantime, however, it may be justifiable to encourage fishing effort to expand beyond the limits of MSY if the primary goal is to increase employment opportunities. Whether this were appropriate would depend on the nature and status of the resource and on whether surplus fishing effort was the result of capital- or labor-intensive fishing technologies.

Summarizing the argument advanced to this point, fisheries development depends on resource management, an inherently political process that calls for a balancing of diverse and sometimes

116

conflicting social goals. The concept of optimal yield was introduced as a means of visualizing the interplay between social, economic, and biological parameters of fisheries development. In the remainder of this chapter, community-based resource management systems will be discussed as an alternative to government control over resource management and allocation.

COMMUNITY-BASED RESOURCE MANAGEMENT

Over-exploitation of fisheries resources generally is attributed to the lack of clear property rights and the consequent efforts of individual fishermen to maximize benefits even at the expense of resource sustainability and long-term societal good (Christy & Scott 1965; Gordon 1954). Under conditions of free and open access, no limits are placed on the entry of individuals who wish to share in exploitation of the resource, and no restrictions are placed on how the resource is to be exploited. Under these conditions, competition between fishermen for a finite resource may be likened to a zero-sum game, where technological advantages enjoyed by a few translate into declining shares of the total harvest by all others.

The opposite of an open access system is one where some form of enforceable property rights exist that serve to exclude outsiders. It is natural for those raised in free-market societies to think of property rights as something that are vested in an individual or business firm. Less frequently recognized are community-based property systems where members of a community or locality-based group have the authority to exclude outsiders and allocate access to individual members (Christy 1982). This is the essence of a common property resource system.

In common property resource systems, boundaries and limits to entry do exist and are imposed by the community or group which controls or "owns" the resource in question (Ciriay-Wantrup and Bishop 1975). Common property systems combine both exclusionary property rights and a particular kind of social arrangement that provide a basis for sustainable resource management.

117

There is a rapidly growing literature describing the workings of common property institutions in a variety of natural resource settings around the world (National Research Council 1986). The South Pacific appears to be a particularly fertile environment for establishing marine common property management systems (Iwakiri, 1983; Johannes, 1981; Ruddle and Johannes, 1985). Cooperatives among Japanese fishermen also exert common property rights over coastal fishing grounds and enjoy government support for their legal rights (Asada et al. 1983; Comitini 1966; Ruddle 1985). In the United States, lobster fishermen in Maine have enforced their own exclusive rights to local fishing grounds through less formal means -- destroying the traps of outsiders (Acheson 1975).

Common property systems not only persist under a diverse set of situations, they offer important advantages where the goals of resource management include long-term sustainability of yields and distributional equity among users. Runge (1986) persuasively argues that common property systems are particularly advantageous to rural, small-scale producers in the Third World because these systems tend to reduce uncertainty in both resource and social systems. Uncertainty in harvests is reduced through finely tuned use restrictions based on precise local knowledge of the resource in question and on a set of values which emphasize long-term stability over short-term gain. Uncertainty in the social environment is reduced at two levels: at the community level by specifying rights of access to local resources which put a premium on cooperation and reciprocity; and at the societal level by providing a legal basis for excluding outsiders.

Third World governments have not yet committed themselves to support of local control over natural resources, although interest in community-based resource management is increasing.[6] There is good reason why this is so. Governments anywhere find it very difficult to enforce fisheries restrictions along thousands of kilometers of coastline. In many cases, the effective capacity of government agencies to regulate what goes on in widely scattered fishing

118

grounds is almost nonexistent.   The costs of enforcement (boats, airplanes, personnel, etc.) are prohibitive and success stories are few and far between (but see Bailey 1986).

Under these conditions, devolution of major resource management and allocation decisions to the local level may be more effective than central government efforts.   To accomplish this shift in responsibility, it would be necessary to vest local communities with property rights that provide the authority to exclude outsiders and allocate resource access to individual members of the community.   Authority of this kind would provide a solid basis for participatory development.

Fishermen generally have a clear conception of resource scarcity and understand intuitively the basic principles of fisheries management (Morril 1967; Pollnac 1980).   The problem is to obtain their acceptance, which often means achieving agreement among all members of the community on the goals of resource management and a willingness among all individuals involved to restrain themselves rather than to maximize personal gain at the expense of the collective good (the essence of the "Tragedy of the Commons"; Hardin 1968).

Common property resource systems will not work under all conditions.   Just as powerful individuals and groups may dominate under conditions of open access and come to control resources that are classified as private property, so too local elites could position themselves within the power structure of a community to take advantage of a common property system.   An understanding of community dynamics is of fundamental importance to determining the potential role of local communities in programs of natural resource development and management.   Not all communities have sufficient internal cohesion or the traditions and values to be effective in enforcing common property rights.   This is particularly the case where communities are riven by factions or where local elites have the economic and political power to take advantage as "free riders" of a locally managed common property system.

Restrictions placed on access to finite resources entail allocational decisions which are inherently political. It can be expected that common property systems will be opposed by those who benefit most from an open access system; generally, this refers to economic elites with the capital to invest in the most powerful technologies. Frequently, these elites exploit renewable natural resources in an extractive manner with little regard for long-term sustainability, and utilize capital-intensive production technologies that minimize employment opportunities. Individual small-scale fishermen often are powerless in defending their interests against highly organized entrepreneurs who occupy the inside track in influencing natural resource bureaucracies. These elite interests also can be expected to oppose the formation of common property resource management systems, as recently occured in the Philippines (Flores & Silvestre 1987; Maclean 1986; White 1984; see also Thomson et al. 1986).

Common property systems are not a universal panacea to problems of resource management and allocation, but they do provide an ethically and practically sound conceptual framework for achieving sustainable development based on local participation in decisions of fundamental importance. Achieving this goal will put a premium on our knowledge of social institutions and their relation to natural resource systems. Policies based on these concepts will give precedence to community-based resource management strategies which emphasize local rather than governmental control of development activities (Korten 1986). This, of course, is the antithesis of the non-participatory, top-down approach to development.

The common property model of resource management holds great potential as a basis for sustainable and socially beneficial fisheries development. Local small-scale producers generally have a vested interest in long-term resource sustainability. The labor-intensive nature of small-scale fishing technologies is such that local control over fisheries resources will support greater employment opportunities than under open-access conditions and competition with large-scale fishing units. In short, common property systems are likely to be supportive of resource sustainability and distributional equity, key components of fisheries policy under the principle of optimum yield.

SUMMARY AND CONCLUSIONS

Over the last two decades, the introduction of powerful new technologies, coupled with increasing demand for fisheries products by both developed and developing nations, has led to significant increases in pressure on a resource vulnerable to overexploitation and depletion. Despite mounting evidence of resource scarcity, national policymakers and international development agencies continue to promote production-oriented programs based on capital-intensive fishing technologies. These programs increase pressure on the resource and have a negative impact on small-scale fishermen, who lack the means to adopt these new technologies.

Third World fisheries development efforts need to be balanced with resource management programs which address a clearly defined set of policy goals. This paper offers a conceptual framework -- optimal yield -- for fisheries policies that are by nature holistic, balancing biological, economic, and social parameters of development. What constitutes an optimal balance between these factors will vary, but the issues of sustainability and distributional equity are central to policy equations generated under the rubric optimal yield.

Public policy regarding the allocation of limited resources is an inherently political process. Small-scale fishermen generally have had limited ability to influence fisheries policy. Lacking the ability to control access to their traditional fishing grounds, they have been unable to protect their traditional resource use rights against the encroachment of wealthy outsiders equipped with powerful technologies. Most Third World governments have, but lack the ability to enforce, regulations which restrict large-scale fishing units from operating in areas where they will compete with small-scale fishermen.

Common property resource systems, where property rights are vested in a community or community-based group, were discussed as a means of shifting resource management responsibility away from the central government and towards the local community. Government support and legal recognition of common property rights and resource management efforts offer practical advantages where governmental capacity for resource management is limited -- which is to say, nearly everywhere. Common property systems have the further advantage of supporting participatory approaches to development that emphasize resource sustainability and distributional equity -- key elements of optimal fisheries development policy.

NOTES

Preparation of this paper was supported by the Alabama Agricultural Experiment Station at Auburn University and by a strengthening grant to Auburn University by the U.S. Agency of International Development to support fisheries development research.

1. See, for example, Allsopp (1985); Bailey (1985, 1987a); Bailey, Cycon, & Morris (1986); Emmerson (1980); Kent (1987); Lawson 1984; Royce (1987); and Smith (1979).

2. See, for example, Allsopp (1985:140), who argues the need to eliminate small-scale fisheries as a means of increasing efficiency.

3. A team of approximately 20 researchers worked over a period of two years documenting the social, economic, and biological aspects of this fishery in the Bicol Region of Luzon Island. Five volumes have been published (Bailey 1982a, 1982b; Pauley & Mines 1982; Smith & Mines 1982; Smith, Pauly & Mines 1983). See also Bailey (1984, 1985), and Smith & Pauly (1982, 1983).

4. Commercial fishermen, processors, and recreational fishing interests, among others, are highly organized in the United States, and have a strong influence over government policy. Similar organizational strength and policy influence

cannot be assumed to exist in most Third World nations. Obviously, how the US Magnuson Act has been implemented will provide little practical guidance elsewhere. The focus on OY here, therefore, is at the conceptual level.

    5. Fishing effort is a technical term is used to measure levels of resource exploitation. Fishing effort is increased through the entry of additional boats and nets to a fishery, through the introduction of more powerful types of fishing units, by the cumulative expenditure of more time spent fishing by the existing fleet, or by some combination of these factors.

    6. During 1987, the government of Malaysia and the FAO (which alone among international development agencies has been actively supporting such initiatives) began a project directed towards community involvement in fisheries management.

REFERENCES

Acheson, J.M. 1975. Fishery management and social context: the case of the Maine lobster fishery. Transactions of the American Fisheries Society 104(4): 653-668.

Allsopp, W.H.L. 1985. Fishery Development Experiences. Fornham, Surrey, England: Fishing News Books, Ltd.

Asada, Y., Y. Hirasawa, and F. Nagasaki. 1983. Fishery management in Japan. FAO Fisheries Technical Paper 238. FIPP/T238. Rome: FAO.

Bailey, C. 1982a. Small-scale Fisheries of San Miguel Bay: Occupational and Geographic Mobility. ICLARM Technical Reports No. 10. Manila and Tokyo: Center for Living Aquatic Resources Management; Institute of Fisheries Development and Research, College of Fisheries, University of the Philippines in the Visayas; and the United Nations University.

Bailey, C. (ed.). 1982b. Small-Scale Fisheries of San Miguel Bay, Philippines: Social Aspects of Production and Marketing. ICLARM Technical Reports 9. Manila and Tokyo: Institute of Fisheries Development and Research, College of Fisheries, University of the Philippines in the Visayas; International Center for Living Aquatic

Resources Management; and the United Nations
University.
Bailey, C. 1984. Managing an open access
resource: the case of coastal fisheries.
D.C. Korten (ed.), People-Centered Development:
Contributions Toward Theory and Planning
Frameworks. West Hartford, Conn.: Kumarian
Press. pp. 97-103.
Bailey, C. 1985. The Blue Revolution: the
impact of technological innovation on Third
World fisheries. The Rural Sociologist
5(4):259-266.
Bailey, C. 1986. Government protection of
traditional resource use rights: the case of
Indonesian fisheries. In D.C. Korten (ed.),
Community Management: Asian Experience and
Perspectives. Hartford, Conn.: Kumarian
Press. pp. 292-308.
Bailey, C. 1987. The political economy of
fisheries development in the Third World.
Agriculture & Human Values (forthcoming).
Bailey, C., D. Cycon, and M. Morris. 1986.
Fisheries development in the Third World:
the role of international agencies. World
Development 14(10): 1269-1275.
Bailey, C., A. Dwiponggo, and F. Marahudin. 1987.
Indonesian Marine Capture Fisheries. ICLARM
Studies and Reviews 10. Manila and Jakarta:
International Center for Living Aquatic
Resources Management; Directorate General of
Fisheries, Ministry of Agriculture, Indonesia;
and the Marine Fisheries Research Institute,
Ministry of Agriculture, Indonesia.
Christy, F. T., Jr. 1982. Territorial use rights
in marine fisheries: definitions and
conditions. FAO Fisheries Technical Paper
No. 227. Rome: FAO.
Christy, F. T., Jr. 1987. A re-evaluation of
approaches to fisheries development: the
special characteristics of fisheries and the
need for management. Paper prepared for
the Agriculture Sector Symposium, The World
Bank, 8-9 January 1987. 15 pages, mimeo.
Christy, F.T., Jr. 1986. Special characteristics
and problems of small-scale fisheries management
in developing countries. E.Miles, R. Pealy,
and R. Stokes (eds.), Natural Resources

Economics and Policy Applications. Seattle:
University of Washington Press. pp. 118-151.

Christy, F.T. and Scott, A. 1965. The Common
Wealth in Ocean Fisheries: Some Growth and
Economic Problems. Baltimore: Johns
Hopkins Press.

Ciriay-Wantrup,S.V. and R.C. Bishop. 1975.
"Common property" as a concept in natural
resources policy. Natural Resources Journal
15:713-727.

Comitini, S. 1966. Marine resources exploitation
and management in the economic development of
Japan. Economic Development and Culture
Change 14(4):414-427.

Emmerson,D.K.1980. Rethinking Artisanal
Fisheries Development: Western Concepts, Asian
Experiences. World Bank Staff Working Paper
No. 423. Washington, D.C.: World Bank.

Flores, E. and G. Silvestre. 1987. Community
based coral reef fishery resource management
in the Philippines: the Balicasag Island
experience. Proceedings, Symposium on the
Exploitation and Management of Marine
Resources in Southeast Asia. Indo-Pacific
Fisheries Commission, Darwin, Australia,
16-19 February 1987.

Floyd, J. 1984. International Fish Trade of
Southeast Asian Nations. East-West
Environmental and Policy Institute, Research
Report No. 16. Honolulu, Hawaii: East-West
Center.

Fricke, P. 1985. Use of sociological data in the
allocation of common property resources: a
comparison of practices. Marine Policy
9(1):29-52.

Gordon, H.S. 1954. The economic theory of a
common-property resource: the fishery.
Journal of Political Economy 62:124-42.

Hardin, G. 1968. The tragedy of the commons.
Science 162:1243-1248.

Iwakiri, S. 1983. Mataqali of the sea -- a study
of the customary right on reef and lagoon
in Fiji, the South Pacific. Mem. Kagoshima
University Research Center for the South
Pacific 4(2):133-43.

Johannes,R.E. 1981. Words of the Lagoon:
Fishing and Marine Lore in the Palau District

of Micronesia. Berkeley: University of California Press.

Kent, G. 1987. Fish, Food, and Hunger: The Potential of Fisheries for Alleviating Malnutrition. Boulder, Colorado: Westview Press.

Korten, D.K. (ed.). 1986. Community Management: Asian Experience and Perspectives. Hartford, Conn.: Kumarian Press.

Lawson, R. 1984. Economics of Fisheries Development. New York: Praeger.

Maclean, J. 1986. End of a marine reserve: Sumilon revisited. Naga, ICLARM Quarterly 9(1):13.

McEvoy, A.F. and H.N. Scheiber. 1984. Scientists, entrepreneurs, and the policy process: a study of the post-1945 California sardine depletion. Journal of Economic History 44(2):393-406.

Morril, W.T. 1967. Ethnoichthyology of the Cha-Cha. Ethnology 6: 405-416.

National Research Council. 1986. Proceedings of the Conference on Common Property Resource Management. Washington, D.C.: National Academy Press.

Panayotou, Theodore. 1980. Economic conditions and prospects of small-scale fishermen in Thailand. Marine Policy 4(2):142-146.

Paulik, G.J. 1981. Anchovies, Birds, and Fishermen in the Peru Current. M. H. Glantz and J. D. Thompson (eds.), Resource Management and Environmental Uncertainty: Lessons from Coastal Upwelling Fisheries. New York: John Wiley & Sons.

Pauly, D. 1979. Theory and Management of Tropical Multispecies Stocks: A Review with Emphasis on the Southeast Asian Demersal Fisheries. ICLARM Studies and Reviews No.1. Manila: International Center for Living Aquatic Resources Management.

Pauly, D. and A.N. Mines. 1982. Small-Scale Fisheries of San Miguel Bay, Philippines: Biology and Stock Assessment. ICLARM Technical Reports 7. Manila and Tokyo: Institute of Fisheries Development and Research, College of Fisheries, University of the Philippines in the Visayas; International

Center for Living Aquatic Resources Management; and the United Nations University.

Pollnac, R.B. and J.C. Sutinen. 1980. Economic, social, and cultural aspects of stock assessment for tropical small-scale fisheries. P.M. Roedel and S.B. Saila (eds.), Stock Assessment for Tropical Small-Scale Fisheries. Proceedings of an International Workshop, September 19-21, 1979, University of Rhode Island. Kingston, R.I.: International Center for Marine Resource Development, University of Rhode Island. pp. 48-59.

Robinson, M.A. 1982. Prospects for world fisheries to 2000. FAO Fisheries Circular No. 722, Revision 1. June 1982. Rome: FAO.

Royce, W. F. 1987. Fishery Development. New York: Academic Press.

Ruddle, K. 1985. The continuity of traditional management practices: the case of Japanese coastal fisheries. K. Ruddle and R.E. Johannes (eds.), The Traditional Knowledge and Management of Coastal Systems in Asia and the Pacific. Jakarta: UNESCO, Regional Office for Science and Technology for Southeast Asia. pp. 157-180.

Ruddle, K. and R.E. Johannes (eds.). 1985. The Traditional Knowledge and Management of Coastal Systems in Asia and the Pacific. Jakarta: UNESCO, Regional Office for Science and Technology for Southeast Asia.

Runge, C.F. 1986. Common property and collective action in economic development. World Development 14(5): 623-636.

Smith, I. R. 1979. A Research Framework for Traditional Fisheries. ICLARM Studies and Reviews No. 2. Manila: International Center for Living Aquatic Resources Management.

Smith, I. R. and A. N. Mines (eds.). 1982. Small-Scale Fisheries of San Miguel Bay, Philippines: Economics of Production and Marketing. ICLARM Technical Reports 8. Manila and Tokyo: Institute of Fisheries Development and Research, College of Fisheries, University of the Philippines in the Visayas; International Center for Living Aquatic Resources Management; and the United Nations

University.

Smith,I.R.and D. Pauly. 1982. Simple methods for the multidisciplinary investigation of tropical multispecies multigear fisheries. Paper presented at the Sea Grant Seminar and Workshop on Coastal Living Resources in Malaysia, 25-28 May 1982. Universiti Pertanian Malaysia, Kuala Trengganu, Malaysia. Mimeo, 45 p.

Smith, I.R. and D.Pauly. 1983. Resolving multigear competition in nearshore fisheries. ICLARM Newsletter 6(4): 11-18.

Smith,I.R., D. Pauly, and A. N. Mines. 1983. Small-Scale Fisheries of San Miguel Bay, Philippines: Options for Management and Research. ICLARM Technical Reports 11. Manila and Tokyo: Institute of Fisheries Development and Research, College of Fisheries, University of the Philippines in the Visayas; International Center for Living Aquatic Resources Management; and the United Nations University.

Thomson,D. 1980. Conflict within the fishing industry. ICLARM Newsletter 3/3: 3-4.

Thomson, J.T., D. Feeny, and R.J. Oakerson. 1986. Institutional dynamics: the evolution and dissolution of common property resource management. National Research Council. 1986 Proceedings of the Conference on Common Property Resource Management. Washington, D.C.: National Academy Press. pp. 391-425.

Villafuerte,E.D. and C. Bailey. 1982. Systems of sharing and patterns of ownership. C. Bailey (ed.), Small-Scale Fisheries of San Miguel Bay, Philippines: Social Aspects of Production and Marketing. ICLARM Technical Reports 9. Manila and Tokyo: Institute of Fisheries Development and Research, College of Fisheries, University of the Philippines in the Visayas; International Center for Living Aquatic Resources Management; and the United Nations University. pp. 25-41.

White, A. 1984. Effects of protective management on coral reefs in the Philippines. ICLARM Newsletter 7(4): 9-11.

7

Southeast Asia: Some Perspectives on Marine Policy

Joseph R. Morgan

INTRODUCTION

Complexity is a word that best describes Southeast Asia. Land and sea meet in intricate patterns, forming bodies of water of varying sizes and shapes, as well as countries with widely differing characteristics regarding orientation to the oceans. There are nations with long coastlines convex to the sea, as well as archipelagic states with their numerous islands and intervening water bodies. Countries of relatively large size are found side by side with mini-states, and nations with various degrees of geographical disadvantage from the standpoint of what they gain from the new Law of the Sea are in sharp contrast to the two largest archipelagic nations in the world. A single landlocked nation exists in the region; it has its own, albeit limited, concerns with the marine environment. There are some commonalities among the countries, however. Most are clearly in the category of developing states, and may be classed as part of the "South". However, it might be argued that Singapore, for instance, as a newly industrializing country (NIC) should be considered part of the "North".

Despite intraregional differences among countries and to some extent in the water bodies making up Southeast Asia, there is in this vast area a distinct sense of regionality. There is homogeneity in both physical and cultural features and a certain unity, due in part to the activities of regional organizations.[1]

There are differing definitions of what constitutes Southeast Asia. In this paper the following countries are included: Brunei, Burma, Indonesia, Kampuchea, Laos, Malaysia, Philippines, Singapore, Thailand, and Vietnam (see Map 7.1). These 10 nations can be divided into four distinct classes from the standpoint of marine policy.

1) The archipelagic states of the Philippines and Indonesia are entitled to claim the waters between their numerous islands as well as territorial seas and exclusive economic zones (EEZs) measured to a distance of 200 nautical miles seaward from straight baselines connecting the outermost extremities of the islands.[2]

2) States with long coastlines and relatively distant neighbors are able to claim large EEZs.[3] In Southeast Asia, the best example is Vietnam. To a more limited degree Malaysia qualifies as well, although lines of equidistance must be drawn with Indonesia and Vietnam in the South China Sea and with Indonesia in the Strait of Malacca.

3) States with severely limited EEZs include Kampuchea, with its short coastline and neighboring Vietnam and Thailand on the Gulf of Thailand, and Thailand itself, which must share waters with Vietnam and Kampuchea in the Gulf of Thailand and with Indonesia and India (Andaman and Nicobar Islands) in the Andaman Sea.

4) The final classification is that of mini-states, such as Brunei and Singapore, which are restricted from claiming sizeable EEZs due primarily

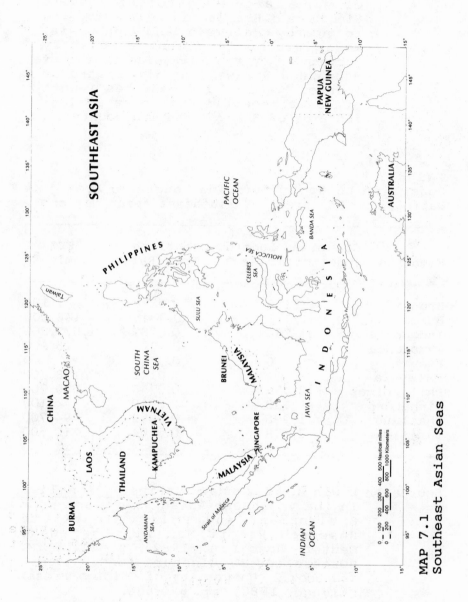

MAP 7.1
Southeast Asian Seas

131

to their small size and the proximity of very large neighboring states. Singapore's EEZ is miniscule compared to nearby Malaysia and Indonesia, while Brunei is almost completely surrounded by the Malaysian states of Sabah and Sarawak, on the island of Borneo. Table 7.1 summarizes length of coast, coastline to area ratios, and area of EEZ for the ten countries.

TABLE 7.1
Coastline Length, Coastline Length to Area Ratios, and EEZ Areas of Southeast Asian Nations

Country	Coastline Length (nautical miles)	Coastline to Area Ratio	EEZ (nmi^2)[a]
Brunei	100	0.0279	7,100
Burma	1,897	0.0045	148,000
Indonesia	35,784	0.0287	1,577,300
Kampuchea	275	0.0024	16,200
Laos	0	0.	0
Malaysia	2,899	0.0141	138,700
Philippines	13,975	0.0750	520,700
Singapore	120	0.3310	c.100
Thailand	1,996	0.0063	94,700
Vietnam	2,828	0.0104	210,600

Sources: Lewis M. Alexander, Marine Regionalism in the Southeast Asian Seas (East-West Environment and Policy Institute Research Report No. 11, East-West Center, Honolulu, 1982), p. 21. E.M. Borgese and N. Ginsburg (eds.), Ocean Yearbook 2 (University of Chicago Press: Chicago, 1980), pp. 690-694.

[a] Area enclosed by 200-nmi territorial sea and EEZ.

TABLE 7.2
Dimensions of Some Southeast Asian Seas

Water Body	Area (nmi^2)	Perimeter (nmi)
South China Sea	959,160	5,901
Gulf of Thailand	85,521	1,241
Gulf of Tonkin	46,961	1,050
TOTAL	1,091,642	
Andaman Sea	190,762	1,830
Celebes Sea	128,352	1,628
Makassar Strait	55,951	1,231
Malacca Strait	45,882	1,252
Sulu Sea	93,460	1,508

Source: Calculation by Dr. Everett Wingert and
           Peter Matsunaga, University of Hawaii
           Department of Geography. Limits of
           Oceans and Seas   (the International
           Hydrographic Bureau, Special Publication
           23, 3rd ed.: Monaco, 1953).

SOUTHEAST ASIAN SEAS

     From the standpoint of political geography
and marine resources, Southeast Asian seas (Table
7.2) can be divided into four broad categories.[4]
First is the South China Sea which with the Gulf
of Thailand and the Gulf of Tonkin as appendages
or sub-regions is bordered by ten states and two
dependencies.   Second are the important   straits,
which include Malacca-Singapore, Lombok,   Sunda,
Makassar,   Ombai-Wetar, Surigao, San Bernardino,
and Verde Island Passage. The third category
consists of the archipelagic waters of the
Philippines and Indonesia. Finally there are the
Celebes and Sulu seas (considered as a single
unit) and Andaman Sea,   which have certain
characteristics in common. Each is bounded by
three or more countries, which must share the
resources and the problems of preserving the

marine environment. Unlike the South China Sea, the problems in these smaller semi-enclosed seas are more manageable and amenable to cooperative solutions by the coastal states. It is logical to discuss the marine policies of Southeast Asian countries in the context of the four general types of marine regions, rather than on a country-by-country basis.

The South China Sea

The large number of nations bordering the South China Sea and the resource potential of this large marine region are factors that influence national marine policies. Several countries make conflicting and overlapping jurisdictional claims, particularly to the Spratly Islands.[5] This group of small islets, rocks, reefs, and shoals is claimed entirely or in part by China, Taiwan, the Philippines, Vietnam, and Malaysia. The claims are based on history (in the cases of Vietnam, China, and Taiwan), proximity and need in the case of the Philippines, and geology in the case of Malaysia, which correctly points out that some of the southern islands in the group are part of the continental shelf of the Malaysian states of Sabah and Sarawak. Brunei, which thus far has made no claim to any of the Spratly group, has an equally valid case, however.

Terrestrial resources in the Spratly group are of no consequence, but possession of the islands entitles their owner to large claims to EEZs and continental shelves. There are fishery resources in the South China Sea that could fall within EEZs based on ownership of the Spratly Islands, and, more important, the ocean bottom around the islands may contain commercial quantities of hydrocarbons. Finally, important sea routes, particularly the tanker route from the Middle East to Japan, pass close to the islands.[6]

Some have suggested that control of the Spratly group could have strategic value, as the islands could serve as bases for naval forces. Although none of the islands is large enough or has enough infrastructure to support a large

naval base, any   presence in the Spratly
islands could serve to counterbalance the presence
of the important bases at Cam Ranh Bay and Subic
Bay.   These bases respectively support Soviet and
U.S. interests in the South China Sea and the
nearby Malacca-Singapore Straits.   They thus can
be viewed as "foreign" from the standpoint of the
regional countries, who might be desirous of
exercising more local influence in the region.
"The Zone of Peace, Freedom and Neutrality, to
which all ASEAN nations and Vietnam subscribe, can
be realized only if sufficient military power,
including naval force, is maintained to provide
for a degree of regional security without
excessive help from outside powers."[7] Some
elements of this naval force might be exercised
from bases in the Spratlys.

Of the countries bordering the South China
Sea we might single out four for particular
attention: Indonesia, the Philippines, Thailand
and Vietnam.

<u>Indonesia</u>.   The largest and most populous
country in Southeast Asia is an important oil
producer, with most of its production from
offshore wells.   As the largest oil producer in
Southeast Asia, Indonesia is concerned both with
exploitation of the hydrocarbon resources under
its control and their transport to markets.   Dumai
on the east coast of Sumatra is Indonesia's
largest crude oil port.   Despite its hydrocarbon
resources, the nation is definitely a member of
the South.

Fishery resources are also extensive and are
regulated by the government with two objectives in
mind: promoting industrial fisheries in the EEZ
and maintaining small-scale, artisanal fisheries
in the archipelagic waters.   In some aspects of
living resource management in Indonesia, the
objective of industrially-oriented economic
development is balanced by a desire to maintain
traditional ways of life among coastal fishermen.
For instance, trawling has been banned in many
areas of the archipelagic waters in order to
reduce competition between the more highly
capitalized trawling fleets and the fishing
activities carried out on a semi-subsistence basis
by families with small, outboard engine-powered

135

boats.[8] Efforts to profit from joint-venture operations, particularly with Japan, have not been notoriously successful.

Indonesia has immense problems in maintaining national unity in the face of considerable diversity among its people and the far-flung nature of the archipelago. The strongly held archipelagic nation concept, in which the waters between the islands as well as the islands themselves are important and equal parts of the national territory, is important to the government in maintaining the unity of the nation-state. In some parts of Sumatra and the eastern archipelago there are dissident groups, and there is a general feeling throughout the nation that people outside the core sub-region of Java and Madura do not fare as well as they might compared to their countrymen in the more highly populated areas.[9]

Indonesia's navy is configured for multiple purposes: to exercise some measure of control over important straits through the archipelago; patrol the extensive EEZ and archipelagic waters to prevent poaching, smuggling, and illegal barter trade; and act as a marine police force to enforce the national laws in far-flung parts of the archipelago. The fleet is not configured to act as a "Blue Water" navy of any consequence, although the location of the country athwart important sea lanes and its dominance in Southeast Asia might entitle it to do so.

As might be expected in a country that feels its archipelagic status so keenly--the phrase Wawasan Nusantara implying that "the seas and the straits must be utilized to bridge the physical separations between the islands, regions, and manifold ethnic groups"[10] is used--Indonesian shipping among the various islands is carried out solely by Indonesian registered vessels. Maintaining communication and adequate cargo and passenger services to all parts of the country is difficult, and the lack of effective transportation hampers economic development. Air service helps to alleviate the problem, particularly for passenger transportation, but air transport of cargo is prohibitively expensive.

In summary, Indonesia makes the most effective use of ocean resources in its offshore oil industry. It is less effective in its fisheries, and shipping and naval defense are largely a drain on the economy, rather than an asset.

The Philippines. The Republic of the Philippines is a more compact archipelago than Indonesia, but in many respects problems of maintaining national unity and an adequate state of national and human welfare are more difficult. The Philippines does not possess offshore oil in exploitable quantities as yet, although there are some promising developments. One of the important reasons why the country claims most of the Spratly Island group and includes it within the Philippine archipelago on its official maps is that a successful claim to the group would entitle the nation to resource sovereignty over important continental shelf areas which may have exploitable oil and gas fields.[11]

The Philippines, although a signatory to the Law of the Sea Convention (UNCLOS) in 1982, makes what many would consider bizarre claims to maritime jurisdictions.[12] It bases its ample claims to territorial seas on straight lines used to establish limits in the Treaties of 1898 and 1930. The former treaty ceded territory to the United States at the conclusion of the Spanish-American War, and the latter established the boundary between the U.S.-owned Philippines and the then British territories of North Borneo (now the Malaysian states of Sabah and Sarawak and the nation of Brunei). The claim to the Spratly group, which the Philippines calls Kalayaan, adds an additional 70,150 nm^2 to the territorial sea claim; the government does not make claims to the islands individually but to a hexagonal area bounded by six specified points. It is reasonable to conclude that the Philippines needs marine resources and makes extraordinary claims to marine territory accordingly. The claims have brought it into disagreement with Taiwan to the north, Indonesia to the southeast, and the four other claimants of the Spratly Islands to the west: China, Malaysia, Taiwan and Vietnam.

The Philippines' navy is far less well equipped to deal with its several missions than is Indonesia's fleet. Philippine naval vessels are

137

frequently less well armed and are slower than boats engaged in piratical activites in the archipelago, and most naval analysts rate the navy as the weakest among the ASEAN countries.[13] Inter-island shipping is generally a problem, although the smaller size of the archipelago (7,000 islands as compared to Indonesia's 13,000) makes the task of transporting cargoes less difficult.

In the Philippines there are important commercial fisheries for demersal species in nearshore waters above the shallow continental shelf. The various species are fished by small boats, many of them unmotorized. However, production from these bottom fisheries, particularly the trawl fishing areas, has declined recently, perhaps because the easily trawlable areas have been overexploited. On the other hand, a greater catch of small pelagic fishes can be obtained, with the estimated catch in recent years well below the estimated sustainable yield. An offshore tuna fishery has developed rapidly over the last several years, and catches in the EEZ could greatly increase the economic potential for the country of these highly migratory fish. However, the capability of the Philippine fishing fleet is still not sufficient to make good use of the extensive EEZ living resources. The relatively high cost of fuel is another factor limiting Philippine exploitation of its EEZ, since the fishermen are generally undercapitalized. Writing in 1985 one Philippine fisheries specialist said:

> In the short run, responsibility for the EEZ poses more costs than benefits for the country. Upgrading of monitoring, control, and surveillance capabilities and exploratory research on resources would entail massive expenditures. Since local fishing companies are not financially able to expand, foreign participation with capital and equipment will play a major role in the exploitation of the EEZ. The immediate impediments to expanding the fishing effort farther from shore enhance the

138

attraction of aquaculture activities. There is burgeoning interest in commercial scale aquaculture for high-value species in brackish, fresh, and salt water.[14]

Thailand. Inasmuch as the Gulf of Thailand is considered part of the South China Sea, Thailand becomes an important country in this sub-region. A glance at the map of Southeast Asia points out some of Thailand's problems. It has extensive coasts on both the Gulf of Thailand and the Andaman Sea, which, but for the proximity of neighbors, might entitle it to extensive claims to maritime areas. However, in the Gulf of Thailand Kampuchea and Vietnam overlap claims of Thailand to exclusive economic zones. The concave nature of the Thai coast in this area makes its geographical location disadvantageous from the standpoint of claims to EEZs and continental shelves.

Thailand is an important fishing nation, both in its home waters and as a distant water fishery power. However, the northern part of the Gulf of Thailand has suffered grievously from marine pollution, reducing the catch of the Thai fishing fleet. The development of a highly capitalized, distant-water fishing industry was an obvious partial solution to the problem of reduced catches close to home. However, since the signing of the Law of the Sea Convention, countries in Southeast Asia have generally forbidden access of Thai vessels to their EEZs. Hence, Thailand has diminished fishery resources in its claimed waters, due to both pollution and overfishing, and is greatly hampered in its overseas operations.

The small Thai navy is designed to patrol its extensive coastline and to protect the fishing fleet from nearby countries, as some have attacked and confiscated Thai boats. The navy, of course, is also responsible for surveillance and control over the Thai EEZ.[15]

The Thai shipping industry is hampered by lack of good port facilites. Bangkok, the principal port, is located well up the Chao Phraya River, providing it with good protection from the elements. However, the port is limited in the size of vessels it can accommodate both by the depth at the river bar (8.25 m) and the tortuous nature of the channel. The latter limits the length of vessels to 171 m (565 ft), since longer ships cannot navigate the bends in the river.[16] Hence, large tankers cannot discharge at the port of Bangkok, due to both length and draft limitations. New ports need to be developed to take advantage of modern tankers and containerships, since both ship types exceed the length and draft limitations of the Chao Phraya. Port development, while clearly needed, is nevertheless expensive. Moreover, Thailand's location is well off the principal trade routes in Southeast Asia, which precludes any use of Thai port facilities as transshipment points and reduces the possible additional revenues a good port might generate. For these reasons Thailands's merchant fleet and its ports are not revenue producers of any consequence, although they do serve the immediate needs of the country adequately.

In common with other Southeast Asian countries, Thailand is searching for offshore oil. Thus far its efforts have been to no avail, although there have been some promising natural gas discoveries.

Vietnam. The conclusion of the Vietnam war left the country reunited, making Vietnam a country with a long coastline and potentially important marine resources on the South China Sea. Capitalizing on these resources, however, is difficult for a number of reasons. The lengthy war left the nation in a state of relative poverty, with much of its infrastructure damaged. Marine resources exploitation is expensive, particularly exploration and production of offshore oil resources. Vietnam has not yet sufficiently recovered from the many years of conflict to be able to devote sufficient capital to offshore activities.

Vietnam still has a number of potential enemies in Southeast Asia, and many of its neighbors view it as a military threat.[17] The use of the important port facilities at Cam Ranh Bay as a large Soviet naval base makes Southeast Asian countries such as Indonesia, Malaysia, the

Philippines, and Thailand uneasy. Many Southeast Asians view Vietnam's military activities in Kampuchea as threatening; Thailand, in particular, has been adversely affected by combat activities near its borders. Cooperation with Vietnam in a Southeast Asian regional context may be a long time in coming. The ASEAN countries of Brunei, Indonesia, Malaysia, the Philippines, Singapore, and Thailand form a regional political unit generally at odds with the alignment of Vietnam, Kampuchea, and Laos.

In the Gulf of Tonkin, where there are promising conditions for offshore hydrocarbons, Vietnam has a serious maritime boundary dispute with China.[18] Since the Vietnamese and Chinese have already been engaged in hostilities (in 1979) over a contested land boundary, each side feels constrained to vigorously pursue offshore exploitation activities that might lead the other side to protest that its borders have been crossed. The situation is complicated by the fact that much of the exploratory activity thus far has been carried out by western oil companies acting as contractors. The large oil companies are naturally reluctant to work in areas where their activities might be viewed by one or more countries as provocative.

Initially, reunited Vietnam tended to treat its newly obtained EEZ as national territory. There were a number of incidents involving Vietnamese armed vessels firing on and capturing fishing boats of other Southeast Asian nations.[19] Now, however, Vietnam is exploring suitable arrangements under the provisions of UNCLOS for access by foreign fishing vessels into its EEZ.

It is difficult to assess the quality of the Vietnamese navy, but it might reasonably be assumed that large numbers of small ships are available for patrol duties.[20] Much of the former Republic of Vietnam naval fleet fell into North Vietnam's hands when the war ended, and the U.S. departure from Vietnam undoubtedly left a large number of small craft in the new government's hands. The Soviets have been providing Vietnam with naval units, further increasing the size of the fleet. However, there have been assessments of the quality of the naval forces which indicate

141

that the state of training of personnel and
material readiness of the ships is at a low level.
How many ships and of what types Vietnam can
really utilize effectively is uncertain; many of
the vessels might not be capable of at-sea
operations without extensive overhauls and
repairs, and there might not be sufficient numbers
of trained personnel to man more than a fraction
of the available ships. If the principal mission
of the Vietnamese navy is to patrol and carry out
surveillance of the extensive EEZ, the fleet might
cope. If, on the other hand, Vietnam intends to
use the navy for offensive operations (against one
of the other claimants to the Spratly Islands, for
instance) most observers would have serious doubts
about the navy's capabilities.

In summary, Vietnam is making progress in
utilizing its marine resources to foster recovery
of the country from the long wartime drains on the
economy. However, progress has been slowed by the
Gulf of Tonkin dispute with China, conflicting
claims to the Spratly Islands, and a general
uneasiness about Vietnam's intentions by the ASEAN
countries. The economy of Vietnam is still
greatly dependent on Soviet aid, which may be
insufficient to permit a rapid rate of economic
growth and development. Furthermore, military
activities in Kampuchea are ongoing, creating a
further drain on the Vietnamese economy. Marine
resources can be important, but only if the
country can find sufficient capital to exploit
them.

The Malacca-Singapore Straits

The Straits connect the Indian Ocean with the
South China Sea and are an extremely important sea
route for tankers carrying cargoes of crude oil
from the Persian Gulf to Japan and other East
Asian nations. Although there are some important
navigational restrictions in the waterway, due
primarily to shoals and the narrow width of the
navigable channels, large numbers of vessels
navigate the route without incident.[21]

Ocean-going ships in the Straits must follow
specified traffic lanes, with eastbound and
westbound traffic separated from each other.

142

Passage is restricted to vessels of shallow enough draft to permit an underkeel clearance of 3 1/2 meters. These traffic regulations were established through the efforts of the three coastal states: Malaysia, Indonesia, and Singapore. Although the underkeel clearance requirement effectively limits the Strait to ships of about 220,000 dwt or smaller and very large tankers must use alternate routes,[22] the management scheme is generally beneficial to the three countries. The cooperative efforts of the three countries to establish a sensible management regime for navigation in the Straits is noteworthy and indicative of the possibility that the three countries might further cooperate with each other in governance and management of the marine territory under their control.

Of the three, Singapore benefits most from its location at the narrowest constriction of the Singapore Strait. However, both Indonesia and Malaysia also have important ports in the region and are concerned with both the smooth flow of seagoing traffic and the prevention of pollution due to collisions or groundings of tankers.

Indonesia. Although Indonesia has already been discussed in the context of its location on the shores of the South China Sea, it is also an important Straits state. Its large size and population make it the most important country in Southeast Asia in a number of respects. Hence, describing it as part of more than one marine region is appropriate.

Freedom of navigation in the Straits and regulated passage of vessels into the ports of the three states is a matter of considerable importance to the country. Of equal concern is prevention of pollution, since there is also a fishing industry of considerable size operating in the Straits. The activities of fishing vessels frequently are a navigational menace to large tankers, and control of all ships is important.

Indonesian naval units patrol the straits to prevent or control smuggling, illegal fishing in the state's waters, and other illegal activities. The navy is supplemented by units of a marine police force, which operates large numbers of small patrol boats.

The underkeel clearance requirement of 3.5 meters resulted in the initial diversion of the extremely large tankers from the Malacca-Singapore Straits route to the Lombok Strait, which is completely within Indonesian-controlled seas. Later, most of the very large ships were determined to be uneconomical to operate, and most tankers now are built to size limits largely dictated by the Malacca-Singapore navigational restrictions.

Malaysia. As a nation with a long coastline on the South China Sea, Malaysia could have been discussed in the context of that marine region. However, it is generally considered as one of the three Straits states. The west coast of penisular Malaysia is heavily industrialized, and two important oil ports, Port Dickson and Port Kelang, are located on the Straits. Both serve primarily to receive imports of crude oil, despite the fact that Malaysia is also an important crude oil producer and exporter. The exports are from an oil terminal more than 100 miles offshore in the South China Sea. Malaysia, too, has an interest in controlling ship traffic in the Straits, since the country has a fishing industry and other reasons to prevent pollution from oil spills or tanker accidents.

The Malaysian navy has a good deal of marine area to cover, since the national territory is split between peninsular Malaysia, with the capital at Kuala Lumpur and the two ports previously mentioned, and the Malaysian states of Sabah and Sarawak on the north coast of the island of Borneo. Hence, the fleet has larger vessels such as frigates to operate farther offshore as well as a number of small, fast well-armed patrol craft to help control the Straits.[23]

Malaysia is in direct competition with nearby Singapore in the field of shipping. The port of Pasir Gudang is on the Johore Strait and should be important in both imports and exports to populous peninsular Malaysia. However, it does not compete successfully with Singapore, and most cargoes bound for the capital city of Kuala Lumpur, for instance, do not enter the region via a Malaysian port, but rather are transshipped over the causeway from Singapore. Malaysia does have

144

important exports of products such as palm oil, which the country produces efficiently, and Malaysian ports on the Straits are suitably equipped to ship this material from liquid bulk terminals.

Singapore. There is no country in Southeast Asia that apparently has gained less from the provisions of the Law of the Sea, while at the same time there is no country whose location is more strategically placed for capitalizing on the seas. Singapore has for more than 100 years served as an important entrepot in Southeast Asia. Its port is among the busiest in the world, with modern cargo-handling, repair, provisioning, and processing facilites. The port can handle crude oil from the largest tankers that can safely navigate the Malacca-Singapore Straits, and there are also extensive facilites for loading and offloading containers. Ships with cargoes not bound for Singapore frequently stop at the port for refueling, repairs at one of the large drydocks, or transfers of cargo either to trucks bound for the large cities of Malaysia or to other ships which will take the cargo to ports such as Bangkok, which as mentioned previously cannot handle vessels of great length.

Singapore was initially reluctant to agree with Indonesia and Malaysia that traffic controls and a restriction on tanker size in the Straits were necessary or advantageous. However, the grounding of a large tanker, the Showa Maru, in the Malacca Strait in 1975, demonstrated that a regulated traffic regime in the Straits would be to everyone's advantage.

Singapore's economy is diversified, and on a percentage basis the port is only moderately important. Other components of the economy, however, are marine-related. Oil refining is important, a commercial activity which would not be successful were it not for the strategic location of the port and the huge quantities of crude oil which pass through it. Singapore also maintains a large merchant marine and has in the past allowed an equally large number of foreign ships to be registered under a Singapore flag of convenience. In recent years the flags of convenience have been progressively phased out.[24]

Other components of Singapore's economy are wholesale and retail trade, tourism, and a booming construction industry. All are in some way a function of the small nation's strategic location at the narrowest point of the Straits.

A Straits Maritime Defense Force? Since the three countries have demonstrated that they can and should cooperate with each other for their mutual benefit in regulating shipping in the Straits, and since all three are members of ASEAN, it is worthy of speculation as to whether or not it would be possible for them to band together in some sort of military alliance to insure control of the Straits in the event of hostilities.[25] Each has a small but relatively efficient navy. Sinagpore's is the smallest, but best configured for its limited missions -- control of the Straits to insure that they are kept open for traffic by friendly nations. If the three countries were to pool their naval and air resources they collectively could become a power to be reckoned with, and even powers such as the United States and the Soviet Union might be concerned about their ability to use the Straits for naval vessel deployments without fear of damage.

ASEAN, of course, is not a military alliance, but on many occasions the three Straits states have conducted joint naval and military maneuvers and training exercises. All three countries have good relations with the United States, and visits from U.S. Navy ships to Singapore are not uncommon. Just what form such a joint defense force might take, and whether or not it is feasible at all, is a matter for conjecture. However, the possibility and desirability of some sort of cooperative arrangement seems obvious.

The Other Marine Regions

There are other important straits in Southeast Asia. However, almost all of them are in either Philippine or Indonesian-controlled waters. Hence, their resources and the management of them are under the control of those two countries. Passage of ships through Indonesian and Philippine archipelagic waters and the important straits leading to them produce no

146

tangible benefits for the archipelagic nations, since there are no important ports on the routes that would attract ships to stop for fuel, repairs, or tranfers of cargo. Both archipelagic nations are entitled to establish archipelagic sealanes, which transiting ships are obligated to follow. These routes, however, should wherever possible follow the normal routes and must be approved by the competent international authority, usually considered to be the International Maritime Organization. Archipelagic sealanes might protect a country's waters from the threat of pollution, but it is difficult to see how they can enhance the economic development of the country or enable it to gain more in the way of marine resources.

The Celebes[26] and Sulu Seas. These two connected bodies of water are semi-enclosed seas surrounded by parts of the Philippines, Indonesia, and Malaysia. There are some moderately productive fisheries in them and both are on important shipping routes. The tankers that are too large to transit the Malacca-Singapore Straits go via the Lombok Strait, thence to the Makassar Strait and the Celebes Sea on their way to Japan. The Sulu Sea is a throughway between the various straits separating the Philippine Islands and the South China Sea. It is perhaps most well known, however, for the widespread presence of pirates. The Philippine navy is hard pressed to control them, since in many cases the pirate vessels are both faster and better armed than the navy units attempting to control them.

The Andaman Sea. The Andaman and Nicobar Islands, which are under the control of India, form the western boundary of this sea. The eastern shore is shared by Burma and Thailand. The Irawaddy River flows into the northern part of the sea, and its nutrient-rich waters lead to high biological productivity.[27] Hence, fisheries are important to Burma and Thailand, both of which are important fishing nations. The Burmese normally exclude Thai fishing boats from waters under Burma's control and have been known to capture Thai vessels that were presumably merely transiting the region. The Burmese navy has a number of fishery protection vessels, configured

147

to both protect Burmese fishing boats and intercept foreign fishermen who are deemed to be poaching in Burmese waters. Thailand's navy operates in the area primarily to protect Thai fishermen and to patrol the Thai EEZ. India maintains a number of coast guard vessels at Port Blair, in the Andaman Islands.

There are overlapping claims in the Andaman Sea, which are under negotiation. Settlement of the claims to EEZs and continental shelves would do much to foster amicable relations among the three countries and the sensible management of resources.

CONCLUSIONS

The fact that Indonesia has been mentioned in connection with the South China Sea, the Straits of Malacca and Singapore, and as an archipelagic nation is indicative of the importance of this country in the Southeast Asian marine region. It is by far the largest and most populous of the nations in the area, and its archipelagic nation status and very large EEZ magnify its impact even further.

Other countries in Southeast Asia capitalize on their marine resources more or less efficiently. Singapore tops the list for making best use of its strategic location. Malaysia is an important oil producer, as is Brunei. Vietnam is only now making strides toward economic development based on marine resources.

The other countries -- the Philippines, Burma, Thailand, Kampuchea, and Laos -- lag in their utilization of marine resources for various reasons. Laos is landlocked and therefore has the least chance to make much of the surrounding seas. Kampuchea is hampered both by a small EEZ and political difficulties that leave little time or energy for other concerns. Thailand, with long coastlines on both the Gulf of Thailand and the Andaman Sea, nevertheless has a geographic configuration that puts it into potential conflict with a number of its neighbors. Among the Southeast Asian countries, it has gained least from the Law of the Sea. Burma has potentially rich fisheries and hydrocarbon resources; it needs

to "come out of its shell" and capitalize on them.
The Philippines, as the second largest of the
world's archipelagic nations, should be able to
make more out of its ocean resources.   Its
performance in this regard has been disappointing,
as the nation struggles with unrest at home and a
lagging economy.
     The ten Southeast Asian nations, all but one
clearly part of the South (if we discount
Singapore because of its rapidly industrializing
character), would do well to pay more attention to
their marine resources; to do so would enhance
their prosperity and provide a more pleasant way
of life for their citizens.

NOTES

     1.   See Lewis M. Alexander, Marine
Regionalism in the Southeast Asian Seas,
(Honolulu: East-West Environment and Policy
Institute Research Report No. 11, East-West
Center, 1982), for a discussion of regional
organizations and arrangements in maritime
Southeast Asia.
     2. Law of the Sea Convention, articles 47,
48.
     3. Ibid, article 57.
     4. See Joseph Morgan, "Marine Regions and
Regionalism in South-east Asia," Marine Policy,
(Oct. 1984) for a categorization of Southeast
Asian marine regions, from which the following has
been adapted.
     5.   A thorough analysis of the Spratly
Islands jurisdictional claims and disputes is in:
J.R.V. Prescott, Maritime Jurisdiction in
Southeast Asia: A Commentary and Map (Honolulu:
East-West Environment and Policy Institute
Research Report No. 2, East-West Center, 1981),
pp. 29-39.
     6.   See Joseph R. Morgan and Mark J.
Valencia, Atlas for Marine Policy in Southeast
Asian Seas (Berkeley: University of California
Press, 1983), pp. 54, 81 for maps of these routes
considered from the standpoints of maritime
defense and navigational hazards.
     7.   George Kent and Mark J. Valencia, Marine

Policy in Southeast Asia (Berkeley: University of California Press, 1985), p. 263.

8.   Ibid, p. 118.

9.   Ibid, p. 250.

10.   Y.L. Lee, "Offshore Boundary Disputes in Southeast Asia," Journal of Southeast Asian Studies, vol. 10 (1979), p. 178.

11.   Morgan and Valencia, p. 115-116.

12.   See Prescott pp. 13-21 for an analysis of Philippine maritime claims.

13.   J.E. Moore, ed. Jane's Fighting Ships, 1978-79, (London: Jane's Publish. Co., 1978), Foreword and M.N. Vego "The Potential Influence of Third World Navies on Ocean Shipping," Proceedings U.S. Naval Institute, vol. 107(5) (1981), p. 111.

14.   Kent and Valencia footnote 7, pp. 126, 127.

15.   Ibid, p. 259.

16.   Morgan and Valencia, footnote 6, p. 92.

17.   Kent and Valencia, footnote 7, p. 236.

18.   Prescott, footnote 5, pp. 11-13.

19.   Kent and Valencia, footnote 7, p. 360.

20.   Ibid, p. 261.

21.   See Joseph R. Morgan, "Strait Talk," Proceedings U.S. Naval Institute, vol. 111(3) (March 1985), pp. 122, 123 for a description of navigational problems in the Malacca-Singapore Straits.

22.   See Morgan and Valencia, footnote 6, pp. 95-97 for an analysis of tanker traffic through Malacca-Singapore and alternate routes (Lombok Strait).

23.   Morgan, footnote 21, p. 124, 125.

24.   Kent and Valencia, footnote 7, p. 202.

25.   Morgan, footnote 21, p. 125.

26.   Morgan, footnote 4, p. 307 and 310 discusses marine regionalism in the Celebes Sea.

27.   Ibid, pp. 306, 307.

PART 3

North-South Perspectives

8

Coastal Area Management and Conflict Management

Kem Lowry, Jens Sorensen and Maynard Silva

INTRODUCTION

Generally the coastal areas of most nations in the world are more richly endowed with renewable natural resources than inland environments. The most notable coastal resources are fisheries, soils, forests, wildlife habitat, hydrocarbons, and recreational quality beaches and shorelands. The concentration of resources in coastal areas appears to be particularly true for the world's tropical and semi-tropical latitudes within which the great majority of the developing nations are situated. The concentration of resources and amenities in conjunction with the vital interface connection between marine and land transportation systems has lead to a disproportionate concentration of development and urbanization within the coastal zone. Two thirds of the world's cities with a population over one million are located on the coast or estuaries (United Nations 1982). Population growth rates are generally greater in coastal than inland communities (United Nations 1982).

It can also be argued that coastal areas have the highest concentration of hazards to human health and safety. These include coastal erosion, subsidence, earthquakes and tsunamis, ocean born storms such as hurricanes and typhoons, flooding of coastal rivers, migrating dunes and landslides.

The most distinctive and challenging characteristic of the coastal zone is the concentration of interconnected environmental and physical systems in a relatively compact area. No other geographic area -- mountains, intermountain valleys, high plateaus, lakes, deserts, or the deep ocean -- has so many systems concentrated in one area. Within most nations' coastal zones, eight complex systems are both functioning as a discrete unit and interacting with one another. The eight systems are large-scale geomorphic processes such as the evolution of barrier beaches or coral reefs; estuary watersheds; estuary circulation systems; oceanic circulation systems -- particularly basins; longshore circulation cells; air basins; populations of sport and commercial species; and public service systems such as water supply, sewage or highways. Recognition that the coastal zone is an aggregation of at least eight interacting systems is important because most conflicts among competing social interests arise from impacts generated by the functioning of these systems.

The aggregation of coastal resources, development, population growth, hazards, and environmental and physical systems produces a concentration of conflicts among virtually all segments in society with a vested interest in coastal resources or environments. The study and practice of coastal management was born out of the need for government to resolve intensifying conflicts among competing interests. In 1965 the San Francisco Bay Conservation and Development Commission ("BCDC") was created to develop and implement a plan to resolve conflicts associated with filling of tidelands, public access to the shore, and the degradation of the shoreline's visual quality (Swanson 1975). A year later in the State of Victoria, Australia, the Port Phillip Authority was created (Cullen 1977). Remarkably the three major issues that led to the formation of the BCDC program were also the motivating forces for creating the Port Phillip Authority and planning program. In two short years coastal area management and planning (or CAMP) had become an international practice.[1]

In the twenty-three years since the creation of BCDC, coastal area management programs and feasibility studies have been undertaken in all regions of the world and by all levels of government (international regions, nations, multi-state regions, states, and local jurisdictions). During the last decade the interest and practice of coastal area management spread out from developed nations or sub-national units to developing nations. A review of the programs initiated in developing nations indicates that international assistance institutions are a primary factor in the diffusion of the practice. This influence usually occurs in two ways: support of information exchange vehicles such as meetings and reports, and the direct funding of feasibility studies or pilot projects.

A total global number of past and present coastal management programs is difficult to ascertain because it depends on how one defines the practice. Previous research has defined a coastal area (or zone) management program as an effort characterized by the following six attributes.[2]

* It is initiated by government in response to issues -- usually resource degradation, exposure to coastal hazards, multiple use conflicts, or socioeconomic development needs.

* The effort has continuity over time, it is not a one-time project.

* There is a governance arrangement to establish the policies for making allocation decisions and, if the program is implemented, a governance arrangement for making allocation decisions.

* The governance arrangement uses one or more management strategies to rationalize and systematize the allocation decisions.

* The management strategies selected are based on a systems perspective which recognizes the interconnections among coastal environmental systems as well as public service systems. The systems perspective usually requires that the design and implementation of management strategies be done as a multi-sectoral effort.

155

* It has a geographic boundary that defines a space which extends from the ocean environment across the transitional shore environments to some inland limit. (There may be an exception for small islands where there may be no meaningful inland boundary.)

In most cases, the fifth and sixth attributes serve to distinguish a coastal management program from other efforts to manage coastal resources or environments. In other words, if a country has defined a coastal area and is planning it from a systems perspective, the other four attributes will be present.

Applying the definition, national programs have been developed in Colombia, Costa Rica, Ecuador, Sri Lanka, France, Greece, Peoples Republic of China, Sri Lanka, Sweden, Thailand and the United States (Sorensen et al. 1984; Olsen 1987). Far more countries have conducted national studies or conferences to assess the feasibility of initiating a program. This latter group includes: Argentina, Australia, Brazil, Canada, Ireland, Israel, Italy, Netherlands, New Zealand, Philippines, Saudi Arabia, South Africa, and the United Kingdom.

In the United States, 34 coastal states initiated programs, largely in response to the Federal Coastal Zone Management Act of 1972.[3] Although Australia has no federal program, the states of Victoria, New South Wales, South Australia, and Queensland have initiated their own programs (Cullen 1982). At the regional level, examples of notable programs are the Great Barrier Reef Marine Park Authority, the San Francisco Bay Plan, the Port Phillip Plan, Hackensack Meadows Commission, the Columbia River Estuary Plan, Master Plan for Galapagos Islands, Bilateral (Argentina and Uruguay) Administrative Commission of the Rio de la Plata, the coastal general development plan for the Iguape-Paranagua region (Brazil), the Waddenzee (Netherlands) plan and the Kuwait waterfront development plan.

Defining what constitutes a coastal area management program ("CAMP") is important for at least two reasons. A definition is needed both to provide semantic clarity and to identify criteria for comparative assessment of national or sub-national programs.

In contrast to the definition of a CAMP effort, the term coastal management has been broadly applied to almost any effort to manage one or more coastal resources or environments. All nations have sectoral programs -- at least on paper -- for managing most of their coastal resources and environments.[4] For example, all coastal nations have some governance structure and management strategy for the exploitation and allocation of fishery resources. Similarly, nations usually have sectoral programs to manage parks and tourism, oil and gas development, ports and shipping, and water pollution control. Table 8.1 lists the sectors that are often coastal zone or ocean specific.

Achieving the development or management objectives of any one sector will almost invariably produce conflicts with other sectors. Two primary reasons for the conflict-prone nature of sectoral development in the coastal zone is the web of interconnections among the eight coastal systems previously outlined and the competition for scarce resources, particularly ownership or lease of coastal land or water areas. Generally the forces motivating the initiation of a coastal area management program are the conflicts among two or more sectors.

A definition of coastal management also serves to distinguish a set of attributes that can be used for the comparative assessment of programs. Previous work has identified and applied five criteria for comparative assessment: issues motivating program initiation, geographic boundaries, the stage in program evolution, governance arrangement, and management strategies. The international spread of CAMP has led to a number of international comparative assessments using these attributes.[5]

This chapter is divided into five sections. The first three sections briefly describe three comparative criteria: motivating issues, governance arrangements, and coastal management strategies. These criteria are followed by a discussion of conflicts and management techniques for dealing with these conflicts. Specialized

157

TABLE 8.1
Sectoral Planning and Development in the Coastal Zone

Sectors that are often coastal zone or ocean specific	Sectors that are rarely coastal zone specific but have direct impacts
1. Naval and other national defense operations (e.g., weaponry testing, Coast Guard, customs)	1. Agriculture-Aquaculture
	2. Forestry
	3. Fish and wildlife management
2. Port and harbor development (including shipping channels)	4. Parks and recreation
	5. Education
3. Shipping and navigation	6. Public health -- mosquito control and food
4. Recreational boating	7. Housing
5. Commercial and recreational fishing	8. Water pollution control
6. Mariculture	9. Water supply
7. Tourism (especially in island nations)	10. Transportation
8. Marine and coastal research	11. Flood control
	12. Oil and gas development
9. Shoreline erosion control	13. Mining
	14. Industrial development
	15. Energy generation

explanations of most of these five topics have been done elsewhere. (United Nations 1982, Mitchell 1982, Sorensen, et al., Sorensen and Brandani 1987). A synthesis and interpretation will be provided here.

MOTIVATING ISSUES

A review of documents that describe the initiation of coastal management programs reveals a strong pattern of repetition and similarity among motivating issues. Virtually every coastal nation with a major metropolitan area bordering an estuary has an estuarine pollution problem. Similarly, nearly every coastal nation that actively harvests its coastal fishery has an over-fishing problem (predictable consequence of common property exploitation). Coastal nations with substantial mangrove acreage invariably burden this ecosystem with sedimentation, pollution, and over-harvesting. Almost all discussions of a nation's institutional arrangements recite the same litany of policy-making problems such as inadequate information, lack of intergovernmental coordination and inadequate budget and staff resources.

Although comparison of the issue-lists from developed and developing nations reveal a far greater similarity than dissimilarity, there are a few notable differences. One expected difference is the emphasis developing countries place on issues concerned with resources and infrastructure development, in contrast to the priority developed nations place on issues concerned with the conservation or preservation of resources and environments. Developing nations generally will not attempt to resolve issues that cannot be expected to yield net socioeconomic benefits that are both evident and occur in the near-term -- unless international assistance institutions are willing to subsidize the effort.

Most of the South is in the tropics -- and numerous issues are tropic specific such as mangrove conversion and degradation or stresses on coral reef systems. Also, in the industrialized North, the issues are usually formed by major impact generating activities such as coastal residential or hotel developments, energy facilities, or other large-scale industrial activities. While such large-scale activities are important in the less-developed countries, many of the most significant resource degrading or depleting activities are the cumulative result of hundreds of individual resource use decisions by economically-marginal coastal inhabitants. Management in the South necessarily involves influencing the behavior of hundreds of thousands of people; people whose behavior is not easily influenced by the conventional regulatory tools of coastal management.

In respect to the institutional issues, inadequate information and staff capability are much greater problems in the South than in the North. The existing data base in most developing nations is usually sparse, scattered, and of questionable validity. Often the data base does not include basic topographic maps or resource surveys such as vegetation composition and soil types. Maps and aerial photography are often restricted by the military. Without international assistance, the technology and staffing costs to gather the information necessary for CAMP development commonly become prohibitively expensive.

The poor information base in most developing nations also leads to another characteristic that distinguishes the North from the South. The relative amount of time and budget spent on information collection and analysis -- the initial steps of program development -- generally is far greater in the South. The greater information gap in the South requires a relatively greater investment in time and resources than in the North. Nonetheless, the information collection and analysis step is assisted in the South by both the willingness of international assistance institutions to fund this process and the lack of domestic political opposition (Who can argue against a good information base for policy making?). Building an information base is a politically safe activity in comparison to the volatility and opposition inherent in the subsequent steps of policy articulation and implementation. Accordingly, CAMP directors are

160

not usually eager to move out of the information building stage, particularly if international assistance will not be available or will be substantially diminished for program implementation. International assistance institutions show an understandable reluctance to get entangled in the national politics associated with program implementation.

GOVERNANCE ARRANGEMENTS.

There is a high degree of similarity among types of governance arrangement selected for coastal area management programs. (Sorensen, et al.). Table 8.2 presents this pattern of similarity. The table indicates that the governance arrangement selected depends on the purpose of the coastal management effort. Five purposes for creating an arrangement can be distinguished:

* To study the issues and consider the feasibility of CAMP initiative;
* To design the program;
* To formulate the policy that will structure and guide the program;
* To implement the policy through the direct application of management strategies; and/or
* To review and comment on the actions taken by others.

The ordering of governance arrangements by purpose in Table 8.2 reflects the usual sequence of occurrence in the policy-making process and, accordingly, also reflects their stage in the usual evolution of CAMP effort. The fifth and sixth purposes (review/comment) can occur either separately or concurrently.

Most developing nations that have studied the feasibility of coastal area management (or progressed on to program design) have used an ad hoc and interagency arrangement, such as a task

TABLE 8.2
Governance Arrangement Options Used in Coastal
Management Efforts

	Purposes: Study feasibility or problem	Design Program Policy	Formulate Policy	Implement Policy	Review/ Comment
Ad hoc arrangments					
One agency and no adjunct interagency unit.	x	x	x		
A lead agency and an adjunct interagency unit.	x	x	x		
Interagency task force.	x	x	x		
Interagency commisssion or panel.	x	x	x		

162

Permanent Arrangements

Arrangement				
Centralized powers in a new or existing agency. No adjunct interagency unit.		X	X	X
Centralized powers in a new or existing agency and form an adjunct interagency unit.		X	X	X
A lead agency to direct an interagency coordination network.	X	X	X	X
Interagency commission or council of equals or near equals.	X	X	X	X

163

force, commission, or panel. There appear to be at least three good reasons why developing nations select an ad hoc and interagency arrangement for the feasibility study or the program design stages. Interagency participation broadens the information base at a minimal cost. Because there is no clear idea of what coastal area management is in relation to the nation's or sub-national unit's existing governance, an interagency arrangement keeps the governance options open. The arrangement also avoids (or at least defers) jurisdictional battles by not placing any new authorities or resources in the hands of any one agency. The governance arrangement can (and often does) change when the CAMP effort reaches the stage of policy formulation or implementation.

By the implementation stage, is it necessary both to create a permanent institution and to centralize authority in one agency or a commission if coastal area management is to become a reality. While this step is politically volatile in both the North and South, most developing nations have the added problem of keeping a new implementation arrangement intact through changes in presidential administrations. CAMP initiatives have been mortally wounded by the massive turn-over in personnel and the critical examination of programs created by the former regime.

MANAGEMENT TECHNIQUES.

International comparison of coastal area management efforts reveals a pattern of similarity among the management strategies chosen by nations or sub-national units to implement their programs (Sorensen, et al., 1984). The strategies selected are usually a reflection of two factors: (1) what the governance arrangement is presently doing to implement environmental or natural resource management programs and (2) what is perceived as being successfully employed by other nations with analogous conditions.

Thirteen U.S. states require that proposed developments within the coastal zone be evaluated according to general guidelines or management techniques governing types of permissible activities and impacts. National or regional

164

economic development plans or broad sectoral plans, such as fishery management plans, have obvious coastal implications, but do not have the geographic focus or the impact or hazard management emphasis of such techniques. These management techniques are:

* shoreland restrictions;
* permits;
* special or critical area management;
* acquisition; and
* land use plans and zoning schemes.

Shoreland restrictions usually refer to programs which specifically prohibit or significantly limit uses within a strip or band in the coastal zone. The areas subject to shoreline restriction are typically landward of the high water mark. The boundaries of shoreland restricted areas are sometimes of a fixed depth, such as Hawaii's 40 feet shoreline setback area. In other countries or jurisdictions shoreland restrictions may extend inland to variable depths depending on coastal characteristics. Sri Lanka, for example, has a shoreland restriction area of variable size depending on the erosion rates in the affected area.

In developing nations the shoreland exclusion technique commonly arises from three concerns: blockage of public access; degradation of views; and erosion of shorelines (Sorensen, et al.). Shoreland restrictions are an attractive management technique for developing nations because they are inexpensive, geographically precise and administratively simple.

Permits are a second popular management technique. In the typical permit system, specific coastal uses within a specified coastal zone or area are subject to a permit. Applications for permits usually require information about the proposed activity and the nature of the impacts likely to be generated by the activity. Sri Lanka is probably the primary example of a developing country with a coastal zone permit system. Sri Lanka requires a permit for all "development activities" within a three hundred meter coastal zone. A "development activity" is defined as:

> ...any activity likely to alter the
> physical nature of the Coastal Zone in any
> way, and includes the construction of
> buildings and works, the deposit of wastes,
> or other materials from outfalls, vessels or
> by other means, the removal of sand, coral,
> shells, natural vegetation, seagrass or other
> substances, dredging and filling, land
> reclamation and mining or drilling for
> minerals, but does not include fishing.[6]

Between 1983 and 1987 Sri Lanka's Coast
Conservation Department approved 764 permits for
development activities, about 98% of the total
applications.[7] Many of these permits were
approved on the condition that the development
activity be modified in some way to minimize the
impacts of the activity. Indeed, the major
advantage of permit systems is that they allow the
management agency to discourage undesirable
projects before they are submitted and to attach
conditions to other proposed uses or activities
that will reduce or mitigate potential adverse
impacts.

Critical or protected area plans have been
developed to conserve sensitive environments and
habitats, or to prevent development in hazard-
prone areas such as eroding coasts or flood
plains. Critical areas are not established on a
coast-wide basis.

Critical area plans are part of the
management strategy in the U.S. coastal resource
management program. Eighteen U.S. states have
used critical area designation as a key component
of their coastal management programs (Healy and
Zinn, 1985).

On a global scale, international non-
government organizations such as the International
Union for the Conservation of Nature, World
Wildlife Fund, International Council for Bird
Preservation, the Royal Society, and The Nature
Conservancy have been active in securing special
area status for sensitive coastal habitats. A few
notable examples are IUCN's efforts for protected
areas in Indonesia and the Seychelles (IUCN 1982).

The International Council for Bird Preservation and the Royal Society have also helped establish protected areas in the Seychelles.

The designation of protected areas is used as a preservation strategy by almost all countries in all regions of the world. A common expression of this approach is the designation of coastal or marine parks (Silva and Desilvestre 1986). Usually, the parks or reserves are created to protect both inland resources and coastal resources. In many such cases, the park or reserve happens to have a coastal border, and the concern for protecting non-coastal resources appears to be the dominant factor (Silva and Desilvestre).

Acquisition programs refer to organized efforts, usually over an extended period, for systematic land purchase as distinguished from a one-time acquisition project. Acquisition programs are usually the single most reliable -- as well as expensive -- way to insure the future of a sensitive resource or to insure that a resource or area is available for a specific public purpose such as a park. International non-governmental organizations also strongly influence this strategy.

In developed countries, land use planning is a common strategy used to allocate coastal resources and environments. Comprehensive land use plans, regional plans, special area management plans, and development plans are all expressions of land use planning. Such plans tend to differ in four respects: the degree of detail with which allocations among uses are made, the number of elements included in the plan (such as transportation), the time horizon of the plan, and the degree to which the plan is meant to be an explicit guide to future resource uses and public expenditures.

In the 34 former British Commonwealth countries, land use planning is a legacy from the English institution of Town and Country Planning. In the U.K., the Town and Country Planning Act requires local planning authorities to make careful surveys of their areas and to undertake estimates for the next twenty years for housing, schools, industry and roads (Sorensen, et al.).

Sri Lanka, a former British colony, has declared all areas within one kilometer of the coastline as "urban areas" subject to planning and regulatory requirements similar to those in 20th Town and Country Planning Act.

In the United States, California's requirement that all 53 coastal cities and 15 coastal counties draw up a Local Coastal Program (LCP) is one of the most ambitious coastal programs in the United States. Land use planning is the primary element of the California program. An LCP must reflect state policies in the local jurisdiction's land use plan and zoning ordinance. Local governments, however, do have some discretion over which goals to emphasize.

CONFLICTS IN COASTAL GOVERNANCE

One of the most striking features in the governance of coastal areas is the intricate web of government agencies and programs which exercise authority over coastal areas and activities affecting resources in that area. This proliferation of management programs and activities is not surprising.

Governments have long chopped policy problems into small pieces, eschewing comprehensive solutions in favor of more incremental approaches. The narrower the focus, it has been widely argued, the more manageable problems become. Indeed, some analysts have gone so far as to suggest that more comprehensive efforts in public policy are not viable intellectually, politically, or administratively (Rabe 1986).

Even the most cursory global examination of coastal area management programs will reveal that in most countries, coastal governance is characterized by multiple sectoral agencies at one or more levels of government using different coastal management approaches or techniques (see Table 8.1). Not surprisingly, there are frequently differences that arise among agencies over how resources are to be managed or who is responsible for management.

168

The complexity of coastal area governance often gives rise to a variety of conflicts. In discussing "conflict" in coastal governance, most treatments tend to stress use conflicts at very local levels or sites. For example, siting of a power plant near a popular recreation area may impair or prevent the use of the recreation area. Review of case studies that portray incompatibilities among competing uses and users instead indicates that three types of conflict can be distinguished: jurisdictional conflicts, policy conflicts, and use conflicts.

Jurisdictional conflicts are those which arise when more than one governmental entity has or claims management responsibility over a particular coastal resource, activity, or impact. In virtually every case, jurisdictional conflicts result from the passage of laws or development of programs at different points in time at the same or different levels of government. Such conflicts may be manifested through discord or non-cooperation between administrative units or they may be latent. Several varieties of related jurisdictional conflicts can be identified.

First, jurisdictional conflicts can be of a geographic nature. In this instance, one or more agencies have the mandate to oversee the regulation of the same geographic unit (e.g., near-shore waters). Second, jurisdictional conflicts can result from more than one management entity having or claiming responsibility over a given resource such as wetland. Such conflicts can be between agencies of the same level of government or between agencies at different levels of government. Since many of the resources found in the coastal zone are mobile living resources, they usually cross spatial or geographic boundaries.

The third source of jurisdictional conflict is found in overlaps or redundancies in the management of coastal <u>activities</u> as distinct from coastal <u>resources</u>. That is, there are "events" (e.g., facility construction, dredging) occurring in a coastal setting (but not necessarily so) which are managed or regulated in order to reduce or eliminate potential adverse impacts on coastal conditions. Jurisdictional conflict of this type

169

arises from one or more agencies, at one or more levels of government, exerting or attempting to exert its authority over the activity in question.

Policy conflicts are generated by inconsistencies which exist in the laws, regulations, programs, or court decisions authorizing or structuring management activities pertaining to coastal resources. In part, these conflicts are the legacy of a policy making process that is reliant upon or dominated by single-purpose legislation. Policy conflicts typically pit resource conservation objectives against resource development objectives, but it is also common for resource development objectives to be in conflict with one another such as the exploitation of oil and its adverse effects on fisheries management.

Three distinctions can be made among policy conflicts. First, the conflict can be the result of inconsistent directives in the legal and regulatory structure. In this case, the management entity or entities are confronted by policy prescriptions which <u>may</u> work against one another. The inconsistencies are not necessarily mutually exclusive, and there is the potential to fulfill both policies if the conflicts can be overcome.

Second, policy conflicts arise from directives that are contradictory. In this case, the policy prescriptions <u>do</u> work against one another. Typically, the agency or agencies are faced with administrative obligations which are mutually exclusive. Regardless of what is done, the policy conflict will not allow for the satisfaction of both set of directives. This is exemplified by the common situation in which some administrative agencies are directed to maximize port and commercial development of an estuarine system while other agencies are charged with maximizing the preservation of the estuary's wetlands.

Resource use conflicts are the third type of resource conflict. This type of conflict represents a fundamental and immediate incompatibility between two or more uses of a coastal space or resource. That is, the contending uses, by their very nature or impacts

170

they create, must be considered to be mutually exclusive.

With use conflicts, a locational dimension must be recognized. When analyzed, this locational dimension breaks down into two sources of use conflicts. First, locational use conflicts arise because it is impossible for the contrary uses to occupy the same physical space. Second, locational conflicts can arise between neighboring uses when an activity produces impacts that are incompatible with another activity. It should be noted that in terms of coastal environments and processes, "neighboring" uses may refer to those which are quite some distance apart but are part of one or more of the same eight coastal systems outlined in the introduction.

Use conflicts, whether they be of the "same space" or "adjacent" variety in terms of the locational dimension, are either incompatible or antithetical. Incompatible use conflicts are such that the competing uses will not allow for the other. For example, oil and gas development platforms cannot utilize the same location with fishing boats towing trawl nets (a same space problem). Likewise, a recreational beach would not be placed downstream from a sewer outfall (an adjacency problem).

Antithetical use conflicts refer to that class of conflicts where uses are not mutually exclusive but where the presence of one implies a lessened value of the other. Here the uses can coexist in close proximity, but the value of at least one of the activities is substantially reduced. For example, a port facility could be situated offshore from a coastal nature reserve or park. The existence of the port facility would detract from the aesthetic experience of those visiting the reserve or park. Similarly, the operations of the port facility could possibly be constrained by concerns about the reserve.

CONFLICT MANAGEMENT TECHNIQUES

Management of conflicts in coastal governance has taken several forms. One invokes the familiar repertoires of conflict management in government: legislative decisions, executive orders to

subordinate agencies, judicial action and the
like. A second approach has been to call for
"integrated" or "comprehensive" management.
Genuinely integrated management has at least three
requirements: management objectives are made
precise, specific and non-competitive; lines of
jurisdictional responsibility are clearly drawn;
and legal authority for management is distributed
among agencies commensurate with management
responsibility. In practice, such integrated
management has proved difficult to achieve.

A third general approach has been to fashion
administrative structures and processes to deal
with governance conflicts on a case-by-case basis.
Six such mechanisms are outlined below. While
some of these mechanisms are not new, their
application to the resolution of coastal conflicts
has not been widely discussed. The mechanisms
are:

* Permanent and/or ad hoc inter-agency
arrangements
* Joint permitting
* Mandatory plan review
* Consistency review
* Facilitated policy dialogue
* Mediation

Developing nations commonly use permanent or
ad-hoc arrangement for conflict resolution. With
few exceptions, the other five mechanisms have not
diffused from the North to the South.

Some jurisdictional conflicts can be dealt
with by means of permanent and/or ad hoc interagency arrangements such as those described in the
section on coastal governance. In the
Philippines, for example, where more than fifty
agencies are directly or indirectly involved in
coastal area research and management, the
establishment of jurisdictional boundaries has
been a major concern (Tolentino 1983). Until a
few years ago, issues involving the scope of the
authority of the Bureau of Fisheries and Aquatic
Development in managing activities affecting coral
reefs brought it into conflict with both the
Bureau of Mines and Geo-Sciences and the Bureau of
Forest Development. Jurisdictional disputes

involving mangroves pitted the Bureau of Forest Development against the Bureau of Fisheries and Aquatic Resources and, to a lesser extent, the Bureau of Lands. Jurisdictional conflicts over marine parks involved the Philippines Tourist Authority, the Bureau of Forest Development, the Bureau of Fisheries and Aquatic Resources, the Natural Resources Management Center and the National Environmental Protection Council.

To deal with these and similar jurisdictional conflicts, the National Environmental Protection Council established a Coastal Zone Management Inter-Agency Task Force in 1979. Twenty-two agencies with management or research responsibilities in coastal areas are members of the task force. The task force identifies and addresses jurisdictional conflicts in proposed plans, programs and projects.

Ad hoc committees and interagency commissions are also used in the policy-making phase of coastal management, as noted in the governance section. An ad-hoc panel was formed in the 1970s by the International Oceans Institute and UN agencies to summarize "the state of marine pollution in the world's oceans." The Group of Experts on Scientific Aspects of Marine Pollution developed a report titled The Health of the Oceans. A more typical example of the use of commissions in policy conflict identification is the work of the U.S. Commission on Marine Science, Engineering and Resources, known as the Stratton Commission. The Stratton Commission produced a 1969 report titled Our Nation and the Sea which identified jurisdictional and policy conflicts as a major impediment to effective ocean and coastal management. The report was especially critical of the roles of state and local governments in coastal management. This report was one of several critical factors leading to the development and passage of the U.S. Coastal Zone Management Act in 1972. (Ironically, the CZMA and implementing regulations put heavy emphasis on having state governments play a major role in coastal management. As a result, most states now have more agencies involved in coastal management -- and more interagency conflicts.)

Permanent interagency commissions are also

173

used for identifying policy conflicts and
developing strategies for dealing with them.
Several developing countries have created
interministerial councils to identify and resolve
policy conflicts in sectoral plans or in regional
plans for coastal areas. Such councils are formed
not simply for the resolution of conflicts, but
also provide opportunities for insuring that
information and expertise are appropriately
coordinated and integrated. The success of such
councils in resolving conflicts is usually a
function of the urgency of the problem, the
political clout of the convening authority and the
skill of administrative staff.

Indonesia has organized inter-ministerial
councils to deal with jurisdictional and policy
disputes (Koesoebiono, Collier and Burbridge
1982). In Thailand, interministerial councils
have been appointed to coordinate the preparation
of coastal regional plans for the Eastern Seaboard
area, the Songkla Lake Basin and the Upper South
region (Thailand Development Research Institute
1986). In the case of the Eastern Seaboard
region, the committee is chaired by the Prime
Minister. In the case of the Songkla Lake Basin
the committee is chaired by the Secretary General
of the National Economic and Social Development
Board. The primary function of the committees is
to identify primary projects to be included in the
master plans for the regions.

Some Latin American nations have also
organized interministerial councils to broaden the
scope of sectoral planning. In Ecuador, the
Directorate of Maritime Affairs of the Ecuadorian
Navy played a leading role in facilitating an
international seminar for the purpose of
discussing Ecuador's coastal problems and
alternative solutions. In Brazil, the Comissao
Interministerial para os Recursos do Mar (CIRM)
was created in 1974 to assist the Presidency in
the formulation of national coastal and ocean
policy and to co-ordinate research in the marine
sector (Pires and Cycon 1987).

Another method of dealing with potential
jurisdictional conflicts that is growing in
popularity in the U.S. is joint permitting
involving two or more agencies. Joint permitting

174

has at least two meanings. It is sometimes used to describe permit review processes in which two or more agencies agree to use one public notice, hearing and/or application for permits issued separately by each agency. Such a procedure is used in Louisiana, for example, to streamline review processes conducted by the federal Army Corps of Engineers (which issues permits involving dredging of wetlands) and the state Department of Natural Resources (Coastal Management Division). Each agency conducts its own independent evaluation of the permit application and issues its own permit. Such a procedure can be very valuable in promoting efficiency in permit reviews, but does not necessarily deal with conflicts occurring because of overlapping jurisdictional responsibilities.

Another meaning of joint permitting is that the agency actually issues a permit for two or more agencies. In North Carolina, the state coastal agency has arranged with the federal Army Corps of Engineers to conduct joint site visits, public notices, hearings (if required) and permits. Application is made to the state agency which forwards the application to the Army Corps of Engineers which, in turn, solicits comments from other federal agencies and issues a recommendation. If the Corps and the state are in agreement, a joint general permit is issued. If the corps and the state disagree, either may issue its own agency permit.

In recent years mandatory plan review has become a popular technique for coordinating U.S. federal-state policies and programs in air and water quality management, surface mining and coastal resource management. The basic approach is to require states to develop resource management plans or programs that are consistent with general federal standards. For example, the Coastal Zone Management Act of 1972 requires participating states to draw up programs that meet general standards with regard to the designation of a coastal zone, the identification of uses subject to management, and areas of particular concern. There is a host of similar standards. States that are successful in developing programs that meet federal standards are then eligible for both funding to implement the programs and the application of the consistency review process (the next technique to be discussed).

Thirteen U.S. states also use mandatory plan reviews to coordinate state-local activities in coastal management. As noted, California's coastal law requires each local municipality to develop a Local Coastal Program (LCP) for the portion of its jurisdiction that overlaps with the state's designated coastal zone. These LCPs are expected to include a land use plan as well as an implementation plan, including necessary zoning, grading, architectural review and subdivision ordinance (Fischer 1985). According to the law, once the LCPs are in place and approved by the State Coastal Commission, state permitting authority would be delegated to local governments.

The basic assumption of mandatory plan review is that intergovernmental conflicts over planning goals and management techniques can be identified and resolved in the process of interaction involved in developing "approvable" plans. To date, 28 of 35 US coastal states and territories have programs that were approved by the federal government and 98 of 123 planning areas in California have approved LCPs as of mid-1985 (Fischer 1985). However, it is not clear to what extent the number of approved programs constitutes the successful resolution of policy conflicts or whether agreement on policies and management techniques merely delayed or transferred resource management conflicts to a different level or venue.

Consistency review has at least two meanings in natural resource management. The more familiar use of the term has to do with the so-called "consistency doctrine" in U.S. local government land use management. The consistency doctrine holds that local zoning ordinances and other legal techniques of land management (such as subdivision ordinances) should be consistent with local government plans. The purpose of such consistency requirements is to provide a degree of certainty and predictability in the amount, location and density of future community development through explicit congruence of planning and regulatory mechanisms. Such consistency requirements are

176

also sometimes intended to limit the discretion of city legislative officials in reviewing proposed planning and regulatory changes. The degree to which such consistency is either practical or desirable has been widely debated among analysts of local government.

The U.S. Coastal Zone Management Act offers an altogether different application of the concept of consistency. Under the CZMA, certain classes of activities undertaken by federal agencies in designated coastal zones (or affecting coastal zones) must be consistent with state coastal resource management programs. These activities include federal licenses and permits, federally-supported activities, construction, off-shore mineral development and some federal planning grants to state and local government agencies.

Since the federal government is engaged in such a wide range of activities in coastal areas with such enormous potential impacts, the consistency provision allows state governments important leverage over federal activities. The process involves a determination by the applicant or federal agency (depending on the type of federal activity) that the proposed activity is consistent with the state program. The state then has a specified period, usually no more than six months, to concur or object. In cases in which the state finds that the proposed activity is not consistent, the relevant state and federal agencies try to resolve the conflict informally. Cases which cannot be resolved informally are forwarded to the national Secretary of Commerce for mediation and, failing resolution at that level, to the courts. Analysis of all consistency determinations in 1983 revealed that coastal states concurred on 93% of the approximately 400 direct federal activities reviewed, and concurred on 82% of the 5,500 federal licenses and permits (Lowry and Eichenberg 1986).

Facilitated policy dialogues are another mechanism for dealing with policy conflicts at the policy-making or plan-making stage. Policy dialogues involve facilitators in the following process:

When parties in dispute encounter substantial differences in their views or anticipate confrontation, nonpartisan facilitators often can play an important role in structuring discussion or managing meetings. Before the parties have reached an impasse, trained facilitators can help to transform incipient disputes into occasions for collaborative problem solving. Facilitated negotiation has been especially successful at the early stages of policy formulation (e.g., legislative drafting or the formulation of regulations). (Susskind and McCreary 1985).

The job of the facilitator is particularly important in facilitated dialogues. The facilitator helps the group structure an agenda and guide discussion in an orderly fashion. Recorders are sometimes used to chronicle the discussion on newsprint or other large paper. This record is posted in the room so that the group has a public "memory" of the process as it proceeds.

In Massachusetts, a facilitated policy dialogue was used to identify ways to revise the Massachusetts Waterway Statute in ways that harmonized developers' interests in harbor development and waterfront revitalization with other public interests in navigation, fishing and hunting. A policy dialogue was organized by the Massachusetts Coastal Zone Management Program and fifty participants were invited. Two highly respected facilitators were selected. The participants engaged in a day-long process at the end of which consensus was reached on a number of issues.[8] This dialogue provided a basis for revisions to the law. Facilitated dialogues were also used in drafting regulations to implement the law.

In Sri Lanka, a facilitated dialogue was used to identify management priorities for coastal habitats. Almost forty participants representing several agencies and non-governmental groups met over a four day period to try to reach consensus about management issues for mangroves, seagrass beds, coral reefs, salt marshes, lagoons, and estuaries.

Mediation is particularly important in multi-party resource use or site use disputes. Mediation involves the use of a nonpartisan third party who can design a process that insures that all the relevant parties are represented, that allows all parties to identify their interests, that invents options that deal with the interests of each party, and that designs agreements.

In the U.S., organizations such as the Conservation Foundation and the National Institute of Dispute Resolution have done much to promote the use of mediation in disputes involving resource uses. A substantial amount of research and training on mediation and other forms of alternative dispute resolution is now occurring at several universities, thanks in large part to foundations, such as Hewlett, which have given large grants to support mediation practice, training and research. In the U.S., mediation has been used in a number of resource use disputes, including coastal resources (Bingham 1986; Susskind and McCreary). Mediation is also used in some developing countries. Mediation was successfully used in Sri Lanka in dealing with a dispute in which fishermen were unable to beach their boats because of construction of a sewage outfall and in another dispute between fishermen and hotel owners (Sadacharan and Lowry 1987).

CONCLUSION

The number of coastal area management programs is increasing -- particular in the South. All five criteria used to make international comparative assessments among programs demonstrate there is a high degree of similarity among the efforts made by developed and developing nations. The similarities are largely the result of the diffusion of the idea of comprehensive coastal management from North to South. In general, less developed countries have perceived and adopted the concept of coastal management in much the same way as they incorporated the environmental impact statement process, initiated by the U.S. a decade earlier. The financial aid and information exchange provided by both international assistance agencies and non-governmental organizations have been the primary means supporting the diffusion process.

Coastal programs in the North and South nations are motivated by the same general types of concerns: resource degradation and depletion, hazard mitigation, and resource development. The specific motivating issues and their relative priority rankings vary among countries. The relative North-South priority among issues is different in one expected aspect. The South places far more concern on the development of resources in contrast to the North's focus on resource conservation and preservation.

The general stages of program development are similar in the North and South. There appears to be more concentration in the South on the initial stages of program development, particularly information collection and mapping. Budget resources and staff capabilities are usually much less in the South, so that program development and implementation have been more problematic.

The general types of governance and management techniques are similar in the North and South. However, many of the similarities in these two comparative criteria are more apparent than real. Administrative structures and procedures that have the same label in the North and South may involve different practices in particular countries. For example, administrative arrangements such as an inter-ministerial council may involve very different expectations about the role of participants, sharing of authority and commitment to action depending on the locale and administrative traditions. In general, developing nations show a strong preference for inter-ministerial councils with responsibility and authority evenly distributed among the participants.

Finally, a central theme of this chapter is that the governance of coastal areas in both North and South is characterized by multiple agencies whose management efforts are frequently redundant and sometimes in conflict. Strategies for coping with inter-agency and inter-governmental conflict are evolving in both the North and South. While some of the techniques of conflict management are diffusing from the North to the South, it is very likely that the diffusion will eventually be two-way. While comprehensive coastal management as currently conceived is fairly new, conflict management is not. It is likely that in at least some countries of the South, traditional methods of conflict management will be used to resolve coastal conflicts and will be found to have potential applicability elsewhere.

NOTES

1. The acronym CAMP stands for coastal area management and planning. The six-part definition of coastal area management (see note 2) incorporates planning as a component since this is the means by which the coastal systems perspective is implemented. The acronym is also used to be congruent with the international newsletter, the Bulletin of Coastal Area Management Planning. The quarterly Bulletin is a product of the U.S. National Parks Service's Office of International Affairs. To date, 6 issues of the bulletin have been published. The mailing list consists of over 1,200 names from 100 nations.

2. See Sorensen et al., Coasts: Institutional Arrangements for Management of Coastal Resources, 1984 and Sorensen and Brandani, "Coastal Management Efforts in Latin America," Coastal Management Journal, vol. 15, no. 2 (1987).

3. For a comprehensive review of the U.S. national program, see the special issue of the Coastal Zone Management Journal, vol. 6, no. 4, (1979).

4. The phrase coastal resources and environments is used to include natural hazards as an important component of a coastal management program. It is common for the CAMP literature to describe programs as coastal resources management initiatives. However, the definition of the term, coastal resources, does not include hazardous environments such as flood plains, tsunami run-up areas, and coastal storm wash-over areas.

5. Criteria for comparative assessment are identified by United Nations, 1982; Mitchell,

1982; Sorensen et al., 1984; and Sorensen and
Brandani, 1987.

6. Democratic Socialist Republic of Sri
Lanka, Coast Conservation Act, No. 57 of 1081.

7. Personal communication from Sri Lanka
Coast Conservation Department staff.

8. The issues included: the overarching
importance of water dependency in screening new
uses of tidelands, the principle that substantial
fees should be charged to site new developments on
tidelands and that these fees should be used to
purchase and protect the most ecologically
sensitive portions of the coastal zone (Susskind
and McCreary).

REFERENCES

Bingham, G. 1980. Resolving Environmental
    Disputes. Washington,.D.C.: The
    Conservation Foundation.
Cullen, P. 1977. Coastal Management in Port
    Phillip. Coastal Zone Management Journal
    3 (3): 291-305.
Cullen, P. 1982. Coastal Zone Management in
    Australia. Coastal Zone Journal 10 (3):
    183-305.
Fischer, M. 1985. California's Coastal Program:
    Larger-Than-Local Interests Built Into Local
    Plans. Journal of the American Planning
    Association 51 (3): 312-321.
Healy, R.G. and J. Zinn. 1985. Environment and
    Development Conflicts in Coastal Zone
    Management. Journal of the American
    Planning Association 51 (3): 299-311.
International Union for the Conservation of
    Nature. 1982. The World's Greatest Natural
    Areas. For World Heritage Committee.
Koesoebiono, W.L. Collier and P.R. Burbridge.
    1982. Indonesia: Resources Use and
    Management in the Coastal Zone. C. Soysa,
    L.S. Chia and W.L. Collier (eds.), Man, Land
    and Sea. Bangkok: Agricultural Development
    Council.
Lowry, K. and T. Eichenberg. 1986. Assessing
    Intergovernmental Coordination in Coastal

Zone Management. Policy Studies Review
6 (2): 321-329.
Mitchell, J.K. 1982. Coastal Zone Management: A
Comparative Analysis of National Programs.
E. Borgese and N. Ginsburg (editors), Ocean
Yearbook 3. University of Chicago Press.
Pires, L. and D. Cycon. 1987. Planning and
Managing Brazil's Coastal Resources. Coastal
Management Journal. 15 (1): 61-74.
Olsen, S. Report: A Collaborative Effort in
Developing the Integrated Coastal Resources
Management for Ecuador, Coastal Management
Journal 15 (1):   97-101.
Rabe, B. 1986. Fragmentation and Integration in
State Environmental Management. Washington,
D.C.: The Conservation Foundation.
Silva, M. and I. Desilvestre. 1986. Marine and
Protected Areas in Latin America:
A Preliminary Assessment. Coastal Zone
Management Journal 14 (4):   311-347.
Sorensen, J., McCreary, S. and Hershman M. 1984.
Institutional Arrangements for Management of
Coastal Resources. Prepared for the
International Affairs Office of the U.S.
National Park Service and the U.S. Agency
for International Development.
Sorensen J. and Brandani, A. 1987. Coastal
Management Efforts in Latin America.
Coastal Management Journal 15 (1).
Susskind, L. and S. McCreary. 1985. Techniques
for Resolving Coastal Resource Management
Disputes Through Negotiation. Journal of
the American Planning Association 51 (3):
365-374.
Swanson, G. 1975. Coastal Zone Management from an
Administrative Perspective: A Case Study
of the San Francisco Bay Conservation and
Development Commission. Coastal Zone
Management Journal 2 (2).
Thailand Development Research Institute. 1986. The
Status of Coastal and Marine Resources
of Thailand, Bangkok.
Tolentino, A.S. 1983. Philippine Coastal Zone
Management: Organizational Linkages and
Interconnections. Honolulu: East-West
Center Working Paper.
United Nations. 1982. Coastal Area Management and

Development. Prepared by the Ocean
Economics and Technology Branch.   Pergamon
Press.

9

Strategic Tensions and Minerals Management in the International Seabed Authority

Robert E. Bowen and Timothy M. Hennessey

INTRODUCTION

In 1982, the participants of the Third United Nations Conference on the Law of the Sea signed what has been called "the new constitution of the oceans."[1] Perhaps the most interesting new concept and entity developed during the nearly fifteen years of conference preparation and deliberation is the International Seabed Authority (the ISA or the Authority), an institution with the potential to evolve into a unique international organization.

The Authority will have the power to regulate the extraction of nickel, copper, cobalt, manganese, and perhaps other minerals from the deep seabed beyond national jurisdiction. It will be unique in that it will be the first cooperative international body whose purpose is the development, management, regulation, and production of resources from areas outside national laws. The Authority is expected to develop its own capital by way of fees, taxes and royalties from the mining activities it is to oversee. It will have the authority to establish its own rules and regulations and to sanction violators.[2]

In short, the International Seabed Authority is a fascinating example of an emerging institution with potentially important implications for global resource redistribution. For students of international organizations and international political economy the ISA presents a challenge to reason through the behavioral implications of ISA structure and rules. This paper is an initial step in that direction.

The paper explores the utility of institutional analysis as an analytic devise to specify some central concepts for assessing the structure and operation of the ISA. Following others, such as Ostrom and Oakerson, we focus on (1) the organizational structure of the ISA, (2) the degree of understanding and shared principles between decision-makers, (3) the nature of the goods to be managed, (4) the strategic behavior of decision-makers, (5) the sets of rules specifying relationships among decision-makers, and (6) expected outcomes.

These factors are viewed in light of the strategic tensions created by disagreements between proponents of "new order" economic relations and those of the developed "old order". These contrasting North-South approaches permeate the ISA at almost every level and threaten to constrain its effective operation.

THE LAW OF THE SEA AND MINERALS MANAGEMENT

It was the convening of the 1930 Conference for the Codification of International Law that began a process of negotiating marine boundary and jurisdictional rules, and that process has continued unabated for more than 50 years. Indeed, the international community has been deliberating the law of the sea for as long as it has formally negotiated international law.

With the founding of the United Nations, law-of-the-sea debates have been focused in multilateral fora under UN sponsorship. Issues relating to the regime of the high seas and the territorial sea were among the first topics considered for codification by the International Law Commission (ILC) in 1949. The work of the ILC on these topics led to the convening of the First United Nations Conference on the Law of the Sea (UNCLOS I) in 1958. A second conference, UNCLOS II, continued these debates in 1960 on some unresolved issues. However, all three of these meetings (the 1930 Hague Conference, UNCLOS I and II) focused primarily on questions of the

186

delimitation of national marine boundaries, the nature of coastal state jurisdiction and high seas freedoms. With advances in technology and interest, debate began to shift toward the minerals, and perceived wealth, of the deep sea outside of national jurisdiction -- resources whose legal status was broadly questioned.

In August of 1967 Ambassador Arvid Pardo of Malta spoke before the General Assembly requesting that the United Nations carefully consider the adequacy of the existing marine legal regime. It was in this speech that Pardo first formally suggested the adoption of the concept of the common heritage of mankind to govern the legal regulation of the seabed beyond national jurisdiction. The full adoption of this concept would mean that this area would not be appropriated by any state and would be exploited primarily in the interests of mankind with special regard to the needs of poor countries.

That historic speech caught the imagination of many and drew general attention to the resources of the deep ocean floor. Pardo went on to request the establishment of a committee to negotiate a comprehensive treaty that would: (a) precisely define the limits of national jurisdiction; (b) safeguard the interests of the world community and the international character of the seabed beyond national jurisdiction; and, (c) establish an agency, linked to, but not necessarily part of, the United Nations system to assume jurisdiction, not as a sovereign, but as a trustee for all countries, over the seabed beyond national jurisdiction.[3]

With this newly heightened awareness of the potential value of deep seabed marine resources and of the need to consider how best to manage the future exploitation of those resources, the international community established, in 1967, a 35 state ad-hoc committee to study the peaceful uses of the seabed and the ocean floor beyond the limits of national jurisdiction. This committee,[4] which served as the primary preparatory and study group for the Third United Nations Conference on the Law of the Sea (UNCLOS III), initiated twenty years of nearly continuous negotiation on the status and functioning of international machinery to regulate minerals development in the deep sea.

From these negotiations has emerged a clear blueprint for future international marine relations and a framework on which the International Seabed Authority will be built. UNCLOS III only established a framework, since ongoing negotiations at the Preparatory Commission of the ISA (PrepCom) are defining the future rules and regulations by which the Authority will operate. The primary role of this paper is to characterize the factors influencing those negotiations and to anticipate the nature of those future rules.

THE INTERNATIONAL SEABED AUTHORITY

Attributes of the ISA include: (i) the basic organizational structure of the Authority; (ii) the general system of exploration and exploitation set up under the ISA; (iii) commodity production controls and limits; (iv) provisions governing technology and information transfer; (v) the Preparatory Investment Protection program; and, (vi) the Preparatory Commission of the ISA.

Structure

An examination of the Authority's structure reveals a complicated, if not convoluted, melange of organs, procedures, and functions. The principal organs of the Authority are the Assembly, the Council (with the Economic Planning Commission and the Legal and Technical Commission), and the Secretariat. The treaty further creates the Enterprise, which serves as the operating arm of the Authority. (Figure 9.1 depicts the organs of the ISA, while the appendix to this chapter summarizes the composition, powers and functions of each).

In general, the Assembly is the body establishing broad policies of the Authority, and on which all states parties to the convention are represented. The Council is the executive organ and principal rule-making body of the Authority, and is comprised of 36 member states (the membership selection criteria are detailed subsequently in this chapter). The Secretariat is

188

the administrative organ, with staff selected on the basis of administrative and geographic criteria. The Enterprise is the organization that would carry out actual mining operations in the Area.

FIGURE 9.1

The International Seabed Authority

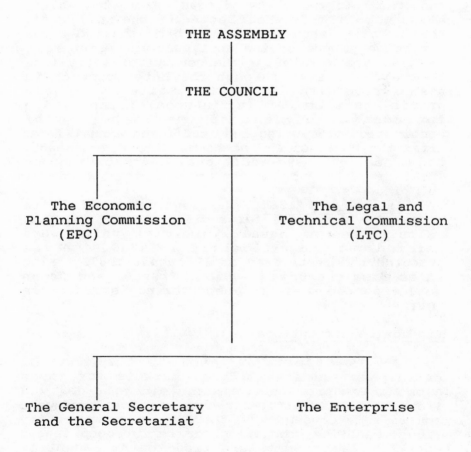

Exploration and Exploitation under the ISA

Mineral development will be conducted by means of a parallel or banking system. The convention confers development rights to both the Enterprise and to state and state-sponsored entities. Under the guidelines set forth in the treaty, prospective miners shall apply to the Authority for a "plan of work" to carry out exploration and exploitation activities in the Area. After having determined the commercial exploitability of a given area, the applicant passes on to the Authority coordinates dividing the area into two parts of equal estimated value, along with all data collected by the applicant. The Authority then decides which of the two areas may be developed by the applicant and which will be "reserved solely for the conduct of activities by the Authority, through the Enterprise or in association with developing States."[5] These provisions also define financial terms, which include the payment to the Authority of application processing fees and fixed annual fees. After the commencement of commercial development, the miner must make additional contributions in the form of production charges and proportions of net proceeds.[6]

In July of 1987, the government of India proposed a mine site for registration by PrepCom. Calculations of equal commercial value were carried out and a slightly amended site was accepted and registered on 19 August 1987.[7] Mine sites from the Soviet Union, France, and Japan were expected to be proposed for registration in November of 1987.

Production Limitations

In an effort to "promote the growth, efficiency and stability of markets for those commodities produced from the minerals derived from the Area, at prices renumerative to producers and fair to consumers,"[8] the ISA has reserved the right to define production limits for deep seabed miners. Such limits are tied to the amount of nickel produced by mining operations, as nickel is assumed to be the most valuable metal found in manganese nodules.[9] If the ISA develops exploration and exploitation rules for resources other than manganese nodules, the criteria for production limits will change.[10]

Technology Transfer

The treaty also provides that the Authority take measures to acquire technology and scientific knowledge related to activities in the Area. The term technology is defined as the specialized equipment and technical know-how, including manuals, designs, operating instruction, training and technical advice and assistance, necessary to assemble, maintain and operate a viable system and the legal right to use these items for that purpose on a non-exclusive basis.[11]

Preparatory Investment Protection

One of the more intriguing compromises arrived at by UNCLOS III was the Preparatory Investment Protection (PIP) program. Late in the negotiations representatives of deep seabed mining states argued that because of their historic commitment and investment in seabed exploration, they should be accorded preferential treatment in the development of mining regulations. The result of those requests has been the development of a mining regime that is effectively separate from, but interim, to that of the ISA. The PIP resolution defines the rights and obligations of these "pioneer investors." A pioneer is defined, essentially, as a state or state-sponsored enterprise that spent $30 million dollars in "pioneer activities" before 1 January 1985 (ten percent of which must have gone toward the location, survey, and evaluation of a mining area). Each pioneer must apply to the ISA for a plan of work and pay to the Authority registration, administrative, and fixed annual fees. Pioneers must also pay "periodic expenditures", in amounts determined by PrepCom to be equal to the expenditures of a bona fide operator intending to bring an area into production.[12] The registration of sites proposed by the governments of India, the Soviet Union,

France and Japan will be carried out under the provisions of PIP.

Preparatory Commission

In order to "take all possible measures to ensure the entry into effective operation without undue delay of the Authority and the Tribunal and to make the necessary arrangements for the commencement of their functions," the treaty establishes the Preparatory Commission of the International Seabed Authority. The PrepCom is obliged, among other things, to: (1) draft rules of procedure for the Assembly and Council; (2) make recommendations concerning the relationship between the Authority and the United Nations and other international organizations; (3) prepare draft rules, regulations and procedures, to enable the Authority to commence its functions, including draft regulations concerning the financial management and the internal administration of the Authority; and, (4) exercise certain regulatory powers as regards pioneers investors. The rules and regulations drafted by PrepCom will apply provisionally, until adopted by the Authority.[13]

The preceding characterization of the ISA structure and regulatory competence, while admittedly limited, is sufficient to begin our analysis of critical institutional design concerns.

INSTITUTIONAL DESIGN AND ANALYSIS

A fundamental challenge facing those who seek to understand the evolving International Seabed Authority is to rely on appropriate theory for reasoning through the behavioral consequences associated with the institutional structure of the ISA. Such analysis should yield both diagnostic and prescriptive information.

Recent work by scholars associated with a particular variant of public choice theory offers considerable promise as a systematic guide to the development of empirically testable hypotheses concerning institutional behavior. This approach views various forms of organization as alternative instruments of public policy. The essential problem of such organizational analysis is to "(1) anticipate the consequences which follow when (2) self-interested individuals choose maximizing strategies within (3) particular organizational arrangements when applied to (4) particular types of goods."[14]

Types of goods constitute the basic ingredients of the problem. The management of goods for joint net benefit requires a particular set of decision-making arrangements which, in combination with goods, act as constraints or opportunities for decision-makers. Both the structure of the goods and the set of decision-making arrangements produce high levels of interdependence among decision-makers. What one decides to do is dependent on what others decide to do. Strategic considerations become inevitable, and outcomes are a function of these interactions. Hence, it is important to characterize certain geopolitical relations that serve to focus the strategic response of individual sovereign actors to alternative organizational proposals.

An understanding of these basic principles and values is essential to any evaluation of national preferences, positions and choices. We suggest two fundamental dimensions that distinguish state perceptions on the appropriateness and acceptability of proposed organizational arrangements for the International Seabed Authority. Outcomes are a function of the combined choices of all relevant decision-makers in relation to the (i) goods and (ii) decision-making arrangements.

Types of Goods

Particular goods can be arranged along a continuum in terms of three basic attributes: (1) jointness in use of consumption (i.e., your consumption of the good will not detract from and is available to me); (2) non-exclusion; and, (3) indivisibility. Private goods occupy one end of the continuum and are highly divisable and exclusion is relatively easy. On the other end of the continuum, we have pure public or collective consumption goods which have no potential for exclusion and are highly indivisible or "lumpy". In the case of pure public goods, what is available for anyone is available to all. The majority of goods, however, are located somewhere between these two end points; that is, they are partially divisible but jointness is possible within limits which circumscribe the behavior of individuals.

The major issue which underlies future ISA operations is the task of determining, as precisely as possible, the limiting conditions under which jointness is feasible. Such a task requires giving close attention to patterns of subtractability among diverse users. Indeed, one of the ISA's charges is to apportion the potential value of deep seabed minerals so that the activity of the developed countries will not excessively subtract from the joint net benefits to other, especially developing nations.

In the case of the ISA, goods have been characterized as belonging to a common pool, a "common". A commons is a resource shared by a community of producers or consumers. Some commons are fixed while others are fugitive, some are renewable while others are not. The problem with a commons is that it is a resource subject to individual use but not to individual possession, i.e., there are no property rights. Hence, individuals have a tendency to overconsume resources and ignore the social consequences of such actions, leading to a "tragedy of the commons." The issue becomes, "how to coordinate individual users in order to attain an optimal rate of production or consumption for the whole community."[15]

In the common, the total rate of consumption varies with: (1) the number of users; (2) the type of use; and, (3) the degree to which several individuals share the same resource. The attributes of such goods, namely, jointness, excludability and divisibility can serve as variables in helping us understand the particular commons in question. The deep sea minerals situation is a case where the international community has determined such minerals to be the "common heritage of mankind." In this sense they are owned by everyone and yet by no one -- they are held to be common property resources.

Open access or non-excludability is, in fact, present in the case of deep sea minerals and could lead to congestion and conflict as each miner seeks to derive benefits. Such conflict would be very likely if there were no exclusive rights to un-mined deposits. It should be clear, in addition, that exclusion is possible; that is, access could be rationed or limited by an appropriate authority. Non-excludability is not an inherent characteristic of deep seabed minerals as, for example, is the case of a national common defense. It is, rather, a choice to be made by the community of nations.

Moreover, deep seabed resources are divisable or packageable. The resource could, in principle, be priced and divided up among private property holders. Deep seabed resources, having only partial jointness, condition and can be subject to exclusion and divisibility. Owing to these particular features such resources are much more susceptible to optimal management than those characterized by jointness, non-exclusion and non-divisibility.

The case for the common-heritage regulation of deep sea mining by an international regulatory agency on purely efficiency grounds (i.e., there will be over-investment, in search, development and production) would therefore, seem weak.[16] But the political case for redistributing wealth remains strong -- at least to a large number of states, especially in the developing world. Given this political desire, the precise form of the regulatory decision-making system is not necessarily clear.

Decision-Making Arrangements

Decision-making arrangements refer to the allocation of authority to decision-makers, where the authority to act is derived from a number of functionally separate decision structures. The focus of analysis is upon the rule-ordered relationships that govern individuals in this interorganizational context. The ISA is a fertile ground for such analysis given the complexity of its organizational arrangements.

We assume that individuals use a cost calculus to determine their preferences in relation to goods and organizational structure. Obtaining information to select preferences is a costly process and perceptions of the situation are imperfect. The operating assumption is that individuals will choose the least costly alternative (or one maximizing net benefit).

North-South national differences regarding the role of international law and organization drive much, if not most, of the debate on the structure and design of ISA rules. These principles lie at the center of many existing geopolitical tensions and are enhanced by a perception of historic inequities among developing countries.

During the past quarter century, the international community has witnessed sweeping changes in both the structure and nature of international politics. The processes that contributed most to these changes, namely the rise of nationalism and the process of decolonialization, were certainly not unique to this period; but the speed and scope of their influence, were, in fact, quite unique. The dramatic increase in the number of nation-states entering the international system transformed most of the basic rules and operating principles under which international politics had been functioning. Shifts in international political and economic norms make it clear that North-South tensions have become a dominant international pattern.

Attendant with these shifts was a growing dissatisfaction on the part of developing states with the appropriateness of international law to their set of concerns. As Professor Verzijl has stated, "now there is one truth that is not open to denial or even to doubt, namely, that the actual body of international law, as it stands today, is not only the product of the conscious activity of the European mind, but has also drawn its vital essence from a common source of European beliefs, and in both of these aspects it is mainly of Western European origin."[17]

International law, it was said, not only reflected a European origin but was too protective of European and colonial interests. Developing states perceived, and argued, that "law is not a constant in society, but is a function. In order for it to be effective, it ought to change with changes in views, powers and interests in the community."[18]

The existence of an international forum such as the United Nations, where such views could be heard and acted upon, helped bring these issues to the fore. The structure of the United Nations system, particularly the one-nation/one-vote rule, afforded developing states an opportunity to generate new, more equitable rules for international relations.

Indeed, these efforts to generate new international legal norms were at the center of much of the debate at UNCLOS III, and remain critical concerns in the design of the operating rules, regulations and procedures for the International Seabed Authority. For many observers of the law of the sea, the question has become one of "new order" versus "old order" rule-making.

In general terms, new-order issues have revolved around efforts to maximize the effective participation of developing states in the Area, while old-order efforts have attempted to maximize the influence of states with sufficient existing capital and technology to exploit Area resources. With specific reference to the International Seabed Authority, these differences have led to two rather distinctive sets of policy preferences. New-order advocates support generally an ISA with strong, if not proprietary rights, and the competence to coordinate, regulate, supervise, control, sanction, and enforce. Alternatively, old-order advocates emphasize the need to protect private and national interests, and tend to stress economic and efficiency questions over those focusing on equity and redistribution.

This North-South contrast can be elaborated further regarding the question of the international legal standing of the International Seabed Authority. Specifically, questions have been raised as to whether the ISA is a "proprietor" or "trustee" of resources in the international area.

Reference to several relevant provisions of

the convention would aid in the following
discussion.

Article 136 - Common Heritage of Mankind

The Area and its resources are the common heritage
of mankind.

Article 137:2

All rights in the resources of the Area are vested
in mankind as a whole, on whose behalf the
Authority shall act.

Article 157 - Nature and Fundamental Principles
of the Authority

The Authority is the organization through which
States Parties shall, . . ., organize and control
activities in the Area, particularly with a view
to administering the resources of the Area.

Discussion on these and related issues have
questioned, in rather fundamental ways, the nature
of sovereignty in the Area. For example, several
representatives have characterized the issue in
terms of property rights. They have suggested
that the concept of property is inextricably
linked to that of control. With administrative
and regulatory control centered in the ISA, one
argument holds that the Authority is then a
"proprietor" - a holder of property rights. This
position has broad support within the delegations
of many less developed states, and acts as an
underlying dimension in a wide range of other
PrepCom discussions.
    The counter argument, held by most developed
states, is that the Authority is no more than a
"trustee" for the wealth and resources of the
Area. The mineral rights of the international
seabed are vested in humankind as a whole, while
rights to organize and control activities in the
Area are held by states parties to the convention.
The Authority functions to administer those
rights. Positions on this question clearly and
directly influence preferences for the building of

198

the rules and regulatory structure of the ISA.

In important ways the negotiations on the law of the sea have incorporated, if not centered around, these general questions of international political economy and foreign policy. Indeed, Arvid Pardo noted recently that the law of the sea negotiations have become, together with questions of disarmament, the New International Economic Order, and others - a part of the contemporary global problematique of peace.[19]

DESIGN RULES FORMULATION

The clearest manifestation of these strategic considerations is in the design and evolution of operational rules. Emphasis is placed here on the role and influence of strategic tensions on the structuring and development of institutional frameworks.

Rules can be viewed as the functions most directly influential in structuring a given situation or environment. In particular, there is continuing influence of strategic tensions on the development of ISA rules at PrepCom.[20] Drawing in some measure from Elnor Ostrom, we propose to focus on two primary rule sets:

(1) Boundary Rules that specify how participants are chosen to hold positions and how participants leave these positions; and

(2) Information Rules that authorize channels of communication among participants in positions and specify the language and form in which communication will take place.

This topology provides a useful vehicle to examine and evaluate the design of the International Seabed Authority.

Boundary Rules

The more convoluted negotiations both at UNCLOS III and at PrepCom have concerned the establishment of entry, exit, and domain conditions for individual mining participants. These rules become particularly important in

multilateral bargaining context, in part, because
of the sheer size of the forum. The cumbersome
qualities of a body comprised of 160 sovereign
actors can be modified by a set of rules
restricting entry and constraining decision-making
competence. In the case of the ISA, several
boundary conditions can be detailed.

Of the four interdependent bodies of the
International Seabed Authority -- the Secretariat,
Assembly, the Council, and the Enterprise -- the
Council provides the most intriguing example of
boundary limits. The Council has been designated
"the executive organ of the Authority." It is the
Council that is granted the power to establish the
specific policies to be pursued by the Authority.
In an effort to increase effective decision-making
and to acknowledge developed state concern over
the one-nation/one-vote system, membership in the
Council is limited to 36 states. Further, members
are drawn from set categories. Members are
elected by the Assembly to the Council in the
following fashion:

(1) four members from among those States
Parties which during the last five years have
either consumed more than two percent of total
world consumption or have net imports of more than
two percent of total world imports of the
commodities produced from the minerals to be
derived from the Area (including at least one
state from Eastern Europe and including the
largest consumer);

(2) four members from among the eight
states with the largest investment in deep seabed
mining (including at least one state from Eastern
Europe);

(3) four members from among the major
exporters of minerals to be derived from the Area
(including at least two developing states whose
exports of such minerals have a substantial
bearing on their economies);

(4) six members from among developing
states with "special interests" (e.g. states that
are land-locked or are otherwise geographically

200

disadvantaged, are importers of Area minerals, are potential exporters of Area minerals, or are from among the world's least developed economies); and

(5) eighteen members elected according to the principle of ensuring an equitable distribution of Council seats.[21]

Effective decision-making is thus vested with 36 states chosen generally to: (1) concentrate power in countries with a substantial interest in the issues under debate; (2) achieve geographical balance; and (3) develop a set of essentially preordained bargaining coalitions. Thus the number of decision-makers is reduced to a more manageable number, and the concern that decisions would be made by states with insufficient economic interests has been resolved. This latter question was one that dominated much of the UNCLOS III debate, and one that drove the development of another set of critical boundary rules -- those of the Preparatory Investment Protection plan (PIP).

As previously described, this provisional PIP regime is designed for the first generation of seabed mining activities. It is important to note, however, that under present economic conditions all of the most reasonable prospects have already been claimed and would be regulated by the provisions of PIP. While there are other areas outside those presently under negotiation, they are either of distinctly lower quality or are highly speculative. Broadus has suggested that, given certain assumptions, there may be as many as 23 economical sites in the Pacific, or as few as three or four.[22] The long-term impact of PIP on the scope of ISA operations could be substantial.

The major function of these boundary rules has been to acknowledge, and to a degree meet, developed states' concerns over the protection of their economic interests in the Area, and the development of efficient regulatory machinery.

Information Rules

Rules establishing information channels, creating common nomenclature, and prescribing measures and methods for evaluation, are critical in this environment for two reasons. First, the size, complexity and duration of the negotiations meant that the creation of a generally acceptable language and relatively efficient communication channels was essential to any degree of successful bargaining (both at UNCLOS III and in the subsequent building of the ISA). Second, the scientific, technical and economic uncertainties surrounding these negotiations have been substantial, if not extreme. Therefore, the communication of information and the identification and resolution of uncertainty assumed much potential importance. Without sufficient information, the degree to which developing states could be expected to participate effectively in these negotiations was much diminished.

The UN Secretariat has produced dozens of technical studies over the past twenty years on the question of the science, technology and economics of deep seabed mining. These studies have characterized the nature of existing technology, the strength and future of international metals markets, and the potential impacts on land-based producers of marine minerals development.

The creation of information channels has proved to be a point of contention, particularly in relation to the technology transfer provisions of the treaty. Questions have been raised, for example, about how the Authority will force the transfer of technology and proprietary information when the developers of the technologies are private corporations and consortia, and not nation-states. Certain developing states have argued that information and technology are part of the common heritage principle. These states argue that seabed resources (as common heritage) have no real economic value until they have been recovered, so that the means to recover those resources must also be part of the universal human heritage.

Indeed, two proposals to PrepCom have addressed the issue in terms of training, research and development. The first came in the form of the Austrian "Proposal for a Joint Enterprise for Exploration, Research and Development in Ocean

Mining (JEFERAD)".[23]   The purpose of the proposal
was to create a joint venture between the
Preparatory Commission and other states and
private mining entities which would facilitate the
early building of technical competence of the
Authority. As proposed, JEFERAD would carry out a
wide range of activities including: (i) the
exploration of the ocean floor and deposit
evaluation; (ii) research and development in
mining technology, transport and processing; (iii)
the institution of appropriate training schemes;
and (iv) participation of developing countries in
the operations from the very beginning, thus
enhancing their active participation in the
Authority. The proposers argue that a joint
venture such as JEFERAD is essential if the
PrepCom is to achieve its goal of taking all
measures necessary for the early entry into
effective operation of the Enterprise.[24]

A second related proposal by Colombia carries
further the reasoning behind the need to establish
an international joint venture.[25] The Colombian
proposal, "The International Venture," argues that
a single inventor or entrepreneur no longer has
the ability to drive technological innovation.
Rather, the proposal asserts that the current
international economy is much more dominated by
large commercial and technical organizations.
However, "less than three per cent of all funds
invested in science and technology throughout the
world is allocated to projects being executed in
the developing countries."[26] This imbalance is
even more pronounced in the area of marine
technology. The joint venture proposed by
Colombia is designed to reduce this gap as quickly
as possible.

The building of information is playing other
roles in the ongoing negotiations at PrepCom. One
particularly interesting example involves the
efforts of the delegates to develop general rules
for "prospecting activities" in the Area.[27] Until
recently, both UNCLOS III and PrepCom had limited
their consideration of mineral resources almost
exclusively to manganese nodules. It had been
thought that the development of a regulatory
structure for other resources would require a
formal request from states party to the

203

convention. It was argued that the ISA could not develop said rules independent of a such a request, nor could they develop a general set of rules for all marine mineral deposits. However, a closer reading of the convention suggests that while this is the case for "exploration" and "exploitation" activities, the ISA could be in a legal position to develop general rules for prospecting.

According to the current working paper on the subject, prospecting regulations would include such obligations as notification to and approval from the Authority, as well as the submission of annual reports. As presently conceived, these reports would include, among other things: (1) the status of prospecting activities, including the amount of material recovered for analysis; (2) information on the degree to which the mission complies with ISA regulations; (3) any information obtained during prospecting relating to the protection of the environment; (4) reports on any training carried out as part of the mission; and (5) observations on any activities affecting safety at sea. Further, the draft provisions include a recognition that the processing of notifications will entail administrative costs on the part of the Authority, and that delegates might want to structure a fee schedule.

Concern has been registered on the part of several PrepCom functionaries that the Authority must be able to carry out its obligations over the full range of mineral occurrences within the Area. The comprehensive effort to regulate prospecting activities is designed to ensure its ability to do so.

One of the critical problems with these draft articles lies in the inability of the PrepCom to distinguish scientific research clearly from inquiry directed solely at developing information for future minerals exploitation. This information-related issue involves the difference between basic and applied marine science.

An additional difficulty arises out of the views of delegates on the question of information transfer. Again, the debate on this issues breaks down along North-South lines. Developed state opinion suggests that the relevant draft article asks for more than the convention obliges. The submission of such data allegedly would constitute premature disclosure and could give substantial economic advantage to actors other than the prospector. The Soviets have suggested that one function of risk capital is to obtain proprietary rights to the information generated by such capital.

A counter argument, while recognizing the need for balance between freedom and regulation, suggests that at least minimum information must be provided to the Authority. This debate will likely spill over to other questions, such as those relating to diligence requirements in manganese nodule mining.

ANTICIPATED OUTCOMES AND CONCLUSIONS

The divergence in the goals of PrepCom representatives along North-South lines will likely be the source of significant difficulties in the design and implementation of Enterprise rules. The resources of the deep seabed can be managed effectively through the ISA only if there is convergence of critical strategic priciples in support of stated ISA economic goals. The examination of key behavioral tendencies and the implications of these tendencies for design rules and policy outcomes leaves little ground for optimism.

Policy clarification hopefully will encourage compromise. From these discussions, one can understand the nature of the goods to be managed, the configuration of rule-ordered behavior within the ISA, and the likely outcomes of strategic behavior responding to these factors.

We expect that the tensions between new- and old-order principles will continue to be reflected in divergence in the conceptual underpinnings of operational rules for the International Seabed Authority. Moreover, the confusion resulting from this North-South split is creating a system with a potential for unreasonably high decision costs. These decision-making costs will be viewed by potential miners as significant opportunity costs. The addition of such costs could alter substantially their considerations of economic viability of deep seabed mining.

NOTES

This research was supported by the Pew
Memorial Trust and the Woods Hole Oceanographic
Institution's Marine Policy Center, and prepared
with funds from the Department of Commerce, NOAA,
National Sea Grant College Program, under Grant
No. NA84AA-D-00033. Additional funds were
contributed by the Environmental Sciences Program
of the University of Massachusetts, Boston. An
earlier version of this paper was presented at the
World Congress of Political Science held in Paris,
France, July, 1985.

1. The United Nations Convention on the Law
of the Sea was opened for signature in Montego
Bay, Jamaica, on December 10, 1982.
2. Decisions of the Sea-Bed Disputes Chamber
of the International Tribunal for the Law of the
Sea, "shall be enforceable in the territories of
the States Parties in the same manner as judgments
or orders of the highest court of the State Party
in whose territory the enforcement is sought."
See, United Nations Convention on the Law of the
Sea, Annex VI: Art. 39.
3. Ibid.
4. Established by UN Resolution 2340, the
ad-hoc Seabed Committee, became a formal
preparatory committee for UNCLOS III in 1968.
5. See, United Nations Convention on the Law
of the Sea (hereafter referred to as Convention),
Annex III, Art. 8.
6. See, in general, Convention, Annex III,
"Basic Conditions of Prospecting, Exploration and
Exploitation."
7. See, "Report of the Group of Technical
Experts . . . on the Application of the Government
of the Republic of India for Registration as a
Pioneer Investor . . .," UN Doc. LOS/PCN/BUR/R.1,
10 August 1987, and "Decision of the General
Committee on the Application of the Government of
India as a Pioneer Investor Under Resolution II,"
UN Doc. LOS/PCN/94, 19 August 1987.

8. See, Convention, Art. 151:1(a).

9. See, Convention, Art. 151:4-7.

10. At present, however, the limits are based on the following:

(1) an initial tonnage equal to the previous five year growth in world nickel consumption;

(2) additional expansion is allocated at 60% of the average annual growth in total world nickel consumption as calculated from a previous 15 year consumption trend; and,

(3) total authorization for any individual operator cannot exceed a quantity of 46,500 metric tons of nickel per year.

11. These provisions are found generally at Art. 144, and at Annex III, Art. 5.

12. See, Convention, Annex I, Resolution II of the Final Act.

13. See, Convention, Annex I, Resolution I of the Final Act.

14. Vincent Ostrom, The Intellectual Crisis in American Public Administration (University of Alabama Press, 1974).

15. Ronald Oakerson, "A Model for the Analysis of Common Property Problems," paper prepared for the Common Property Steering Committee, Board on Science and Technology for International Development, Washington D.C., May 17, 1984.

16. Ross D. Eckert, The Enclosure of Ocean Resources (Palo Alto: Hoover Institute Press, 1979).

17. J.H.W. Verzijl, "Western European Influence on the Foundations of International Law," International Relations, vol. 1 (1955): 137.

18. R.P. Anand, "Attitude of the Asian-African States Toward Certain Problems of International Law," International and Comparative Law Quarterly, vol. 15 (1966): 63.

19. Arvid Pardo, "An Opportunity Lost," in Bernard H. Oxman, ed., Law of the Sea: U.S. Policy Dilemma (San Francisco: ICS Press, 1983).

20. Elinor Ostrom, "An Agenda for the Study of Institutions," paper prepared for the Workshop in Political Theory and Policy Analysis, Indiana University, March 28, 1984.

21. See, Convention, Art. 161.

22. Personal Communication, James M. Broadus, Marine Policy Center, Woods Hole Oceanographic Institution.

23. UN Doc. LOS/PCN/SCN.2/L.2/Rev.1, 10 August 1984, and UN Doc. LOS/PCN/SCN.2/L.2/Add.1.

24. See, Convention, Final Act, Annex I, Res. 1.

25. UN Doc. LOS/PCN/SCN.2/WP.14/Add.1, "The International Venture," 26 March 1987.

26. Ibid.

27. UN Doc. LOS/PCN/SCN.3/WP.6, 15 March 1985.

Appendix to Chapter 9: The Powers and Functions of the ISA Organs

THE ASSEMBLY

The Assembly is referred to as the Supreme Organ of the ISA and is comprised of all States Parties to the Convention. Each member has a single vote with questions of procedure being decided by a simple majority of states present and voting with questions of substance needing a two-thirds majority.

The Assembly will develop the general policies for the ISA, and will consider and approve rules, regulations, and procedures recommended by the Council.

THE COUNCIL

The Council is the executive organ of the ISA. Membership to the Council is limited to 36 states chosen on the basis of certain geographical and interest criteria. Membership to the Council is for a period of four years with re-election possible. Each member is accorded one vote with questions of procedure requiring only a simple majority. Questions of substance are decided on by a three-tiered system of two-third, three-quarter, or consensus requirements, depending on the importance of the issue.

The Council is the body designated, among other things, to set specific ISA policies, supervise and coordinate the implementation of policies, propose candidates for election, approve plans of work, and borrow funds.

THE ECONOMIC PLANNING COMMISSION AND THE
LEGAL AND TECHNICAL COMMISSION

These commissions serve to implement certain policies of the Council. They are comprised of fifteen members each with representation based on criteria of interest, geography and other qualifications, with members serving for five years.

Voting rules for the commissions will be established at a future date by the Authority. They will formulate certain rules and regulations for consideration by the Council, and will serve to supervise activities in the Area.

THE ENTERPRISE

The Enterprise is the organ of the Authority which carries out activities in the Area directly. These activities include prospecting, exploration, exploitation, transportation, processing and marketing of minerals. In developing the resources of the Area, the Enterprise must operate on the basis of sound commercial principles. The Enterprise must act in accordance with the general policies of the Assembly and the directives of the Council.

The Governing Board of the Enterprise is comprised of 15 members elected to a four-year term with re-election possible. Each member has a single vote, with questions of procedure and substance decided by a simple majority. The Governing Board of the Enterprise will direct the business operations of the Enterprise; draw up and submit formal written plans of work to the Council; prepare and submit applications for production authorizations; authorize negotiations on the acquisition of technology; and approve the annual budget of the Enterprise.

The Director General is the legal representative and the chief executive of the Enterprise. The Director General and the staff must be international officials responsible only to the Enterprise.

10

The Great Naval Powers
and the Third World

David L. Larson

NAVAL RANKINGS

The various maritime states may be grouped
into five power levels: 1. Superpowers; 2. Major
Powers; 3. Regional Powers; 4. Minor Powers; and
5. Developing Powers. (Refer to the appendix of
this chapter for detailed identification). The
United States and the Soviet Union clearly fit in
the Superpower category; Great Britain, France and
China fit into the Major Power category;
Argentina, Australia, Brazil, Canada, West
Germany, Italy and Japan fit into the Regional
Power category; North Korea, Norway, Netherlands,
South Korea, Saudi Arabia and Sweden fit into the
Minor Power category; and the Congo, Kuwait,
Qatar, Singapore, Sri Lanka, Nicaragua, and many
other countries from the Third World fall into the
Developing Powers category.

The dominant naval powers are the United
States and the Soviet Union, since they are the
only powers which have global capability and
sustained global power projection. For example,
defined just in terms of sub-launched ballistic
missiles (SLBMs), the nuclear capabilities of the
US include 640 deployed with a total of 6,656
warheads while the counterpart figures for the
USSR are 944 and 3,216.

The only other naval powers that have SLBM
capability are Great Britain (64 launchers),
France (96 launchers), and China (24 launchers).[1]
Insofar as we know from public sources, the rest
of the world's naval powers have no nuclear SLBM

capability and probably no other nuclear capability. This rather starkly divides the naval powers into nuclear haves and nuclear have-nots.

INTERNATIONAL STRAITS

The superpowers have been concerned for some years that the mobility of their strategic ballistic missile submarines (SSBNs) might be restricted or restrained by the creeping jurisdiction of coastal states out into the world ocean. In fact, one of the primary forces behind superpower interest in convening the Third United Nations Conference on the Law of the Sea (UNCLOS III) in 1973 was to counter this apparent trend. Access through straits was of particular concern. Of the 205 international straits in the world, 153 are between 6 and 24 nm. in width, and could be overlapped by 12 nm. territorial seas authorized by Article 3 of the United Nations Convention on the Law of the Sea (hereafter the UN Convention).[2] This could seriously constrict and constrain commercial transportation and naval navigation through these straits if the strait states would not accept customary international law as interpreted by the United States or would not accept the new concept of transit passage through international straits outlined in Articles 37-45 of the UN Convention.

The superpowers made it clear that their first priority in regard to the law of the sea was unimpeded and unrestricted transit passage through international straits, and freedom of navigation on the high seas. These objectives were fundamentally achieved in the Informal Single Negotiating Text of May 1975,[3] and have been actively and positively asserted by the superpowers since that time, such as by the United States in the Gulf of Sidra in 1981 and 1986.[4] Although the basic objectives of the superpowers were achieved in the negotiating process, they have not yet been fully or generally accepted by the international community in view of the rejection of the UN Convention by the Reagan Administration. The UN Convention has also failed to attract the necessary sixty ratifications to bring it into force and effect (only thirty-two states had ratified by March 1987).

Although there are some 153 international straits which might be overlapped by 12 nm. territorial seas, there are probably only sixteen major international straits which are especially important for commercial and naval navigation:

Anglo-America:
Bering Strait, West (U.S./U.S.S.R.); Strait of Juan de Fuca (Canada/U.S.).

Latin America:
Old Bahamas Channel (Cuba/Bahamas); Dominica Channel (France/Dominica); Martinique Channel (France/Dominica); Saint Lucia Channel (France/St. Lucia); Saint Vincent Passage (St. Vincent).

Europe/Middle East:
Strait of Gibraltar (Spain/Morocco); Dover Strait (France/U.K.); Bab-el-Mandeb (Djibouti/Yemen); Strait of Hormuz (Iran/Muscat and Oman).

Southeast Asia and Far East:
Malacca and Singapore Straits (Indonesia, Malaysia, Singapore); Sunda Strait (Indonesia); Lombok (Indonesia); Ombai Strait (Indonesia); Western Chosen Strait (South Korea).[5]

Since numerous major international straits are located in the Third World, North-South issues bulk large in the ongoing debate over straits' states control of traffic.

The problem for the United States, and potentially for the Soviet Union and other major maritime powers, is that international straits are particularly vulnerable to anti-ship missiles such as Exocet, Otomat, Harpoon, Seawolf, Silkworm and others. Vulnerability of surface vessels of even great powers in constricted waters was dramatized in the Falklands war of 1982 and in the Persian Gulf when the USS Stark was hit on May 17, 1987. Missiles attacks, possibly backed up by shore batteries, land-based aircraft, fast patrol boats and mines could conceivably cut off navigation in crucial straits, such as the Strait of Hormuz. The possibility that such interdiction might occur is increased since several major straits states from the Third World have acquired anti-ship missiles including Indonesia, Malaysia, Singapore, Morocco, and Iran.

SUPERPOWER STRATEGIES

There has been great continuity in maritime strategy over the centuries, although the principal actors and the magnitude of the weapons available have changed. Today, only the two superpowers can be regarded as truly global maritime powers.

Although both the United States and the Soviet Union have long maritime histories, they really did not become global maritime powers until after World War II. The United States emerged from World War II as the predominant global maritime power, and still maintains a substantial advantage. However, the Soviet Navy gradually improved in size and quality under Admiral Sergei Gorshov, and by 1973 could be regarded as another maritime power with a global reach and global interests.

In the decline of the British and French colonial empires following World War II, the United States Navy moved the Sixth Fleet into the Eastern Mediterranean where it still remains today to try to fill that power vacuum. And, following the "fall of China," the United States moved the Seventh Fleet to the Western Pacific where it still remains. The United States also developed a naval presence in the Persian Gulf and the Indian Ocean after the Suez Crisis in 1956 and the British decision to withdraw all naval forces "East of Suez."

The Soviet Union also began to compete for power and influence in the Third World after the Suez Crisis, and gradually developed a permanent naval presence in the Mediterranean and the Indian Ocean. Following the withdrawal of the United States from Vietnam in 1973, the Soviet Union took over the enormous US naval base at Cam Ranh Bay and now maintains a substantial naval presence in Southeast Asia. As leading experts of Soviet

214

naval diplomacy put it in 1979, "the Soviets are now universally understood to be fully fledged participants in the Third World."[6]

In support of their global forces, both the United States and the Soviet Union maintain worldwide systems of naval bases and port privileges, as they compete for power, prestige, and prosperity throughout the world. In addition to Hawaii and Guam, the United States has overseas bases in the Philippines, Japan, Great Britain, Iceland, Bermuda, the Azores (Portugal), Spain, Italy, Greece and Diego Garcia (Indian Ocean) as well as port facilities and/or port privileges in several other countries. The Soviet Union has overseas bases in Vietnam, Socotra (Indian Ocean), Dahlak (Red Sea) and Cuba, along with port privileges in several other countries. These global strategic forces and bases cement the position of the US and USSR as the only two global maritime superpowers, and they tend to dominate the strategic agenda. The regional, coastal and straits states do have some local power, but they are usually subordinate to the power of one or both of the superpowers.

WESTERN EUROPE

The navies of Western Europe are of various sizes and shapes, and they do not have a great deal in common except for general location. However, these navies are important in the balance of power for six basic reasons:

1. European naval power is impressive in terms of quality and quantity.
2. European navies are relatively strong in their own home waters, and European waters are among the most strategically important in the world.
3. The level of cooperation between European navies and naval industries is steadily increasing and is substantially higher than forty years ago.
4. There is strength to be found in the diversity of the European navies, which are usually well suited to their own national interests.

215

5. Coordination of European naval strategy
under the aegis of NATO has been steadily
increasing over the past few years.

Some of the basic missions of the European
navies under NATO are to detect, track and
possibly interdict Soviet naval forces stationed
with the Northern Fleet at Severomorsk, the Baltic
Fleet at Kaliningrad, and the Black Sea Fleet at
Sevastopol. There is a relatively greater
emphasis on smaller combatants such as destroyers
and frigates, as well as fast attack craft (FAC)
and mine counter measures vessels (MCMV) for
purposes of detection, anti-submarine warfare
(ASW) and interdiction with the use of mines. The
major regional powers including Great Britain,
France and Italy also have offensive tactical and
strategic capability, which must be a source of
some concern to the Soviet Union.

European countries have been significant
suppliers of naval weaponry to the Third World.
While this does not usually lead to direct
strategic involvement in Third World regions as in
the case of the two superpowers, it does make them
significant actors in Third World armament and
conflict.

THIRD WORLD NAVAL CONSTRUCTION

Although the Third World purchases most of
its naval weapons and equipment from the developed
world, a number of Third World countries have been
able to develop a fairly substantial naval
construction industry. Third World naval
construction is usually based upon licensed
programs, but is occasionally under original
design. A recent survey of Third World naval
construction identified seventeen (17) countries
currently building a variety of naval craft, eight
(8) of which are building sizable warships
including frigates and/or submarines.[7]

Some of the potential advantages of home
based naval construction for Third World countries
are as follows:

1. Lower manpower and materials costs.
2. Higher employment levels.

216

3. Transfer of technology and increased technical skills.
4. Improved naval capability through construction and repair.
5. Enhanced national security.
6. Some exports.
7. Improved balance of payments.
8. Enhanced sense of national pride and identity.
9. Increased independence.

Even though the basic construction may occur in Third World countries, most of the weapons, radar and sonar systems are still purchased from the developed countries. As a consequence, there is still a strong dependent or interdependent relationship between the Third World and First and Second World designers, licensors and weapons producers. In many instances, these dependent and interdependent relationships are conscious and purposeful policy on the part of the superpowers or the major powers as part of an overall national strategy.

Against the perceived advantages of Third World naval construction should be offset the allocation of scarce resources and technical skills, which might otherwise be used for more conventional economic development. However, national security has such a high value in the Third World that conventional cost-effectiveness considerations are often not given priority.

GEOGRAPHIC REGIONS OF THE THIRD WORLD

The geographic regions of the Third World have expanded enormously since World War II in at least four maritime dimensions: the territorial sea (TS), the contiguous zone (CZ), the exclusive economic zone, (EEZ) and the continental shelf (Consh). The UN Convention permits coastal states to extend their national jurisdiction offshore to maximum limits as follows: TS - 12 nm, CZ - 24 nm, EEZ - 200 nm, Consh - 350 nm. These extensions have greatly enlarged the jurisdictions and responsibilities of coastal states, usually with a concomitant expansion of offshore patrol vessels (OPV) to enforce their jurisdictions.

217

In addition to the rapid expansion of OPV, there has also been a similar expansion of other minor naval vessels including fast attack craft (FAC) or fast patrol boats (FPB). These FAC/FPB are often equipped with missiles and torpedoes and can be used to reinforce the more conventionally armed OPV as well as for offensive purposes. These smaller vessels are especially popular in the Third World because they are less expensive, more easily manned and conform more closely to their coastal requirements. Expansion of major naval vessels has been concentrated in leading Third World countries.

The Middle East and North Africa

This region is of closest proximity to Europe and the Soviet Union, and the United States maintains a major naval presence with the Sixth Fleet. The region is of historic, economic and geographic significance to the superpowers and the major powers as well as to other powers outside of the region. The overarching strategic significance of the region is defined largely in terms of oil and gas.

In support of their strategic interests, both the United States and the Soviet Union maintain a substantial naval presence in the region. The United States maintains the Sixth Fleet in the Mediterranean and elements of the Seventh Fleet in the Indian Ocean and the Persian Gulf ("Mideast Force"). The Sixth Fleet normally consists of 40 naval vessels including two aircraft carriers, 20 surface ships, five amphibious ships and several submarines including both SSN attack submarines and SSBN nuclear ballistic missile submarines.[8] The Mideast force has normally consisted of four surface missile ships and a command ship.[9] The United States decision to reflag eleven Kuwaiti tankers in March 1987 and the subsequent increase in hostilities in the Persian Gulf (the "tanker war") contributed to an increase in US naval forces in the Persian Gulf region to about forty vessels including an aircraft carrier, a battleship, and two attack submarines.[10]

The Soviet Union maintains a Mediterranean squadron which normally consists of eight submarines, eight surface vessels, one minesweeper (MCMV), two amphibious ships, and about twenty support ships.[11] It also has a small task force in the Persian Gulf consisting of a frigate, a minesweeper and a command/supply ship.[12] Since the onset of the Iran-Iraq war in September 1980, the United States, Britain, France, and Australia have maintained a naval presence in the Indian Ocean of about sixty warships, while the Soviet Union has stationed about thirty warships in the same region.[13]

The Persian Gulf

The Persian Gulf has been the focal point for much of the superpower competition and conflict throughout the Middle East, North Africa, and South Asia since World War II. The conflict began over the continued Soviet occupation of Azerbaijan Province in Iran, pressure on Greece and Turkey and general interference in the region. This resulted in the Truman Doctrine of March 1947, which laid the basis for the U.S. military commitment to the region over the past forty years.

The Iranian revolution of 1979, and the Soviet invasion of Afghanistan in December of 1979, produced a more specific commitment to the Persian Gulf, the Carter Doctrine, which is still regarded as official U.S. policy. In early 1980, President Carter declared that "[a]n attempt by any outside force to gain control of the Persian Gulf region will be regarded as an assault on the vital interests of the United States of America, and such an assault will be repelled by any means necessary, including military force."

In support of this doctrine the Carter Administration developed the Rapid Deployment Force (RDF), which was designed to be a flexible response to any military challenge in the Persian Gulf. Under the Reagan Administration the RDF was absorbed and replaced by the new Central Command (CENTCOM), which was designed to fill the power vacuum in the Persian Gulf region between the European Command (EUCOM) and the Pacific Command (PACOM). The main headquarters for CENTCOM are in Florida with a forward command post with the

219

Mideast Force at Bahrain. The naval headquarters for CENTCOM are located in Hawaii with PACOM, and in addition to the newly expanded Mideast Force (40[+] ships) it can call upon elements of the Sixth Fleet, Seventh Fleet and Indian Ocean Task Force for support.[14] CENTCOM is organized into four sub-commands for ground, air, sea and special forces, and in the event of a crisis it is estimated that 300,000 men could be called into action.[15]

The Iraq-Iran War which began in 1980 started out as a conventional land war involving large amounts of manpower and support equipment. Iran subseqently tried to grind Iraq down with a war of attrition punctuated by periodic mass attacks, which were designed to overwhelm the less numerous Iraqi ground forces. However, after losing some graound, Iraqi ground forces have been able to stabilize the battle front through a combination of better training, superior firepower and almost complete air superiority. As a result, the ground war largely stabilized and stagnated by mid-1984, when Iraq shifted its strategy to try and interdict oil tankers going to and from Iran, thereby hoping to cut off much of Iran's income and gradually force Iran to end the war and sue for peace. Iran responded by intercepting and inspecting ships headed for Iraq, and attacking others. This strategy and counter-strategy have led to an impasse as well, since neither Iraq nor Iran has sufficient naval forces to conduct such a strategy. As Argentina found out in the Falklands War of 1982, the only way to win a naval conflict is with adequate naval forces.

Partially as a result of the Iraq-Iran War, and the increasingly difficult situation in the Middle East from Lebanon to Afghanistan, the smaller states in the Persian Gulf -- Saudi Arabia, the United Arab Emirates, Bahrain, Qatar, Kuwait and Oman -- formed the Gulf Cooperation Council (GCC) in 1981 for economic, political and social cooperation. Within a year the GCC declared itself to be concerned as well with mutual security and soon evolved into a full-fledged military alliance. As part of this broader orientation, the GCC encouraged a gradual build-up of naval forces of the member states.

When the Iran-Contra scandal broke into the news in November 1986, the United States suffered a substantial loss of credibility throughout the Persian Gulf region as well as among other friends and allies. In a move designed to help restore its credibility in the Persian Gulf, and also to help ensure the continued free flow of oil, the United States offered to protect Kuwaiti tankers from possible attack. Kuwait initially wanted the joint protection of both the United States and the Soviet Union, but the United States tried to preempt and forestall any reliance on the Soviet Union. To further consolidate its position, the United States re-registered or re-flagged eleven (11) large Kuwaiti tankers, and began the naval escort service in July 1987.

This new policy of escorting reflagged tankers and building up the Mideast Force in the Persian Gulf was not without some risk. On May 17, 1987 the USS Stark was inadvertently hit with an Exocet missile fired from an Iraqi jet. Thirty-seven crewmen died in the attack and many others were injured. The incident tested American and Congressional resolve to support the naval buildup in the Persian Gulf and provide escort service to reflagged Kuwaiti tankers, although presidential determination sustained the new policy. A second challenge to the policy occurred in late July 1987, when the USS Bridgeton, the first re-flagged Kuwaiti tanker, struck a mine while under escort by U.S. naval vessels. Nonetheless, the policy continued and gradually gained support from Britain, France, the Netherlands and to a degree even the Soviet Union.

Shortly after the Iran-Contra hearings came to a close in July 1987, the United States used multilateral diplomacy to push a cease fire resolution through the UN Security Council. Iraq agreed to abide by the cease fire, but Iran was non-committal. However, de facto observance of the cease fire involved Iraq temporarily stopping its air attacks and Iran stopping its gunboat attacks.

Just as the uneasy cease fire began to take hold, the tanker war, whose prior emphasis was on air and boat strikes, gained a new dimension through the use of mines. The first ship to

strike a mine was the USS Bridgeton on July 24.
The United States was unprepared for this new
dimension of the tanker war, but quickly responded
with the dispatch of the USS Guadalcanal and eight
helicopter minesweepers. By the end of August,
the United States had dispatched some minesweepers
to the Gulf along with Britain, France, Italy and
the Netherlands. Nonetheless, the ambiguity of
the mine warfare seemed to suit Iran's policy of
punishing Arab states that backed Iraq, and for
Iran had the added advantage of highlighting US
vulnerability in the region.

Toward the end of August the major naval
powers seemed to be getting the mine warfare
problem under control, when Iraq broke the de
facto cease fire and abruptly resumed air strikes
against Iranian shipping. Iran immediately
retaliated by resuming gunboat strikes against
Arab shipping. Within six days over twenty
vessels had been hit, and the tanker war seemed to
resume full intensity. Simultaneously, Iran fired
several Silkworm missiles from the Fao peninsula
in the direction of the Kuwaiti port of Al Ahmadi.
The missiles fell harmlessly on the coast, but
obviously escalated the war and posed a still
greater danger of their potential use in the
Strait of Hormuz.

The prospects for some kind of diplomatic
resolution of the Iran-Iraq war seem rather remote
at this time. The central questions seem to be:
1. What should be done if the Iran-Iraq war does
not end? 2. What should be the response if an
American or allied warship is attacked? 3. What
should be the response if the Strait of Hormuz is
closed? Naval considerations had moved to center
stage.

The Indian-Pacific Ocean Region

The Indian Ocean. The Indian Ocean has
considerable strategic importance for a number of
reasons. First, the Persian Gulf with all its oil
leads into the Arabian Sea, which is part of the
Indian Ocean. Second, the Suez Canal connects the
Mediterranean with the Red Sea, which in turn
leads into the Indian Ocean. This route is
especially important as a trade route for oil from

the Persian Gulf to Western Europe.   Third, the Straits of Malacca/Singapore, Sunda Lombok, and Ombai connect the South China Sea with the Indian Ocean, and constitute the main east-west transit routes from the Persian Gulf to Japan.   Fourth, the Indian Ocean is the main transit route to and from Europe and Australia and New Zealand as well as around Southern Africa.   Fifth, the Indian Ocean connects several continents and regions -- Africa, Asia, Australia, the Middle East, South Asia, and Southeast Asia, which constitute a large portion of the Third World.   Sixth, the Indian Ocean with the Bay of Bengal and the Arabian Sea is reportedly a prime patrol area for United States SSBNs targeting the Soviet Union.   Seventh, as manifestation of this strategic importance the United States, Britain and France maintain about sixty (60) naval vessels in the region, the Soviet Union maintains about thirty (30), and India maintains about eighty-four (84) naval vessels of varying sizes including one aircraft carrier and eight (8) submarines which makes it the only regional power.[16]   Eighth, the United States maintains a major naval base on the Island of Diego Garcia, and the Soviet Union maintains a similar base on the island of Socotra.

From the time of Peter the Great (1689-1725) down to the present, Russia has desired direct access to warm water ports without having to pass through international straits, canals or waterways held by other powers.   Following World War II, it seemed as though Russia might force Greece, Turkey and Iran to make significant concessions involving Soviet maritime access, but the Truman Doctrine seemed to check this drive.   However, when the Soviet Union invaded Afghanistan in 1979 the possibility of direct Russian access to the Indian Ocean was increased.   For example, the Strait of Hormuz is only 350 nm from Afghanistan, and the Indian Ocean is only 650 nm.

For these and other political, ideological and economic reasons, the Soviet Union has moved steadily closer to India and has placed a variety of pressures on Iran and Pakistan to adopt more amenable policies.   If the Soviet Union could gain direct land access to the Indian Ocean and establish a permanent port facility and naval base

223

there, it might be able to exert a great deal more political, ideological and economic influence in the region. However, the United States is fully aware of the strategic and economic importance of the Indian Ocean, and has made substantial military commitments in the region to try and sustain its interests, friends and allies, and offset Soviet influence.

Although India is the strongest regional power in the Indian Ocean, Pakistan and South Africa are important local powers. Pakistan has a total of fifty-three (53) naval vessels including eleven (11) submarines, eight (8) destroyers and twenty-four (24) fast attack craft (FAC).[17] This force is probably sufficiently strong to make a credible deterrent impact upon any potential aggressor (India), and still exert some influence in the region in spite of aging vessels. South Africa has a total fleet of sixty-four (64) vessels including three (3) submarines, two (2) frigates, twelve (12) FAC, and thirty-nine (39) offshore patrol vessels.[18] This is the most powerful naval force south of the Sahara, and is able to maintain a credible posture in the immediate area. The special significance of South Africa is that it lies adjacent to the major transportation route from the Persian Gulf to Western Europe for very large cargo carriers (VLCC) transporting oil. Also, South Africa maintains two naval bases at Simonstown and Durban, which used to be available to Western powers in time of need or crisis.

Southeast Asia. Southeast Asia is of special strategic importance because of its geographic location between the Indian and Pacific Oceans and north of Australia and New Zealand. The major international straits connecting the Indian and Pacific Oceans are Malacca/Singapore, Sunda, Lombok, Ombai, and Makassar. If these straits were interdicted or closed off, the transit passage from Japan to the Persian Gulf around Southern Australia would be extended about 14,000 nm, as opposed to 7,000 nm via Malacca/Singapore and 8,000 nm via Lombok. The same would be true for naval vessels, including submarines, that transit between the Indian and Pacific Oceans.

The geographic and hydrographic features of

224

Southeast Asia make the major straits especially vulnerable to closure or interdiction from within the region or from without by one of the major powers. The small regional navies can have an inordinate effect upon shipping or hostile naval forces if they rely on the unique geographic and hydrographic features of the region, including straits and archipelagoes, as a force multiplier.[19] Also because of the relative confinement and shallowness of Southeast Asian waters, the use of large surface vessels and submarines is not as advantageous as in the open ocean. This is probably the most prominent example of relatively small Third World states making prudent use of limited naval resources to have maximum impact in a region.

Of special interest is the role of the Association of Southeast Asian Nations (ASEAN). ASEAN has attempted to assume a neutralist, non-aligned posture by declaring the region a Zone of Peace, Freedom and Neutrality (ZOPFAN) because of the destabilizing potential of the convergence of geostrategic importance of the region and interest of the superpowers. The concern of ASEAN in not limited to superpower interests, but also extends to Vietnam and China. The concern with Vietnam relates to its invasion of Cambodia/Kampuchea in 1978 and its continued occupation. The current ASEAN policy calls for the withdrawal of Vietnamese forces from Kampuchea and the establishment of a neutral regime. This emphasis on disengagement relates not only to Vietnamese expansionism, but also to the presence of substantial Soviet forces at Cam Ranh Bay.[20] The concern with China relates to its support for the Khmer Rouge Forces in Kampuchea, the historic Chinese role in Southeast Asia, and the conflict over islands in the South China Sea.

Following the withdrawal of the United States from South Vietnam in 1975, the Soviet Union moved in and took over the former United States naval base at Cam Ranh Bay. This port facility is a large, well sheltered deep water anchorage about 2,200 nm south of Vladivostock and 120 nm north of Ho Chi Minh City. It originally had a capacity of about thirty (30) warships but it has now been upgraded to hold forty (40) ships.[21] In addition

225

to the port facility, there is an air strip at Cam
Ranh Bay which supports ten to twelve Badger
Bombers and six to eight Bear Bombers along with
substantial fighter support.[22] The Soviet
headquarters and logistic/support base for Com
Ranh Bay is Vladivostock, and there are periodic
replenishments, force deployments and military
exercises. The military significance of Cam Ranh
Bay for Southeast Asia is considerable, and it
poses a serious challenge to the ASEAN states as
well as to United States and Chinese forces in the
South China Sea.

On the other hand, the United States still
has a substantial naval base at Subic Bay and a
large air base at Clark Field in the Philippines,
which together support about fifty-four ships,
including fifteen submarines and two carrier
groups, and one air force division. However, the
Philippine bases agreements are up for renewal in
1991, and their future is far from certain. If
the United States had to withdraw from Subic Bay
and Clark Field, this would eliminate a strategic
forward position for the United States, and
greatly change the balance of power in Southeast
Asia, the Indian Ocean and the Middle East. Given
this possibility and the legacy of Vietnam, ASEAN
is not altogether certain that the United States
would come to its aid, assistance or support,
which has resulted in greater emphasis on self-
reliance. In recent years, there has been a
definite trend toward closer military cooperation
among ASEAN members.[23]

Northeast Asia. Northeast Asia is a region
of great geographic diversity including the East
Asian landmasses of China and Russia with the
Korean Peninsula and the offshore islands of
Taiwan, Ryukyu, Japan, Kurile, Sakalin and the
Kamchatka Peninsula. The geo-strategic
significance of the region is that mainland China,
Russia and the two Koreas are essentially locked
in by the offshore islands. In order for the
mainland states to gain access to the Pacific
Ocean, they have to pass through one of the major
straits of the offshore island states, principally
Japan. There are about forty (40) international
straits in Northeast Asia of which the most
important are the two Korean straits separating

South Korea from Japan; Osumi Strait between Kyushu Island and the northernmost Ryukyus; Tsugaru Strait between Honshu and Hokkaido; and Soya Strait between Sakalin and Hokkaido.[24] To a large extent, these geographical considerations have shaped the naval forces of the region, although Japan is a notable exception.

The Chinese Navy is clearly the largest naval force in Northeast Asia, as well as the largest naval force in the Third World. Although it has the third largest submarine fleet in the world, including three ballistic missile submarines, the Chinese Navy is still essentially a coastal and regional force without any long range strategic capability. Heavy emphasis on submarines and Fast Attack Craft (FAC) clearly indicates the largely defensive maritime strategy pursued by China. This is probably a function of its large land mass, long coastline and political subordination to the People's Liberation Army (PLA). However, the three ballistic missile submarines do lend a degree of strategic capability and credibility to Chinese Naval Forces. This strategic capability may be augmented in the near future, since it is reported that several ballistic missile submarines are on order.

Japanese naval forces constitute an exception in Northeast Asia. There are both constitutional and political limitations upon Japanese naval forces, and their official title -- the Japan Maritime Self-Defense Force (JMSDF) -- is rather self-descriptive. Clearly, the JMSDF is not today, and will not be in the foreseeable future much more than a local, coastal navy with the primary mission "to defend the nation against direct and indirect aggression."[25] This constitutionally limited role for the JMSDF is rather unusual since Japan now has, or will as soon have, the second largest national economy in the world, and it sits astride some important international straits opposite the major Soviet naval base at Vladivostock and the Chinese naval base at Qingdao. However, to a large extent the US Naval Base at Yokosuka, which is the headquarters for the Seventh Fleet, compensates for Japan's strategic deficiency in maritime forces. The resulting conformation of the JMSDF heavily emphasizes an antisubmarine warfare (ASW) mission in close cooperation with the US Navy.

The Northwest Pacific. The Northwest Pacific is the region where there is the greatest superpower concentration of naval and other military forces in the entire Pacific Basin. The Soviet Pacific Fleet (SOVPACFLT) headquarters is at Vladivostock with additional bases at Petropavlosk, Sovyetskaya Gavan and Cam Ranh Bay and with advanced port facilities at Socotra and Dahlak. The United States Pacific Command (USPACOM) headquarters is Hawaii; and the headquarters for the Third Fleet is Yokosuka, which in turn is headquarters for the Seventh Fleet. US bases are at Subic Bay, Midway and Guam, with advanced port facilities at Diego Garcia and Bahrain. While the areas of responsibility for both the USPACOM and the SOVPACFLT are quite similar, the force structures are rather different.

Although the SOVPACFLT is quantitatively larger than USPACOM (826 to 300 ships) it is qualitatively weaker in terms of modernization, operational days at sea, anti-submarine warfare (ASW), electronic warfare (EW) and general tactical and strategic competence.[26] However, SOVPACFLT does have available to it a highly effective Soviet Naval Air Force (SNA), which could neutralize USPACOM surface forces. This is one reason why USPACOM Seventh Fleet maintains two aircraft carrier battle groups (CVBG) in the Northwest Pacific in time of peace, which would surge to five in time of war.

The basic strategy of USPACOM appears to be offensive, while the basic strategy of SOVPACFLT appears to be defensive. In support of this strategy the US Navy has "concentrated the best half of its resources in the Pacific Theatre."[27] This is somewhat puzzling, since many naval strategists regard the main region of potential US-Soviet naval conflict as the Barents and Norwegian Seas where the Soviet Northern Fleet is expected to send its SSBNs down through the Greenland-Iceland-United Kingdom (GIUK) gaps to attack North America. Some of the possible explanations for this deployment may be that the Pacific-Indian Ocean is a far larger area of

228

responsibility than the North Atlantic and Mediterranean Sea, and that the United States Atlantic Command (USLANTCOM) has the substantial support of Allied NATO forces. However, USPACOM does benefit from significant support from ASEAN and ANZUS forces, as well as possible complementary missions from the Indian and Pakistani navies, in time of need.

Latin America

The Gulf of Mexico and the Caribbean Sea are bounded in the west by the United States and Central America and in the east by the Bahamas, Cuba and the islands of the Antilles. This geography makes the Gulf and the Caribbean a "semi-enclosed" sea which has very limited access in the west through the Panama Canal, and somewhat greater access in the east through the Florida Straits, the Windward Passage, the Mona Passage, the Anegada Passage, the Grenada-Tobago Passage and several lesser passages. The significance of this geography with multiple chokepoints is that in time of conflict or war the Panama Canal might be closed in a matter of hours, and the major transit passages to and from the Atlantic Ocean might be interdicted. The United States alone is able to counter these possible strategic threats.

To provide coastal security, most of the Central American/Caribbean states put almost all of their naval resources into offshore patrol vessels (OPV) or fast attack craft (FAC). This is understandable in terms of cost effectiveness, maintenance, manpower and training.

Cuba is of special importance to the region and the Soviet Union, because it has developed significant military forces with Soviet assistance and it also provides substantial port facilities for the Soviet Navy at Cienfuegos Bay. To help counter this strategic position and to maintain freedom of navigation, the United States maintains its naval base at Guantanamo Bay. Nonetheless, Cuba has proved to be an excellent strategic outpost for the Soviet Union, which maintains a naval presence in the region through periodic naval exercises. Also, in local terms Cuba maintains a significant naval force with three submarines (<u>Foxtrot</u> class), two guided missile frigates (<u>Koni</u> class) and seventy-five (75) large OPV, twenty-three (23) of which are armed with Styx type surface-to-surface missiles. This force could cause serious disruption and possible blockage of the major sea lanes out of the eastern Caribbean.[28] However, the recent loss of Grenada to Cuba with its potential air and port facilities has reduced that capability.

Mexico is another major Caribbean naval power, although the number of vessels (114) is rather misleading, because most of Mexico's naval forces are overage and in need of replacement. The two most modern, major surface vessels are two <u>Gearing</u> class destroyers which do not have any missiles or modern fire control systems. Although the Mexican economy is ten times larger than that of Cuba, the overwhelming external debt of about $100 billion has contributed to obstacles preventing modernization and upgrading of the navy. Since Mexico has no large ship construction capability, it has to rely upon external sources for naval modernization, which would only add to its external debt. As a result, the United States would have to assume a defensive role for Mexico in the event of any external naval threat, which further underlines the overwhelming dominance of US naval forces in the Gulf and Caribbean.

In South America, Brazil is the dominant country, and possesses the largest and the most effective navy. The basic mission of the Brazilian Navy in time of war is to protect the SLOCs in the South Atlantic going to and from the Indian Ocean and the Pacific Ocean. This mission requires a substantial ASW capability backed up by an effective ASW carrier group and attack submarines. The lack of modernization of the entire force structure and the supporting infrastructure on shore may weaken the effectiveness of the Brazilian Navy. Like Mexico, Brazil's inability to modernize its naval force structure is partially a function of its large external debt of $105 billion.

The Southern Cone navies of Argentina and Chile are both quite strong and have some regional capability, but are still largely coastal zone support systems. Both Chile and Argentina have been in territorial conflict for a number of years over the Beagle Channel, but this now seems to be resolved by the 1984 Argentine--Chilean Treaty of Peace and Friendship. The Argentine Navy only played a limited role in the Falklands War of 1982, but did lose the battleship Belgrano and a few other vessels. The Argentine naval air force fought well and effectively in destroying a number of British vessels, although the British were able to maintain sea control and win the war despite a 7,500 nm supply line.

The Anglo-Argentine conflict over the Falklands remains unresolved and threatens to aggravate longstanding, competitive national claims to adjacent sectors of Antarctica. Strategic interests involving the superpowers further complicate these disputes. For example, if in time of war the Panama Canal were interdicted or destroyed, the main route of navigation from the South Pacific to the South Atlantic would be through the Drake Passage.

CONCLUSION

The Superpowers

Both of the superpowers are striving for the maintenance and expansion of ideological, political, economic and social systems that are similar to or compatible with their own. In time of relative peace, the respective navies are major instruments of national policy in support of political, diplomatic, economic and other instruments of national policy. The Third World is one of the principal areas of concern for and competition between the superpowers. The region-by-region survey above indicates that the maritime strategies of the two superpowers, in extending their competition throughout the globe, to a considerable extent may be considered as a mirror image of the other. Many Third World countries try to opt out of or escape from this superpower competition by assuming a neutralist/non-aligned stance, while simultaneously trying to obtain economic, technical or military assistance. A few Third World countries are openly aligned with the Soviet Union (i.e., Cuba, Syria, Ethiopia, South

Yemen, Vietnam, Angola) or with the United States (part of Latin America and some other countries), but they still try to retain some freedom or autonomy of action. Most Third World countries are heavily dependent upon the superpowers, or other developed states linked to one of the two military blocs, for naval vessels, weapons, technology, training and support.

In regard to the law of the sea, the strategies of the two superpowers coincide in supporting freedom of navigation on the high seas and transit passage through international straits, although they depart in regard to deep seabed mining. The United States is flatly opposed to the present regime of deep seabed mining in the UN Convention, while the Soviet Union has been strongly supportive. The Soviet position in regard to deep seabed mining has received considerable approval in the Third World, while the counterpart United States policy has been roundly criticized there.

In terms of the broad naval balance, the United States is once again the dominant naval superpower, with its recent modernization program and 600 ship navy about to become a reality. The United States Navy clearly has global capability, and can probably fulfill its global missions in time of war, peace or crisis, and prevail over the Soviet Navy. By the mid-1970s the Soviet Union also achieved global capability and periodically manifests that capability through regional and global naval exercises. However, the Soviet Navy is aging, and many vessels are not deployed on a regular basis due to lack of maintenance and modernization. For example, in terms of submarines, the Soviet Navy outnumbers the US Navy about 2.5 to 1, and yet many of the Soviet submarines are not believed to be fully operational and fully deployed. In terms of aircraft carriers, the United States is far ahead of the Soviet Union by a ratio of 2.5 to 1, and is able to project power more effectively along strategic lines of communication (SLOCs), international straits, and in local areas of conflict or crisis such as the Persian Gulf. In time of relative peace, the areas of greatest potential conflict are precisely those SLOCs, choke points, and other strategic points of local tension.

The Major Powers

There is a substantial drop in naval forces from the superpowers to the major powers, with a concomitant reduction in capability and strategy. The most significant dimension of the naval forces of the major powers is the capability to deliver SLBMs from SSBN platforms. This capability gives some strategic credibility to these Western powers, and also augments the strategic capability of the United States. They also have close economic, political and military connections with the Third World, and provide naval vessels and substantial amounts of weapons, equipment and training, usually on a straight commercial basis.

The Regional Powers

The regional powers are limited by the range in which they can project, sustain and support naval power, but they can be highly effective and useful within that range. Most of these regional powers are in direct alliance or close association with the United States, which augments or can assist the US Navy in its strategic missions -- especially ASW. Also, many of the regional powers have ship construction, repair or overhaul capabilities along with a strong munitions industry. As a result, these regional powers are emerging as important suppliers to the Third World.

The Minor and Developing Powers

These powers are mostly Third World countries with a primary mission to protect their coastal zone and economic zone. Their concerns are largely to protect and conserve living and non-living resources within their national jurisdiction. They are also concerned about national security and protection of the coastal zone, as well as adjacent international straits and sea lines of communication. As a result, most of these states rely heavily upon fast attack

233

craft or offshore patrol vessels. These vessels
are often equipped with missiles, torpedoes and
large guns, and can be quite effective in short
range.

The Third World countries within these groups
are generally almost totally dependent upon the
superpowers and other developed states for
vessels, weapons, equipment, technology and
training. The adverse economic conditions,
balance of payments, and/or external debts of many
Third World countries make it burdensome to
purchase naval vessels and equipment from outside,
although the Third World naval build-up continues
and in some cases has been supported by local or
regional shipbuilding. As a result, the Third
World is still heavily dependent upon the First
World and the Second World for naval forces,
technology and training.

OVERVIEW

The United States is by far the first naval
power in the world. When this power is augmented
by allies and friends, it is even greater. The
Soviet Union is the second naval power; however,
it is improving, and with its allies is
challenging the United States in several
capabilities and regions of the world. European
navies (NATO and others) constitute the third
largest naval concentration in the world, and can
exert considerable power in the European theatre.
The Third World is still dependent upon the First
and Second Worlds in terms of naval forces as well
as aid, trade and technology, but is slowly
improving its local naval capabilities.

NOTES

1. International Institute of Strategic
Studies, The Military Balance 1986-87 (London:
IISS, 1986), pp. 222, 203, 208.
2. Lewis M. Alexander, Navigational
Restrictions within the New LOS Context:
Geographical Implications for the United States
(Peace Dale, R.I.: Offshore Consultants, Inc.,
1986), pp. 188-203.

3. United Nations, Third Conference on the Law of the Sea, Informal Single Negotiating Text, A/Conf. 62/WP.8/Part I, 7 May 1975.

4. David L. Larson, "Naval Weaponry and the Law of the Sea," Ocean Development and International Law, Vol. 18, No. 2 (1987), p. 138.

5. Robert D. Hodgson, World Straits affected by a 12 mile Territorial Sea, Chart 551036 (Washington, D.C.: Department of State, February 1971); and David L. Larson, "Innocent, Transit and Archipelagic Sea Lanes Passage," Ocean Development and International Law, Vol. 18, No. 4 (1987).

6. Bradford Dismukes and James M. McConnell, Soviet Naval Diplomacy (New York: Pergamon Press, 1979), p. 299.

7. Faroog Husain and Robert Van Tol, "Third World Naval Construction," Naval Forces, Vol. 7, No. 3 (1987), p. 72.

8. Nicholas Wright, "The Middle East and North Africa," Naval Forces, Vol. 8, No. 2 (1987), p. 130.

9. IISS, The Military Balance 1986-87, p. 29.

10. The New York Times, September 6, 1987, p. E3.

11. IISS, The Military Balance, 1986-87, p. 44.

12. The New York Times, September 4, 1987, p. A8.

13. Wright, "The Middle East and North Africa," p. 139.

14. Ibid., p. 130.

15. Ibid.

16. IISS, The Military Balance 1986-87, pp. 154-155.

17. Ibid., p. 165.

18. Ibid., p. 135.

19. Ngoh Lee and Alan Hinge, "The Indian-Pacific Ocean Region," Naval Forces, Vol. 8, No. 2 (1987), p. 163.

20. Alan J. Hinge and Ngoh Lee, "Naval Developments in Southeast Asia," Naval Forces, Vol. 7, No. 1 (1986), p. 30.

21. Ibid.

22. Ibid.

23. Lee and Hinge, "The Indian-Pacific Ocean Region," p. 164.

24. Alexander, Navigational Restrictions...,

p. 302.

25. James E. Auer and Sadao Seno, "Japan's Maritime Self-Defense Force," Naval Forces, Vol. 8, No. 2 (1987), p. 190.

26. Lee and Hinge, "The Naval Balance in the Indian-Pacific Ocean," p. 158.

27. Ibid., p. 160.

28. Ashley J. Tellis, "Latin America's Navies: A Strategic Survey," Naval Forces, Vol. 8, No. 2 (1987), p. 209.

Appendix to Chapter 10:
Naval Rankings

The author has developed a detailed system for ranking navies of both developed and developing countries. A detailed explanation and justification of this naval ranking system was presented in David L. Larson, "Naval Weaponry and the Law of the Sea," Ocean Development and International Law, Volume 18, Number 2 (1987), pp. 125-198. Data have since been updated and refined, and many naval comparisons in my chapter in this book rely on these data. Unfortunately, space does not permit publication here of the revised, updated data.

A summary of the method used for naval rankings is presented below. Power levels were used to specify the more common descriptions, as follows:

Power Level	Description
1	Superpower
2	Major Power
3a,3b	Regional Power
4a,4b,4c,4d	Minor Power
5a,5b	Developing Power

The power levels provide a basis for comparing the relative strengths of the various navies of the world in terms of ships and

237

aircraft that each possesses. The data do not attempt to account for a nation's capacity to produce any or all of its own weapons. Thus, in power level 3a, Italy, a major producer of naval weapons, is grouped with countries that do not have that same level of weapon production capability. These power levels have been set using the following criteria for each category, which may vary slightly in the case of any specific nation-state.

1. Superpowers
   - (a) "Blue-water" capacity; the ability to project combined naval forces world-wide.
   - (b) Possession of a wide range of fleet components across the entire spectrum of naval weaponry categories.
   - (c) Possession of aircraft carriers or air-capable ships.
   - (d) Possession of SSBNs in quantity.
   - (e) Cruisers or Battleships as largest surface fleet combat ships.

2. Major Powers
   - (a) Limited Blue-water capacity; can project forces world-wide on a limited basis only.
   - (b) Some aircraft carriers or air-capable ships.
   - (c) Some SSBNs or SSGNs or SSGs.

3a. Regional Power - Rank 1
   - (a) Non-nuclear attack submarines only; no nuclear or missile-armed submarines.
   - (b) At least one aircraft carrier or air-capable ship.
   - (c) Destroyers as the largest surface fleet combat ship.

3b. Regional Power - Rank 2
   - (a) Non-nuclear attack submarines only; no nuclear or missile-armed submarines.
   - (b) No aircraft carriers or air-capable ships.
   - (c) Destroyers as the largest surface fleet combat ship.

4a. Minor Power - Rank 1
   - (a) Non-nuclear attack submarines only; no

238

nuclear or missile-armed submarines.
- (b) No aircraft carriers or air-capable ships.
- (c) Frigates as the largest surface fleet combat ship.
- (d) Some Corvettes or Fast Attack Craft.
- (e) Possesses both Fixed-wing aircraft and Helicopters.

4b. Minor Power - Rank 2
- (a) No submarines.
- (b) No aircraft carriers or air-capable ships.
- (c) Frigates as the largest surface fleet combat ship.
- (d) Some Corvettes or Fast Attack Craft.
- (e) Possesses both Fixed-wing aircraft and Helicopters.

4c. Minor Power - Rank 3
- (a) Coastal submarines only.
- (b) No aircraft carriers or air-capable ships.
- (c) No Frigates.
- (d) Corvettes or Fast Attack Craft as the largest surface fleet combat ship.
- (e) Possesses Fixed-wing aircraft, but no Helicopters.

4d. Minor Power - Rank 4
- (a) No submarines.
- (b) No aircraft carriers or air-capable ships.
- (c) Frigates as the largest surface fleet combat ship.
- (d) Some Corvettes or Fast Attack Craft.
- (e) No Fixed-wing aircraft or Helicopters.

5a. Developing Power - Rank 1
- (a) Fast Attack Craft as the largest surface fleet combat ship.

5b. Developing Power - Rank 2
- (a) Patrol Vessel as the largest surface fleet combat ship.

11

Conclusions

Michael A. Morris

INTRODUCTION

While all of the articles in this volume
reach conclusions about the particular topic
treated, the interlocking nature of the three
parts of the book suggests broader conclusions.
Overall conclusions, besides synthesizing some
major aspects of the book, may help stimulate
future research. Conclusions relating to each of
the three parts of the book are presented in turn,
and from each perspective relationships between
the parts are explored.

DEVELOPED STATES' PERSPECTIVES

Marine policies of the industrialized states
of the North have been much more researched than
those of the South. The relatively high degree of
affluence and expertise of the developed states
gives them considerable advantage in managing
marine policy. At the same time, there have been
recurring problems on both the domestic and
international fronts, and understanding of these
problems remains tentative.

There have been a variety of innovations in
the organization and implementation of developed
states' marine policies. The European Community
(EC) has added a new supranational marine policy-
making process to long-established national marine
policies of member states (Laursen).
Incorporation in varying degrees of several
sectors of marine policy into the process of

European integration is a generally positive development, but the new EC policy-making dispositions have brought a variety of new problems in their wake. Moreover, the progress or lack of it in transferring each sector from national to supranational control has often resulted from the fortuitous interaction of variety of factors.

There are interesting comparisons between the emerging Blue Europe and US marine federalism, but it is uncertain, Laursen adds, if European integration at sea and on land will lead toward a federal state like the United States. Like the EC, US state and national responsibilities at sea have been evolving, so that comparative appraisals of these and other marine policy innovations by developed states would be useful for all concerned.

The United States may usefully be contrasted as well with European states, especially Britain, with regard to their ability at different times to encourage control of marine environmental pollution in the international arena (Grolin). Their intention -- control of oil pollution from tankers -- has been noteworthy, but positive results have usually depended on great power hegemony. When there was no hegemon or when the hegemonial power was in decline, maritime community in this issue-area was especially weak. The nature of public goods has contributed decisively to the inability of the hegemon to evoke lasting cooperation from lesser powers. Pressure by the strong, even when for a good cause, also tends to appear to the weak as bullying. The precarious nature of international cooperation over a prolonged period when developed states have wielded predominant influence highlights the marine policy dilemmas faced by leading countries.

In an increasingly interdependent world, progress in international management of the seas by developed states must be judged in terms of the kind and extent of Northern domination of the South. Northern marine policies often impinge all too directly on those of the South across an array of issues, from arms transfers (Larson) to tanker pollution (Grolin). Where progress has

242

depended on great power hegemony, as with regulation of tanker pollution, a lasting, stable order has not resulted. The North-South naval arms trade has promoted narrow interests of selected parties on both sides, while also aggravating antagonisms within and between each group. At the same time, a number of critical issues for the North, such as marine federalism and the balance of national/supranational policy responsibilities, are largely irrelevant for the South. Identification of opportunities for constructive North-South marine interaction can help offset these all-too-common trends toward collision or irrelevancy.

DEVELOPING STATES' PERSPECTIVES

Third World states face especially difficult problems in forging marine policies. Their capabilities for meeting multifaceted marine challenges are generally much more modest than those of developed states, and their time frame has also been greatly condensed in fashioning marine policy. Third World management of these problems in the postwar decades may be divided into three stages (Morris). Persistent Third World efforts helped forge a new ocean order in the first two stages, which in the present third stage now provides a firm legal foundation for pursuit of longstanding Third World offshore aspirations. With legal consolidation of the new ocean order, specific problems of policy implementation have moved to center stage for Third World marine policies.

Interlocking problems of offshore security and development continue to burden developing countries (Morris/Pomeroy), and these problems tend to vary by region (Morgan). Problems vary as well by marine sector, so that responses must be tailored to the particular characteristics of the sector as well as to the circumstances of the country in question. Bailey identifies inappropriate responses in one sector, fisheries, and suggests alternatives for more socially responsible management of fisheries.

There is also a need to integrate the various marine sectors into a unified policy, which more

243

fully protects and utilizes offshore areas for national development. Bailey's distinction between appropriate and inappropriate kinds of development suggests that achievement of even this generally laudable policy goal is strewn with obstacles. Moreover, all too often Third World states have been inclined to place excessive emphasis on the security dimension of national marine policy (Morris/Pomeroy). Naval buildups have occurred at the expense of both offshore resource protection and development. Third World marine policies must then cope both with recurring problems of a general nature and a variety of specific obstacles.

Identification of the many problems facing Third World marine policies is not meant to convey a uniformly pessimistic picture. The intention has been to clarify prominent problems as well as policy choices of Third World marine policies, so that appropriate responses can be fashioned. A number of Third World states have been coping with at least some marine sectors as well as can be expected. With greater experience with the many specific, interlocking problems of implementation, they may multiply positive results. The Third World record is still more impressive when account is taken of the generally adverse circumstances faced and the relatively limited time and effort devoted to resolving formidable problems of implementation across a variety of marine sectors.

Juxtaposition of Parts One ("Developed States' Perspectives") and Two ("Developing States' Perspectives") dramatizes contrasting North-South perspectives on marine policy. Marine policies, North and South, are at very different stages of evolution, interests and perspectives often contrast, and there is usually a sizable gap between their capabilities for benefiting from and protecting interests at sea.

While marine policies, North and South, are distinctive, this should not cloud the contribution that some Western concepts and practices may make to implementation of Third World marine policies. Bailey develops this theme with respect to fisheries, and Lowry/Sorensen/Silva elaborate a related theme in Part Three with regard to coastal area management.

244

Moreover, differences between marine policies, North and South, are to some degree relative. Grolin emphasizes the limits to hegemonic Western leadership in ocean affairs as a more multipolar world emerges. The rise of at least some Third World states at sea is contributing to this tendency toward global diffusion of power.

The very complexities of marine policy tend to have a certain North-South levelling effect as well. In spite of the relatively privileged position of developed states, they, somewhat like Third World states, experience continuing difficulties in relating different levels and kinds of policies (Laursen). Moreover, the appropriate relationship depends on specific circumstances. There are sound reasons for different policy prescriptions, simply because the circumstances in which marine policy operates vary so greatly. For example, some marine policy responsibilities in Europe have been shifting from the national toward the supranational level (Laursen); a contrasting tendency in the United States involves the devolution of some counterpart responsibilities from the national to the state level; and Bailey calls for the devolution of control over fisheries in at least some areas from the national and international levels toward the local level. At the same time, regardless of the approach used, policy implementation has proved difficult.

Marine policy is of course not wholly relative. While recurring problems call for different solutions in different settings, the setting not only varies substantially within both the North and South but also between North and South. Comparison of marine policies, North and South, can clarify different experiences in dealing with such problems and help both sides adapt better to current challenges.

NORTH-SOUTH PERSPECTIVES

North-South interaction at sea bulks large for both developed and developing states, but unfortunately the conflictive dimension of this relationship is more prominent than the

245

cooperative dimension. All too often, the conflictive dimension intrudes into the cooperative sphere.

Lowry/Sorensen/Silva do emphasize the cooperative potential of North-South marine relations, but suggest that much more can be done to promote harmonious relations. Morgan's survey of Southeast Asian marine policies also indicates that considerable North-South and South-South (intra-South) collaboration has been possible in some regions, although continuing East-West tension over Vietnam suggests the limits of this cooperation. Similarly, Grolin traces international collaboration in regulating oil tanker pollution, although this collaboration has relied heavily on the hegemonic role of one or another northern power. The end (regulation of oil tanker pollution) may be laudable, but Third World states have long objected to northern domination in this and other areas even when North-South cooperation may enhance the common good. Even the tendency toward greater EC collaboration in ocean affairs resulted in part from North-South and East-West disputes (Laursen).

Some sectors and areas have been especially conflict-prone, such as the deep seabed (Bowen/Hennessey) and naval affairs (Larson). Reconciliation of diverging North-South perspectives and interests there is arduous.

Linkages and interdependencies further complicate resolution of these and other North-South marine disputes. For example, an international seabed authority is only likely to be viable with the collaboration of developed states. At the same time, large-scale investment in deep seabed mining by the private sector may not occur unless effective collaboration can be forged with the International Seabed Authority (ISA) and Third World states associated with it. Each side is also able to escalate the stakes. Third World opposition to some developed states' policies toward the deep seabed (and possibly other issues) could be expressed through constraints on naval access in Third World waters. The maritime powers enjoy global naval superiority and have not hesitated to rely on naval power to support important interests.

246

While there is obvious North-South interdependence at sea, Third World dependence on the North is especially pronounced and is a source of continuing resentment and tension. The various chapters help clarify kinds and degrees of Third World marine dependency. Third World marine dependency varies according to the marine sector (Grolin and Morris/Pomeroy). National capabilities, both marine and non-marine, of the Third World state in question may qualify or heighten dependency (Larson). The nature and diversity of Third World marine and non-marine relationships with developed states is another important factor influencing the degree of marine dependency (Morgan and Bowen/Hennessey).

These complex relationships indicate that overall conclusions about marine dependency must be made with great circumspection. Nearly all Third World states face recurring dilemmas of marine dependency, but national settings for these dilemmas tend to be idiosyncratic and hence possibilities for overcoming them vary greatly. For example, Larson's hierarchy of naval powers dramatizes the great spread of North-South capabilities. Large differences in national capabilities in this and other areas may be cause for despair, insofar as a large number of Third World states cannot realistically aspire to viable marine policies without very significant assistance and collaboration from outside and/or neighboring powers. Such a high degree of assistance may not be forthcoming, and even if it were it could easily evolve into an onerous, dependent relationship.

Even for ascendant Third World states reliance on developed states continues, although their growing capabilities and bargaining power do increase policy options. In these privileged Third World cases, national capabilities can perform some essential tasks and the expertise of various developed states can be tapped to help resolve remaining problems. Selective national assumption of marine responsibilities in combination with judicious diversification of foreign links in the marine sphere can help achieve a reasonable degree of policy autonomy.

Marine dependency raises theoretical

247

considerations as well as more immediate policy-oriented ones. A number of other theoretical concerns in this book have paralleled more practical ones in helping clarify the evolving structure of North-South interests and approaches to marine policy. Historical interpretations can help clarify the degree to which "the past is prologue." The identification of stages in the development of Third World marine policies synthesizes the past and points toward the future (Morris). Similarly, Grolin identifies three periods in the regulation of oil tanker pollution, which are defined primarily by the changing nature of Northern hegemony. Collective action theory is also applied by Grolin to oil tanker pollution, and Bowen/Hennessey rely in part on a related theoretical framework. The same theory could be fruitfully applied to the analysis of a variety of marine issues including other sources of marine pollution, common renewable resources such as fish, and cartel-like arrangments such as liner conferences. A number of other theories help explain how national and supranational marine policies have interacted (Laursen), and could also be applied to other issues.

While the authors rely to one degree or another on theory to guide their research and help generate conclusions, they are uniformily modest about the applicability of theory to practice. Grand theoretical approaches are not tenable, since the applicability of theories varies by marine sector, by country and even over time. Any attempt to derive specific guidelines for marine policy from North-South comparisons would likewise appear to be elusive. The orientation here has been more modest. Greater understanding about similar and dissimilar aspects of marine policies of developed and developing states can be used to help strengthen the collaborative dimension of North-South marine relations. It is hoped that this study will have just this effect and will encourage others to explore the many dimensions of the subject.

Contributors

Conner Bailey is with the Department of Agricultural Economics and Rural Sociology of Auburn University, Alabama. He received his Ph.D. in development sociology from Cornell University and he has extensive international research experience in agricultural and fisheries development. His primary research interests are in the sociology of natural resources and the environment. His publications include The Sociology of Production in Rural Malay Society (Oxford University Press, 1983) and, with A. Dwiponggo and Firial Maruhudin, Indonesian Marine Capture Fisheries (Manila and Jakarta: ICLARM, 1987).

Robert E. Bowen is a member of the faculty of the Environmental Sciences Program at the University of Massachusetts in Boston. His doctorate is in International Relations from the University of Southern California and he spent several years affiliated with the Marine Policy and Ocean Management Center of the Woods Hole Oceanographic Institution. He has published extensively in the areas of international law of the sea, U.S. marine policy, and coastal and estuarine management.

Jesper Grolin teaches international politics at the University of Aarhus in Denmark. He was a postgraduate researcher at the European University Institute in Florence, Italy, 1984-1987, working on theories of collective action and the problem of marine pollution. He is a member of the Board of Directors of the Institute for Global Policy Studies (Amsterdam), and he was a member of the Danish delegation to the Law of the Sea Conference in 1982. He has written extensively about the politics and management of the oceans and other global commons.

249

Timothy M. Hennessey is Chairman of the Department of Political Science at the University of Rhode Island. His Ph.D. is in Political Science from the University of North Carolina, and he has held research positions at the Woods Hole Oceanographic Institution and Dalhousie University. He has published numerous articles in the fields of public choice, political theory, and marine resources management.

David L. Larson is Associate Professor and previously Chairman of Political Science at the University of New Hampshire, past president of the New England International Studies Association and the Northeastern Political Science Association, and currently Vice President of Pi Gamma Mu, the International Honor Society in the Social Sciences. His edited publications include The Cuban Crisis of 1962, The Puritan Ethic in United States Foreign Policy, and Major Issues in the Law of the Sea, and he is the author of numerous articles on security issues and the law of the sea.

Finn Laursen is with the London School of Economics and he has been a visiting lecturer and course director at the College Universitaire d'Etudes Federalistes, Aosta, Italy and a Research Fellow at the Marine Policy and Ocean Management Center, Woods Hole Oceanographic Institution. His publications include Superpower at Sea: U.S. Ocean Policy (New York: Praeger, 1983) and (Edited) Toward a New International Marine Order (The Hague: Martinus Nijhoff, 1982).

Kem Lowry is Chairman of the Department of Urban and Regional Planning, University of Hawaii. He is the author of published articles on evaluation research, coastal area management and land use planning. He has served as a consultant on coastal planning in Hawaii, Sri Lanka and Thailand. In 1985-86, he was a Research Fellow at the Marine Policy and Ocean Management Center of the Woods Hole Oceanographic Institution.

Joseph R. Morgan is Associate Professor of Geography at the University of Hawaii and a

Research Associate at the East-West Center, Honolulu. His principal research interests are in marine geography, and as a retired U.S. Navy Captain with 25 years active service, he also writes extensively on naval strategy, with a particular interest in the navies of developing countries. In addition to published articles, he has co-edited the Atlas for Marine Policy in Southeast Asian Seas (University of California Press, 1983).

Michael A. Morris is Professor of Political Science at Clemson University, South Carolina, and during the academic year 1987-1988 is a Fulbright Exchange Professor at the Hatfield Polytechnic in Great Britain. He is the author or editor of a number of books, the most recent of which is Expansion of Third World Navies (London: Macmillan, 1987). His published books, as well as numerous articles, focus on ocean and foreign affairs of Third World countries. Visiting research appointments include the Stockholm International Peace Research Institute (SIPRI), 1980-82, and the Marine Policy and Ocean Management Center of the Woods Hole Oceanographic Institution, 1984-1985.

Robert S. Pomeroy is with the Department of Agricultural Economics and Rural Sociology, Clemson University, South Carolina. As a marine resource economist, he has research, extension and teaching responsibilities for coastal resource development, aquaculture and marine fisheries. He has done research in the Caribbean and Southeast Asia and has authored several articles on marine resource economics.

Maynard Silva has a Ph.D. from the Political Science Department of the University of California, Santa Barbara. From 1980 through 1986 he was a member of the research staff of the Marine Policy and Ocean Management Center of the Woods Hole Oceanographic Institution, and he is currently a private consultant on economic development and environmental resources. His research interests include economic development and the coastal zone, marine protected areas, the

251

policy implications of sea level rise, and marine fisheries policy. He is the author of numerous articles and book chapters, and he also edited Ocean Resources and U.S. Intergovernmental Relations in the 1980s (Westview Press, 1986).

Jens Sorensen is Principal, Jens Sorensen and Associates, and Adjunct Associate Professor in Marine Affairs at the University of Rhode Island. His Ph.D. is in environmental planning from the University of California and he has specialized in coastal management since 1968. He has carried out numerous studies in the United States (particuarly California), Australia, Mexico and South America, and is the author of 32 articles and reports on coastal management and impact assessment as practiced both in the United States and abroad. He has taught courses in the University of California system and the Massachusetts Institute of Technology in ocean and coastal policy, regional environmental planning and impact assessment.

Index

MSY. _See_ Maximum sustainable yield

National enclosure, 71
  global consensus
    about, 74, 80
  and Third World, 73,
    79, 87
  and transit through
    straits, 76
  and United States, 85
National Environmental
  Protection Council,
  173
National Institute of
  Dispute Resolution,
  179
Nationalism, 72, 74,
  78, 80, 196
NATO. _See_ North Atlantic Treaty Organization
Natuna Island area, 99
Nature Conservancy, 166
Naval forces, 227,
  230, 231-234. _See
  also_ Naval powers
Naval powers
  rankings of, 211-212,
    231-234, 237-239
  of Western Europe, 215-
    216
Naval rankings, 211-
  212, 231-234, 237-239
NEAFC. _See_ North East
  Atlantic Fisheries
  Commission
Neofunctionalism, 47-
  48, 60-61
Netherlands, 22, 40,
  46, 53, 54, 59
New International
  Economic Order, 199
Newly industrializing
  country (NIC), 129
New Zealand, 32, 223
NIC. _See_ Newly industrializing country
Nickel, 190-191
North Atlantic Treaty
  Organization (NATO),
  216, 229
North Borneo, 137
North Carolina, 175
Northeast Asia, 226-228
North East Atlantic
  Fisheries Commission
  (NEAFC), 62
North Korea, 99
North Sea, 56, 57, 62
North vs. South marine
  policies, 78, 80,
  242, 244-245
  and arms trade, 243
  and coastal management
    programs, 159-161
  and confrontations, 72
  cooperative vs. conflictive, 3-4, 245-
    246
  and international law,
    196
  and international
    straits, 213
  and ISA, 186, 196,
    197, 205
  and national
    enclosure, 80
  research on, 241
  and UNCLOS, 73-76, 79
  See also Third World
    marine policies
Northwest Pacific, 228-
  229
Norway, 50, 56, 57
Norwegian Sea, 228

OAU. _See_ Organization
  of African Unity
O.E.C.S. _See_ Organization of Eastern
  Caribbean States
Offshore patrol vessels (OPV), 217-218,

260

Life at Sea Convention
Songkla Lake Basin, 174
South Africa, 224
South China Sea, 133, 133(table), 134-135, 223, 225, 226
Southeast Asia, 99-100, 131(map), 133-134, 224-226
South Korea, 99
Soviet Union
  and Afghanistan, 219, 223
  and antiship missiles, 213-214
  and Cam Ranh Bay, 135, 140, 214, 225-226.
  and Cuba, 229
  and deep seabed mining, 232
  as global naval power, 211, 214, 232
  and Indian Ocean, 223
  vs. NATO naval forces, 216
  naval forces of, 216, 218-219, 228, 229
  Northern Fleet, 228
  overseas base of, 215
  Pacific Fleet (SOV-PACFLT), 228
  SLBM capability of, 211
  SSBNs, 228
  and Third World, 214-215, 231-232
SOVPACFLT. See Soviet Union, Pacific Fleet
Soya Strait, 227
Spain, 46
  Spanish-American War, 137
  Spill-over, 47, 48, 51, 61
Spratly Islands, 99, 134-135, 137, 142
Sri Lanka, 165-166,

168, 178, 179
SSBNs. See Submarines, strategic ballistic missile
Stockholm Conference on the Human Environment, 32
Strait of Hormuz, 102, 222, 223
Straits
  international, 212-214, 224, 226-227, 232
  transit through, 76, 212
Stratton Commission, 173
Subic Bay, 135, 226
Submarine-launched ballistic missiles (SLBMs), 211, 233
Submarines, strategic ballistic missile (SSBNs), 212, 227, 233
Suez Canal, 214, 222
Sumatra, 136
Sunda Lombok Strait, 223, 224. See also Lombok Strait
Sweden, 57

TACs. See Total Allowable Catches
Taiwan, 137
Tanker war, 101, 218, 221-222
Territorial sea(s), 84
  and fishing zones, 49-50
  overflights of, 34
  vs. patrimonial sea, 71, 73
  and submarines, 34
  of Third World, 217. See also Third World; Third World

marine policies
3-mile, 49
12-mile, 2, 34, 50,
52, 58, 73, 217
200-mile, 34, 62, 70-
71, 85, 130
See also Exclusive
Economic Zone(s);
United Nations Con-
ference on the Law
of the Sea I and II;
III
Thailand, 100, 130,
131(map),
132(table), 139-140,
141, 147-148, 174
Thailand, Gulf of, 94,
99, 130, 133,
133(table), 139
Thatcher government, 52
Third World
and Antarctic Treaty,
76
anti-ship missiles of,
214
and common property
systems, 118-119
and European Com-
munity, 61
fisheries of, 30, 85,
89-92, 116
fishermen in, 105
and ISA, 246
joint ventures of, 100
nationalism in, 72,
74, 78, 80
naval construction in-
dustry of, 216-217
naval vessels of, 218
naval weaponry of, 216
navies of, 1, 86-87,
233-234
political independence
of, 72
and superpowers, 231-
232
and UNCLOS, 2, 73-76,

79, 80
and UN Seabed Commit-
tee, 73
See also Third World
marine policies
Third World marine
policies
and common interests,
78
and dependency on in-
dustrial states, 85,
217, 232, 234, 247
and exclusive economic
zones, 74
and fishery regula-
tions, 92-95
and fishery research,
89-92
implementation and in-
tegration of, 75-79,
80, 87-89
literature on, 7
and national
enclosure, 73, 79, 87
and new law of the
sea, 85. See also
United Nations Con-
ference on the Law
of the Sea III
and ocean security and
resource protection,
86-87
and offshore resource
development, 84-86
and optimal yield, 111
problems of, 243-244
and security vs.
development, 83
and 200-mile zones,
70, 85, 86
See also North vs.
South marine
policies; Third World
Timor Sea, 99
Tonkin, Gulf of, 99,
133, 133(table)
Torrey Canyon, 19, 30,

265